I0796815

# A Wheelie AWKWARD Romance

# A Wheelie AWKWARD Romance

The Love Story of a Girl Who Is Definitely Not Touchy-Feely and a Quadriplegic Guy Who Most Assuredly Is

**TESS CAMPBELL**

WITH ~~FOOTNOTES~~ WHEELNOTES BY CORBY CAMPBELL

SHADOW MOUNTAIN PUBLISHING

All interior photos courtesy of Tess and Corby Campbell.

© 2026 Tess and Corby Campbell

All rights reserved. No part of this book may be reproduced in any form or by any means without permission in writing from the publisher, Shadow Mountain Publishing®, at permissions@shadowmountain.com. The views expressed herein are the responsibility of the authors and do not necessarily represent the position of Shadow Mountain Publishing.

Visit us at shadowmountain.com

---

Library of Congress Cataloging-in-Publication Data

Names: Campbell, Tess, 1993– author. | Campbell, Corby, 1986– author.
Title: A wheelie awkward romance : the love story of a girl who is definitely not touchy-feely and a quadriplegic guy who most assuredly is / Tess Campbell with Corby Campbell.
Description: Salt Lake City : Shadow Mountain, [2026] | Summary: "Tess wasn't searching for love—but she still found it in Corby, a man with a power chair, dad jokes, and a heart as golden as his wit. Their unlikely connection becomes a wildly funny, refreshingly honest journey of love, growth, and self-acceptance. Together they prove that love isn't about perfection—it's about showing up, being seen, and rolling with life's surprises"—Provided by publisher.
Identifiers: LCCN 2025029739 (print) | LCCN 2025029740 (ebook) | ISBN 9781639934690 (hardback) | ISBN 9781649335333 (ebook)
Subjects: LCSH: Campbell, Tess, 1993– | Campbell, Corby, 1986– | People with quadriplegia—Biography. | Man-woman relationships. | LCGFT: Autobiographies.
Classification: LCC RC406.Q33 C36 2026 (print) | LCC RC406.Q33 (ebook)
LC record available at https://lccn.loc.gov/2025029739
LC ebook record available at https://lccn.loc.gov/2025029740

---

Printed in the United States of America
Publishers Printing

10 9 8 7 6 5 4 3 2 1

# Contents

# Preface

I met Corby, a wheelie awkward quadriplegic, in 2014. (Yes, we use wheelchair puns all the time. *Roll* with it. *tee hee*) Before going out, I tried to research all aspects of his injury. I had a few questions—if I married a man in a wheelchair, what would our lives look like? What sort of activities would we be able to do together? What would I have to give up?

At the time, there were not very many resources to answer these questions. I dug around on the internet for hours and only found three blogs about wheelchair relationships. The first consisted of a single post proclaiming to the world, "I never saw the wheelchair, only him!" While admirable in a way, I didn't find that post very relatable. The second was depressing and discouraging. That woman mostly complained about her husband's wheelchair and everything they couldn't do. I didn't understand why she agreed to marry him if she hated the chair so much. The third blog was tantalizing. I knew the husband was in a wheelchair and that his injury was very similar to Corby's, but in the dozens of blog posts, there was hardly any mention of the wheelchair at all! It was just . . . there! And they had a normal life! Clearly, this couple had figured out how to make their relationship work. It was possible! But . . . how did it get to that point?

I know there are more wheelchair couples making content now, but those couples have already decided to be with each other. How did they make that decision? Did these people fully accept the disabilities of their partners from day one, with no reservations? What if they weren't sure they could handle it? Were they ever mad or sad?

I am not the only person who has wondered these things. On two separate occasions, a random woman has approached Corby and asked him if he was married. When he confirmed that he was, they asked, "Can I talk to your wife? I'm going out with a man who has a disability, and I would really like to talk to someone who has done this before." I wasn't with Corby on either of these occasions, so I couldn't answer their questions, and now I wonder about these women often. Did their relationships work out? I wished that Corby had been able to hand them a book about my experiences—the good and the bad. So I started writing.

As I wrote, the scope of the story expanded. This was annoying. I didn't want to write about myself. I wanted to write about Corby. But Corby is not the only person in this relationship with disabilities. I have some too. It turns out that everybody has issues they deal with. And everyone in a relationship needs to accept something about their partner that they didn't expect. I obviously had to deal with Corby's wheelchair and the limitations that came with it. But he had to learn about and accept my physical and mental health issues too—things I didn't have a name for when I met him. And I had to accept things about Corby that had nothing to do with the chair. After we chose to communicate about and accommodate these tricky bits, our relationship started to work. That choice is what this book is about. And that choice was hard. It's irritating that it took me so long to figure it out and that I had to write a whole book about a relatively simple concept. But here it is.

I should probably end this preface in some sort of gushy, inspirational way. But I am too pragmatic for that. Please commence your reading.

## Chapter 1

# I Am NOT Delighted

*September 2009*

Calculus.

I do realize that the word *calculus* is not generally a good word to start a book with. For most readers, the word *calculus* probably makes them want to stop reading. Fear not, this book has little to do with calculus, but as a junior in high school, I let calculus take up a large percentage of my brain power. I loved math. Numbers were logical. People were not. I preferred numbers.

I was sitting at a card table in "The Zone." The Zone was in the unfinished basement of my home. It was furnished with a card table, a scrap of leftover carpet, a whiteboard, and a swing-arm lamp screwed to the side of the table. There was a single bulb on the ceiling, operated by yanking on a tattered piece of string. There was also an archaic space heater that made loud, electric groaning noises and glowed bright orange. If I could show you a picture of The Zone now, you might say it looked like some sort of interrogation chamber. All that was missing was a giant man sitting on the other side of the table, glaring at me over my textbook stack.

But I didn't mind the cold cement walls. The Zone was *mine*. I had five younger siblings who avoided the scary basement, so while I didn't have to deal with them down here, I was still aware of my family's existence. I heard their footsteps above me, and I heard water rushing through the pipes when they used the bathroom. At this moment, I heard the muffled sounds of the phone ringing, the distant murmuring of my mom's typical phone greeting, and the clattering of someone putting silverware in the dishwasher.

I stared at the problem in front of me, then dutifully copied the numbers onto the whiteboard, hoping they would make more sense if I wrote them in neon-pink dry-erase marker. I was usually pretty good at math, but trying to figure out how *X* behaved as it reached infinity was a little too abstract for my very literal brain. What was infinity? If infinity was an *impossibly* big number, then why should I care about it?

I heard my mom's footsteps coming down the basement stairs. I knew it was my mom because she wore slip-on shoes that clunked, and she didn't skip stairs. I didn't turn around. She was probably coming to put some leftovers in the downstairs fridge, and chances were we wouldn't even acknowledge each other. I never instigated conversation. Talking was confusing.

Mom wasn't coming down to preserve uneaten lasagna. She had news.

"Cole Hayward just called," she said. "He wanted to know if you had a date for homecoming!"

What? Homecoming? Wasn't that a dance?

I slowly turned on my folding chair to see my mom's excited face. Her oldest child was just about to get asked on her very first date! She had probably been anticipating this event. She would get to help with fun things, like dress shopping. For some reason, people thought that going shopping for expensive dresses was *fun*.

"What!?" I could feel a bubble of panic swelling inside my stomach. "I don't have to go, do I?"

Tears began to trickle out of the corners of my eyes. I did not have time to go to a dance! Saturdays were my most productive homework days! The only reason I knew who Cole was at all was that I took piano lessons from the same lady as his little sister, so we had seen each other at recitals. Being vaguely aware of someone's existence at boring piano recitals did not constitute a relationship, even if it had been going on for years. We did not have the type of relationship where two people got dressed up and danced. What was Cole thinking!?

My mom was not expecting this reaction. Cole was friendly. And sixteen-year-old girls liked dances . . . right?

"What's wrong? Why don't you want to go?" Mom asked.

I stared at my hands, tears dripping onto my shirt. I didn't know how to answer that question. I didn't know why the mere prospect of a date made me react this strongly. I wished I could go back to my calculus homework, blissfully ignoring whatever people my age were "supposed" to do. Figuring out what *X* thought about infinity sounded infinitely more straightforward than spending an entire evening with Cole Hayward.

Mom started her usual routine of trying to convince me that being social was a good idea. For some strange reason, she was worried that I didn't talk very much. I half listened as she said things about how much courage it took to ask someone out and how I needed practice being around people my age.

I didn't like being around people my age. I didn't like being around people in general.

I continued to stare at my hands. Mom wrapped up her monologue with horrible finality. "Look, Cole is a nice young man. You have no reason to say no to him. You need to go, and maybe you will even have fun!"

Fun? There was no way this dance was going to be fun. But I didn't argue. I twisted my marker-stained fingers together, refusing to look up. Mom waited in vain for a response, sighed in resignation, and retreated up the stairs. After her footsteps had moved back to the vicinity of the dishwasher, I crept over to the other side of the basement and stole a roll of toilet paper from the storage shelves, then plowed through a few dozen squares while staring at the problem on the white board. But my brain refused to focus on the numbers. It had a different problem to untangle. The sudden prospect of a dance had generated a list of logistical questions: What kind of dress are you supposed to wear to homecoming? Are you supposed to get him one of those man-flowers with the weird name? Who pays for everything?

The next day, my mom picked me up from school. Instead of driving me home, she drove to a consignment shop a few blocks away from the high school, informing me that we were going to just "run in really quick" to see if they had dresses. I mutely stood by while my social mother greeted the enthusiastic shop lady, informing the lady that I had just been asked to my very first dance and wasn't that so exciting? I attempted to smile as the woman looked at me. It probably looked more like a grimace.

Mom riffled through the rack and handed me two dresses. I shuffled over to the dressing room.

The first dress didn't fit very well, but my mom insisted that I come out and model it anyway. I stepped out and slowly turned in a circle while Mom pointlessly tugged at the sleeves and neckline. I didn't like the tugging—I hated being touched.

The second dress fit much better. It was a deep purple with sparkles accenting the waistline. Mom and the shop lady agreed that it was gorgeous, discussing how serendipitous it was that we had managed to find something so perfect on only the second try! When asked about my opinion, I said it was fine. *Fine* was my go-to word for everything. I would have been fine with any dress that fit because I didn't particularly care. I was just grateful that we had somehow managed to find a dress in ten minutes so I could escape this nightmare and contemplate calculus limits again.

As soon as we got back home, I rushed down to The Zone, where I smashed my head onto a tall stack of textbooks in frustration. How did I get here? I avoided people so things like this wouldn't happen! I wasn't shy, although many people probably thought I was. In reality, I just didn't know how to interact with other humans, so I consciously chose not to say things.

The elementary school counselors had tried to teach me how to talk to the other kids, but their lessons hadn't worked. Usually, any statement I made was met with awkward silence, and the other person's face would crumple together in a way that I couldn't interpret. I felt like my brain was missing a crucial piece that everyone else seemed to have. I was often described as "blunt" or "rude." After years of trying, I had come to the conclusion that human interaction wasn't efficient. I was not designed for talking; I was a robot designed for taking meticulous notes.

But now I had to talk to Cole Hayward. He was on the wrestling team, and the only thing I knew about wrestling was that they wore silly leotards. But telling a date that his wrestling leotard looked stupid didn't seem like a good conversation strategy. Even I knew that.

The night of the dance arrived. Mom curled my hair and pulled part of it up in some fancy, sparkly clips, and I put on a small amount of makeup for the first time ever. I examined my face in the mirror. If there was something wrong with the glittery powder, what would you do about it? Smudge it more? Or smudge the other side so the smudges were at least symmetrical?

There was a knock at the door. Cole stepped in, looking a bit nervous. He slid a big flower onto my wrist, and Mom pinned a boutonniere on Cole's shirt. Cole then offered me his arm, and we walked out the door.

We had to pick up two other couples. As we drove to the first house, Cole and I made an awkward, nervous attempt at a casual conversation.

He asked, "What classes are you taking this year?"

Oh dear, that was a terrible question to ask.

I reluctantly answered, "Uh, AP US history, AP calculus, AP psychology, biology . . ." I wished I had been taking some less ambitious classes just so I would have had something normal to list. I knew Cole was not a school robot, so the sentence I had just uttered must have been intimidating.

Sure enough, he responded, "Oh . . . I'm not really that into school."

After a moment of awkward silence, I said, "I heard that you made the wrestling team?"

Cole confirmed the rumor and said he was planning on trying out for the basketball team as well. Basketball was just as foreign to me as wrestling. This was going to be a long night. We had absolutely nothing in common.

We picked up the other members of the group and went to dinner. Cole's friends were the talkative sort and had asked out talkative girls, so gratefully, I didn't have to say anything. I employed my trusty "just laugh when everyone else does" strategy. I was good at copying people. At the dance, I mimicked everyone else's dance moves, feeling like a gangly bird tripping around a marsh. I tried not to calculate how many calculus problems I could have completed in the last five hours.

Cole finally took me home. He gave me a short hug on the porch and left. My mom had waited up. I informed her that the dance was "fine" and stowed the dress in the back of the closet.

For the remainder of high school, I swiftly squelched any inkling of interest any male showed toward me. I was asked on only three more dates. I considered it a victory.

## Chapter 2

# Rusty Lindy Hopper

*Five Years Later*

I was sitting in The Zone. It had gradually grown throughout college, and I now had *two* tables, which I'd set up in an L-shape. The folding chair had been upgraded to a salmon-colored office chair, and I now had a laptop with a wireless mouse that was constantly getting buried under the ever-present knitting projects.

I submitted a homework assignment and leaned back in my chair to stretch. I had just started my final semester of college. This was an alarming fact. I hadn't *intended* to finish my degree quite so early; it had just kind of . . . happened. I wasn't even twenty-one yet, but I would be done with a biomedical engineering degree in just a few months. I had been accepted to two cognitive neuroscience doctoral programs, but I didn't feel like I was old enough to be making those sorts of life-altering choices.

The Zone wasn't the only thing that had changed in the last five years. After starting college, I had come to the realization that my life was wildly out of balance; I needed to practice things that weren't just homework. Things like talking to people. I had gone on a few dates. I had tried hugging a couple of guys, but I still didn't like it very much. Especially after one of those guys got excited, had the audacity to ask if he could kiss me, and brought up the insane concept of my being his *girlfriend*. I thought I eloquently expressed my misgivings about the situation, but as usual, I must have been too blunt because he seemed upset, and I didn't hear from him again.

My interpersonal skills clearly needed more work, so I decided to try a new approach. I took up a new hobby—Lindy Hop swing dancing. Dancing was a great place to practice both physical contact and talking to other humans. Every week, there were new people whom I had never talked to before. If I said something awkward, it wasn't a disaster—each song lasted only about four minutes, so there were built-in time constraints! I could run off at the end of a song, and it wouldn't be weird at all!

There was a dance tonight. I fished my shoes out from under the table and yanked on the lightbulb string before heading up the stairs.

Even after a year, I was still not a very good dancer. I felt clunky, like an ancient car engine that had potential but had never been greased. Though the warehouse studio was lined with mirrors, I studiously avoided looking at myself, especially while I was dancing. I was aware of my choppy dance style, but I didn't want to confirm just *how* bad I was. I preferred to imagine that I was graceful and smooth.

I was doing better than usual tonight. I hadn't accidentally backed into anyone or smacked my partner with an elbow. I perched myself on a chair at the edge of the dance floor and studied the more experienced dancers, trying to figure out how they twisted their hips so smoothly and spun in place without drifting to one side. I especially liked watching the married couples on the floor. It was obvious they had danced a lot together. They all moved so confidently. I wanted a permanent dance partner to practice with someday. It would be nice to dance in the kitchen on a Wednesday at noon rather than every other Friday at 10:00 p.m.

Was this an absolute must-have in a future partner?

Of course not. But lately, dance was the only place where I met men, and I could only get married after I met someone. Based on statistics, wasn't I extremely likely to marry a dancer?

## Chapter 3

# The Tribulations of Profile Construction

I had about an hour before my next class but not a lot of homework. The classes I was taking for my final semester were relatively easy. I was struggling with having too *little* homework for the first time since ninth grade. Not having a full to-do list was a new experience. It was also dangerous. Instead of working on the few things I had to do, I was more prone to procrastinate.

Take this moment, for instance. Instead of working on a presentation, I was contemplating setting up a dating profile. There was an ad for a dating site on the side of my screen, and I clicked it.

Wait, what?

A dating profile?!

I quickly hit the Back button.

I needed more practice with dating. It was a skill I had not yet mastered. However, it was harder to find dates than I had anticipated. Almost all my potential dates ended before they began. After getting my number, the male subject would ask something like, "Soooo . . . what are you majoring in?"

"Uh, bioengineering?"

"Oh, that's . . . cool? How much longer do you have?"

"Uh, I'm a senior . . ."

*Momentary pause, during which I could tell that the male subject was doing some quick subtraction to verify that I was, indeed, only twenty years old, based on my high school graduation date they had asked about earlier in the conversation.*

"You know what? I don't think I'm going to call you after all. But it was . . . nice . . . meeting you . . ."

And forevermore, all future encounters with this male subject would be very awkward.

Life made no sense. All adults had impressed upon my brain that I couldn't go wrong with being ambitious and obtaining higher education. But from my experience, males were not fond of selecting the female with an above-average intelligence level to bestow ice cream upon.

What did they think I would try to do? Teach them complex math equations? I was just a somewhat socially awkward person who happened to like math, just like they were a mostly competent social person who happened to like . . . sports? Why couldn't two people who liked different things partake of frozen custard together?

I thought back to high school. I had often overheard groups of girls talking about their upcoming dance plans, sighing over things like their date's "strong jawline." What? Did that particular facial feature indicate future compatibility and happiness? That behavior had never made sense. Physical appearance was not important to me. It was a good thing too. I couldn't be picky about jawlines. It would be hard enough to find someone who didn't find knitting a complete turnoff.

The biggest thing I was looking for in a potential mate was someone I was comfortable talking to.

This requirement eliminated everyone.

I had never met anyone who fit that description, and I suspected it had something to do with my bizarre communication style.

It did seem odd to try a dating website when I had hardly been on any dates obtained in the conventional manner. But it was time to try a new approach. So why not a dating website?

I was sitting at a table in a study area in one of the engineering buildings. I shifted my chair and turned my screen brightness down to the lowest setting. I didn't want anyone walking by to see what I was doing.

I created my username and password and then proceeded through the profile creation steps: First, upload some pictures. Next, select appropriate options from the drop-down descriptor menus. These were easy—5'7", slender, brown eyes, brown hair, age twenty. Occupation: student.

The remaining questions were not straightforward. They required me to write about myself. For instance, the first box was labeled "A Little About Me." This label was frustratingly vague. What sorts of things did searchers want to know? After working on it for a while, I came up with a variation on an Old Spice cologne ad:

> Hello, gentlemen,
>
> Look at me, now back at you, now back at me. Sadly, we don't know each other yet . . . but we could. Look down, back up—where are you? You're on a date with me this weekend. What's in your hand? Back at me. You have it—it's a frozen yogurt and two tickets to something awesome. Look again, the tickets are now a diamon . . . You know what? Let's save THAT one for date forty-seven or so. I'm on a flamingo.
>
> I am a professional elbow model looking for a nice, single gentleman, preferably one younger than thirty. He has to be self-confident, and he can't be afraid of an independent, motivated, goal-oriented girl. I will go out with anyone who can fold a fitted sheet. Oh, and I also like guys who wear cologne (but it doesn't necessarily have to be Old Spice).

There. It conveyed my weird sense of humor, and it was interesting to read while hardly divulging any personal details. It would also increase my chances of getting more frozen yogurt.

I looked at the next box. This one was labeled "What I Do for Fun." Ah. My attempt to avoid giving out personal details wouldn't work so well on this one. I decided to mention normal activities while deliberately not listing grandma-esque hobbies, like knitting:

> Sit on the porch and eat ice cream late at night during the summer, ice skate (forward only, in a circle), play the piano, invent awesome stuff with duct tape (especially things related to *Star Wars* or *Dr. Who*), occasional hiking/camping excursions, swing dancing (seriously, spontaneous dances in the parking lot are the best), goofy text debates (the crazier your profile is, the better), strategic board games, and periodic raids on the freezer to steal chocolate chips (I never get caught. Well, not usually).

I thought I'd struck a good balance. I'd included some indoor and outdoor activities. I seemed like a somewhat active person, though I wouldn't actually describe myself that way. I referenced the only two pop-culture shows I had ever seen, so it *looked* like I didn't exclusively watch old black-and-white reruns. I had never actually spontaneously danced in a parking lot, but I had seen other couples do it, and I really wanted to try it. I was positive that it would be "the best," so it wasn't *exactly* a lie. The same sentiment applied to strategic board games—I had never played them, but they seemed like something I would enjoy. That statement was aimed at the nerdy sorts of guys whom I assumed were poking around on this site.

I had been doing this for only an hour, and it already felt like a game.

The site instantly generated a list of "recommended" men based on the answers I had selected. A list of pictures appeared, accompanied by the first sentence of each profile. I looked at the first entry.

> Haha ive always been hesitant with this online dating but my friend said it really helped him! My name is corey and im a great guy to get to know!

What?! This was what he wanted his first impression to be? Not even capitalizing his name? I looked at the next profile. Surely, it would be better.

> Its funny because I thought I would never be on a dating site but why not give it a shot?

Clearly, there was a theme here: Making excuses for being on a dating website. Next:

> i grew up in so cal big USC fan I feel like a split between a sports guy and a super nerd I like to create wether it's in writing drawing sculpting or music my favorites are prob drawing and sculpting

Again with the punctuation! And spelling! And half-words! And this was a guy who claimed that he liked to write! Was I the only person on the planet who used the Shift key when *not* writing an essay for English class?

> i work for a demolition company tearing down buildings and it's a lot of fun. some things about me. i am shy at first buy once i get to know you i start to open up.

Ugh. Dating profiles were so *boring*. And I had only read the first sentence of each one. After going through a few dozen search results, I started to notice patterns. Everyone was looking for a "partner in crime," and everyone liked being outside but was also cool staying in and watching Netflix. It was like they were all using a template that didn't come with spell-check:

> "I am a student at ________, I work at ________, and I am super laid-back and fun loving!"

Whoops. I mean:

> "I am a student at ________ i work ________ and i am super layed back and fun loving"

So far, I was not a fan of online dating.

*Chapter 4*

# The Disappointing Subscription

By the time I got home from school, I had twenty-seven messages from the dating website I had signed up for earlier in the day. I logged in to see why a dating website was sending me updates every three minutes.

After inspecting the various notification boxes, I discovered that I was the proud recipient of a collection of "flirts." There was a button on everyone's profile that said, "Send a flirt." If you clicked it, it sent that person a message that said, "Bob sent you a flirt!" or, "You deserve a flirt!"

Um . . . thanks? What was I supposed to do with these? Was I supposed to send each guy a return flirt? What exactly was the end goal of these randomly selected statements?

Along with the flirts, there were some actual messages. I tried to open one, but the website informed me that reading messages was a feature you had to pay to gain access to. I could see who had sent the message, but I couldn't read the message itself. That was sneaky.

I concluded for the fifth time that online dating was stupid, and I attempted to work on some homework. But the mystery of those messages kept pulling me back.

By the next day, I had enough unread messages to justify paying for a month of the dating website service.

With great anticipation, I opened the first message.

"hey"

That was it?! That was what I'd paid $19.99 for? That was what the modern man considered to be an adequate, well-thought-out message? What was I supposed to say back? "Hi"? Ahem . . . I mean, "hi"?

All in all, I felt like I wanted a refund.

For the ninth time, I concluded that online dating was stupid. Unfortunately, it was also more entertaining than homework. Every few days, I would get on and look at profiles, marveling at how crazy some of them were. For instance, one of the men expected his wife to bear him at least a dozen children and homeschool all of them. I wondered how many flirts he had received. Occasionally, I would completely cancel my account. But the very helpful site remembered all my information and would instantly reactivate my profile the next time I logged back in. The reactivation process was seamless; there must have been a lot of site users who followed the same cancellation cycle.

At the beginning of February, I was once again looking at dumb profiles. At the time, I just thought I was avoiding homework. Looking back, I am convinced there was a squad of angelic cheerleaders encouraging me to get back on over and over and over again. I had looked at so many profiles that I'd reached the inactive ones, which meant that the profile owner hadn't logged on in at least thirty days. This made me question my sanity even more seriously. What was the point of looking at inactive profiles?

I continued to scroll through endless screens of boring sentences. Oh, look, another guy who lived exclusively for football! A guy who didn't bother to write anything at all . . . A guy with a terrible beard holding up a deer head and a gun . . . Yet *another* guy looking for a partner in crime . . . A guy who claimed he shaved regularly . . .

Wait. What?

I stopped and read the sentence again.

> "You probably already know this from my pictures, but I shave my face regularly."

I glanced over to the side of the screen at the picture. This man had heavily gelled dark hair and a slight smirk on a clean-shaven face, as advertised. The picture was inconsequential, but a clever, properly spelled opening sentence with punctuation deserved a brief profile visit. I clicked on the picture and started to read the rest of the profile.

> "You probably already know this from my pictures, but I shave my face regularly. On a less interesting note, you may have noticed I'm in a wheelchair. I broke my neck eight years ago while wrestling a live alligator for a high school fundraiser. Okay, maybe I'm making that up. The wheelchair adventure has been awesomely unique and amazing! It's not a touchy subject, never has been. I get my own set of wheelchair jokes that only I can make. It didn't slow me down either. I finished my bachelor's degree, and I've been working full time for over a year now. I don't live at home, and I even have a van I can drive fully independently.
>
> What *is* different is dating. Experience shows most girls will not read this far after seeing my oh-so-attractive pictures. I love water sports and rock climbing and tickle fights and so on. I'm attracted to outgoing, active people who like such things too. I'm just not very good at them anymore. Wheelchairs offer cuddling perks though.
>
> I'm a social person, so I don't care much about what's being done as long as I enjoy the people it's being done with. I love going to movies, shows, plays. Playing games at home. Going on spontaneous adventures. Talking about everything and anything. I love the feeling of the sun on my skin. Any sort of wheelchair-friendly lake or hike type activities are great but harder to find. Cuddling . . .

> I realize no girl's childhood dream is marrying a guy in a wheelchair, honestly I'm not sure if it's a step I'll get to take (pun intended). I still love meeting people though. I'd be happy to buy you dinner anytime! (no rings attached!)
>
> I don't always respond quickly. If I'm being slow, or you can't send messages, my last name is Campbell. Practice your internet skillz.

I read the entire profile. Then again. And again. Did I really just find a funny, intelligent person who correctly used commas? I looked through the pictures. Corby was definitely in a wheelchair—a big power wheelchair.*

I decided to practice my "internet skillz" and typed "Corby Campbell" into Google. This new male subject who knew about the Shift key deserved some investigation. The first result was a personal website. Its design was old and clunky, and the only thing on the home page was an outdated music player and a playlist of about twenty songs. Apparently, Mr. Campbell was a singer! I clicked on the first one. The recording quality was not the best, but the voice was gorgeous. I pushed my homework aside and knit while I listened to the entire playlist. After the final song was finished, I dug deeper into the website and found the story of how Corby had broken his neck:

---

* *Hey, it's me! The awkward husband! We decided I was going to add footnotes. But my feet are crap, and I use wheels, so it made more sense to call them "wheelnotes."*

*As my first "wheelnote": At one point, I took all wheelchair pictures and references off my dating profile. But I didn't like it; I felt like I wasn't being fully me. Yes, the full me has some limitations most people don't have, but I find it's much better to accept them and work around them than it is to hide my limitations or try labeling them so they sound positive. As you meet me through this book, you'll find I'm unabashed about my circumstances.*

Here it is. The real story of how Corbinealious Brycetholomue Campbelliticus Maxiumus Danger the III (yes, that's me) became GimpMan.

Ever since I was a wee tyke, I've always wanted to be able to do a back flip off a wall. During my 9th grade year, I taught myself how to do a round-off back flip. A few months later, my older brother and amazing mom helped me figure out how to do a standing back flip. I honed my skills to the point where I could do seven standing back flips in a row. My junior year, I tried a wall flip for the first time and kicked myself for not trying it earlier; it was a cakewalk. The point of all this is I had been able to do a back flip off a wall for three years at the point I broke my neck. It wasn't a mistake. It was my destiny :).

During my first semester at college, I had a computer and networking sciences scholarship (yay for being a nerd!). 'Twas almost the end of the semester . . . I was heading to the gas station to buy a 74-cent hot dog before going to the bus stop to go straight from school to work. I decided to expel some energy doing some back flips off the wall like I often did. I was alone and out in front of the school. I did the first back flip just fine. When I went to do a second flip, I slipped.

I don't know how I rotated, but somehow, I hit the back of my neck (because a bone was pushed forward) and ended up facedown on my belly. I believe the first thing I thought was, "Oops." I tried to get up, but nothing moved.

I was probably there for less than a minute before someone came up and asked if I was okay. I told him I couldn't move anything, but besides that, I was fine. He called for help, and the next guy who came over was an EMT, which was nice. The school cop showed up and told me an ambulance was on the way. He asked if there was anyone I wanted him to call, so I had him call my mom and my then-girlfriend. The ambulance arrived soon, and on the way to the hospital, we stopped by Home Depot to get some screws for my neck (just kidding). Everyone felt at peace, especially me. I turned the whole thing into a joke, which was lots of fun. I was in surgery within 1–2 hours after the fall.

I broke the c5 bone in my neck (the fifth bone from the top of the spine), it bruised my spinal cord around there, and now everything below it can't signal from or send signals to my brain.

At the time of this writing, it has been 6½ years since I broke my neck. I lived with my parents, with my mom as my primary caregiver, for about two years. I spent most of that time learning to be as independent as possible. Particularly, figuring out how to sit upright since I was so lightheaded. I also started back at college.

After two years or so, my next step toward independence was switching to home health care. Also around that time, we got the modifications on the van so that I could drive it places completely independently. I could type my own notes and email any assignments to my teachers. I have no use of my fingers, so I used my typing aids. They are basically two plastic sticks that stick out of my hand. It's like typing with your two index fingers.

I finished my bachelor of computer science in December of 2010. School was difficult, and I complained about homework a lot, but it was totally worth it! I was guided to an excellent software developer job and started February 1, 2011. I'm still working there with amazing people who even have similar senses of humor to me. And I get paid a great full-time, salaried, computer-science wage. Note to everyone: Go to college.

Now! In no particular order! Here's a bunch of fun pictures!

A lot of the pictures were the same as the ones from his dating profile: Corby playing rock band with the drumsticks duct taped to his hands, Corby "standing" as he was held up by two friends, Corby dressed up as a roller skate, Corby wearing a life jacket, floating in a lake with a girl. Oh, and one of Corby wearing swim trunks. But instead of having his ribs showing, he covered them with a black box and typed the word *censored* inside.

That was my kind of humor.

*Chapter 5*

# Continued Research (Which Could Be Easily Misconstrued as Stalking)

For the next several days, I read a lot about Corby Campbell. I found his blog, went to the very beginning, and read every single post. He wrote about books he'd been reading, philosophical discussions he'd had with his roommates, and his irritations with nose hair. The posts I found most interesting were about girls—his frustrations with dating and his successes. Mostly frustrations. In the three years he had been writing this blog, he'd had two short-lived relationships. I had never met this guy, but I felt so bad for him. His posts when he was dating were giddy, and then after breaking up, he seemed so sad.

> I'm a big fan of the head nod. It's really nice to have some means of saying, "Hey, friend, I see you're in a hurry, so I won't make you wait for me to come all the way over there just to say hi. Instead, I'll acknowledge your presence from here without even moving my arms." Or even, "Hello, fellow classmate whom I recognize is a classmate but I don't even know your name. Let's share this moment of joint recognition with a head nod."

* * *

Dating can be frustrating. To me, "success" in dating means finding a wife. By that benchmark, thus far, I have "failed." Note that I don't really mind as much lately, despite my sometimes bothered comments about females. But anyway, it seems like there's no straightforward route to earn a wife like there is for buying a car or becoming a black belt. Sometimes, I feel like, "I've put in so much effort! Taken out so many people! Isn't it enough yet?" but feelings like this are based on the mistaken notion that after a set amount of general dating effort, I'll have earned a wife, and this just isn't true. Which kind of sucks because it removes the predictability. It's really easy to know when you'll be able to afford something.

* * *

So, you know how sometimes my leg will shoot straight out and shake around a little, then fall to the ground in front of my foot rest? Well, today it landed right on the off switch for my computer's power strip. Hilarious. But I'm moving that power strip.

* * *

I find it attractive when I see a girl use *you're* correctly. How funny is that? (Addendum, the next three or so times after this that I went to write *you're*, I wrote *your* instead and felt like an idiot.)

* * *

Showed up to work today with no shoes haha. Whoops.

***

Still pretty low on dating. I have an active run-around-type personality, so I tend to be attracted to similar girls. However, girls like that tend to be attracted to similar guys. Since I can't actually run around and play ultimate Frisbee or soccer or go hiking, etc., I can't seem to hold said type of girl's interest. So it feels like I can't have that type of girl. I also don't want to settle for someone though. Whoever I marry deserves to feel like I love everything about them. I'm not good at faking genuineness. Anyway, it adds up to feeling pretty hopeless.

***

A random thing I've noticed from having various CNAs: Different people put very different amounts of toothpaste on their toothbrush. I use relatively little. When you see commercials that put a massive chunk of toothpaste on the toothbrush, is that really how you do it?

***

I'm super cuddly. One of my favorite wheelchair perks is that a girl can sit on my lap. And we can go places without having to quit cuddling haha. I call it permacuddle. On that note, whether a girl can/enjoys sitting on my lap is, like, a big selling point for me with dating potential. If she can't appreciate fun bonuses like that of my wheelchairness, she probably will have a hard time accepting the not fun parts of wheelchairness.

***

I found his blog fascinating. Did all guys think this way? Or just Corby? It all *seemed* genuine.*

I closed the blog and started working on homework again. But I kept thinking about these blog posts. Corby had written an awful lot about cuddling. He loved it. I was in the habit of shunning anything even remotely close to a cuddle. My biggest pet peeve was old ladies who were incapable of speech until they had a firm grip on my elbow. And I hadn't voluntarily hugged anyone for years, not even my parents.

Despite this fact, after reading the blog, all I wanted to do was help Corby. He wanted a girl so badly. A girl who knew what apostrophes were and who could retaliate with wit and sarcasm. One who could challenge him at board games. On paper, I fit all the job requirements! I could be that girl for Corby, and then he wouldn't have to be sad anymore!

The next day, I found Corby on Facebook and read every single status update and looked through all the pictures. Corby had a lot of pictures, many of them had girls in them, and he looked very happy in those photos. He looked *especially* content in the photos where the girl was sitting on his lap.

I started to feel strangely jealous of those girls. What if Corby had a girl perched on his lap at that very moment and just hadn't posted any pictures yet? And if that many girls always hung around Corby, then why wasn't he married? Quite a few girls seemed to regularly post cat memes and cat videos on his wall.** Was that significant? Why was I jealous of these girls? I didn't want to ever sit on anyone's lap! But I wanted to make Corby happy. Even though I hadn't ever met him.

I kept scrolling through the photos. I couldn't decide how I felt about Corby's physical appearance. Corby used the word *maelstrom* in one of his posts, so he was linguistically attractive. But there was

---

* *Seemed genuine!? It was genuine! Head nods, dating, and toothpaste are serious business!*

** *Clearly, these friends understood what the internet is* really *for.*

something decidedly off-putting about the wheelchair. The pee bag strapped to the side of his leg was kind of gross. And he constantly looked like he was melting out of his chair. I supposed that sitting upright in a strong and gallant fashion was just not possible for those who lack functional ab muscles.

My obsessive, overprepared tendencies drove me to look up "c5/6 quadriplegia" on the internet. I knew a bit about spinal injuries, but I wanted to know exactly what it affected. I kept thinking about Corby's sad blog posts when his relationships didn't work out because of the chair. I didn't want to be one of those girls.

My process was completely illogical. It would have been more practical to find out if Corby a) was single and b) wanted to spend time with me before spending hours researching spinal bruising and how it could affect shivering—like I was actually going to go out more than once with this guy!

That wasn't going to happen. I had never, ever contacted a guy I didn't know before. Especially not in a flirtatious, I-found-you-on-a-dating-website-and-stalked-you-for-two-days sort of way. But if I *did* do it, I was going to do it right.

# USEFUL

## What Happens When You Injure Your Spinal Cord?

To prevent random interruptions in the story to explain various wheelchair things, I will instead throw in short educational chapters that you can easily skip over. And because this is not an English paper I am being graded on, I'm not going to provide references. I just know this stuff after hanging around Corby. Sorry to disappoint; I know everyone looks up references. I also apologize to readers with real medical training for these overly simplified explanations.

The spinal cord is encased in the spine, within bones called "vertebrae." The spinal cord is made up of nerves that carry signals—motor signals and sensory signals—between the brain and the rest of the body. Your brain sends motor signals down to muscles that tell them when and how to move. Your muscles and skin send sensory signals back to the brain—information about what you are feeling, temperature, pressure, position, etc.

Every spinal cord injury (SCI) is different. Some injuries are "complete," meaning there is complete loss of sensory and motor function below the level of the injury. Some injuries are "incomplete," meaning there is some sensory or motor function left. Some spinal cord injuries are caused by accidents, others by disease. Currently, there is no way to repair damage to the spinal cord.

There are seven cervical vertebrae (C1–C7, neck), twelve thoracic vertebrae (T1–T12, upper back), five lumbar vertebrae (L1–L5, midback), and five sacral vertebrae (S1–S5, low back). The higher the injury, the more function the person will lose. Injuries to levels C1–T1 result in quadriplegia or tetraplegia. Both terms refer to the same thing (*quadri* means "four" in Latin, *tetra* means "four" in Greek). People with quadriplegia have incomplete use of four things—two arms and two legs. Damage below T1 is called paraplegia because there is incomplete use of two things—the legs. Starting at the top of the spine, here is a quick breakdown of each level and what it controls. An injury at a specific level means everything below that level will be lost or impaired.

C1: Typically fatal. Most sensory and motor function will be impaired.

C2: Sensation to the scalp, ears, and upper neck. Muscles that allow head nodding.

C3: Sensation to the neck. Muscles that tilt the head side to side. Nerves at C3–C5 run to the diaphragm, so injuries to C5 and higher impact the ability to breathe; injuries to C3 and above usually require a ventilator.

C4: Sensation to the shoulders, upper back, and upper chest. Ability to raise the shoulders.

C5: Sensation to the outer upper arm. Ability to raise arms and bend elbows.

C6: Sensation to the outer forearms, thumbs, and index fingers. Ability to bend the elbows and raise wrists.

C7: Sensation to the middle finger. Ability to straighten the elbows and bend wrists.

C8: Sensation to the ring and pinky fingers. Ability to bend the fingers and grab.

T1: Sensation to the inner forearm. Ability to stretch the fingers apart from each other.

T2–T6: Sensation to the chest and upper back and movement of chest muscles.

T7–T12: Sensation to the abdomen and lower back. Movement of the abdominal muscles.

L1: Sensation to the pelvic region.

L2: Sensation to the upper thighs. Ability to move the hip muscles that control upper leg movement.

L3: Sensation to the lower thighs and knees. Ability to straighten the knees.

L4: Sensation to the front lower legs. Ability to move the muscles at the ankles.

L5: Sensation to the front lower legs and big, second, and middle toes. Ability to move the big toe.

S1: Sensation to the fourth and pinky toes, heel, and calf.

S2: Sensation to the back of the legs. Ability to bend the knees.

S2–S4: Functions of the bladder and bowel as well as sexual functions.

S3–S5: Sensation to the buttocks.

Corby has a complete injury, so he does not have any voluntary control or sensation below his injury level. C5/6 quadriplegia means that Corby damaged his spinal cord at the C5 level on the right side of his body and the C6 level on the left. He has no feeling or control from his armpits down. He cannot move his fingers and can feel only his thumbs and index fingers. His biceps still work, so he can bend his elbows and raise his arms halfway. The only big difference between the two sides is that he has more rotation in his left arm.

There are a lot of reasons why someone might be using a wheelchair that have nothing to do with spinal cord injuries.* Even within the realm of just spinal cord injuries, there is huge variation. Try not to make assumptions when you see someone in a wheelchair. Other people with Corby's exact same injury level are able to do different things than he can, so even the injury levels are just a rough guide. There are a ton of variables.

If you want to experience what it is like to be paralyzed, do the following: Make a fist. Extend your ring finger. Rest your hand on a table, palm-side down. Press your hand down firmly, and try to lift your ring finger. Fun, right?

---

* *For me personally, it's always appropriate to ask! Just say, "Can I ask why you're in a chair?" not, "So, what's the matter with you?".*

## Chapter 6

# A Singularly Useless School Day

I felt like my brain had betrayed me. Instead of focusing on very reliable, predictable topics, like homework, it decided to focus on Corby. And wheelchairs. My brain *loved* Wheelchair Guy. Could I be the one making him look so happy and content? Could I deal with the physical challenges? Was this something that I wanted to do? Would he need much help on a date?

I studied the catheter bag in the photos and concluded that he probably couldn't empty it on his own. And I assumed that he would need help with tasks like eating. That didn't sound like a huge deal. I could handle it.

I had invested a lot of time doing research on this guy. A very obsessive, very creepy amount of time—an entire week of afternoons and evenings. And that time couldn't be wasted. Even though his online dating profile was inactive, his personal email address was all over his blog. I decided to email Corby.

> So, a couple days ago, I was reading through dating profiles. (Okay, let's be honest here, I was really inventing ways to avoid homework. I can't decide if such sites are good for anything else.) Anyway, I found your profile with a very intriguing invitation to stalk you, which I simply couldn't resist. Because you were

> so accommodating as to provide free music, I felt obligated to procrastinate a bit longer, work on random projects, and listen to aforementioned music.
>
> Good gravy, you have a fantastic voice! I just had to thank you for posting those songs! I thoroughly enjoyed listening to them. Also, you have a delightful writing voice. That is all. Thanks again, and have a great night!

*Good gravy* was not a phrase I had ever used before. But Corby had said he liked gravy in at least one of his blog posts, so I thought the phrase would be appropriate. I had gone from being extremely skeptical of online dating to becoming a competent and desperate online stalker.

I tried to convince my brain that I didn't want to message Corby. It would be much better to *not* contact him so I could continue to enjoy just thinking about the extremely delightful blog version of Corby.

My brain would not be sidetracked. It convinced my fingers to type "Stalking . . . Not Spam" into the subject line. I was able to resist this evil new brain for nearly an entire day, but my weak index finger finally succumbed at 10:37 p.m. and pushed the Send button. The message was gone. I panicked. Why had I just sent such a forward message to a man I had never met? I gave myself several mental pep talks. I couldn't control what Corby did with the message, and it had already been sent, so I should probably just move on and stop worrying about it.

Yeah right. Like this new and definitely-not-improved brain was going to let me do that.

The late hour made me feel better. There was no way Corby would respond until at least the next morning. I had a few panic-free hours in which I could work on projects and not check my email.

I went upstairs to get a drink. My mom had fallen asleep on the couch while watching TV. The Olympics were on. I wearily stared at the screen while a few crazy athletes deliberately launched themselves off snowy jumps at high speeds while wearing sticks on their feet. During a commercial break, I glanced down at my phone screen.

No way. I had an unread message. From Corby Campbell. I couldn't believe it. He had already responded? It was nearly 11:00 p.m. Was that a good thing or a bad thing? Was he interested in continuing a conversation with a random internet stranger?

I tapped on the email.

> Well I'm happy to accommoda—Wait, did you say, "Writing voice"? I've never heard the term! Although maybe it was an accident. :p
>
> Anyway, I am totally honored that I could be so helpful in helping you be unhelpful to yourself! I think.

Hmm. Well. This message was not really what I'd been expecting. But what had I been expecting? Some super cute, long, I-am-dying-to-meet-you-after-reading-your-one-paragraph message? But Corby's message didn't have anything to respond to. No follow-up questions. Just a "you're welcome" written in a very appealing, conversational, properly capitalized fashion. *He used quotation marks and commas in real life!* Was this just a courtesy reply, and he wasn't interested? Or was he just unable to come up with any questions but was still willing to carry on the conversation?

So much for having a few worry-free hours.

After exhaustively thinking about my options for twenty minutes, I logically decided that if I sent another message and he never responded, I would know *for sure* that he wasn't interested. I decided to thank him some more. Really pile it on. And casually bring up an item that usually appealed to males.

> Yeah, didn't any of your English teachers ever use the term "writing voice"? And can't you identify certain people in texts without looking at their name simply because of the way they write? Everyone has one. You are very good at writing in an entertaining

style. Like joking about going to Home Depot to pick up neck screws. I was laughing at that one.

Oh, you should be honored! I even listened to you last night while organizing a bunch of duct tape! (That sounded really weird. I was listening in a very non-creepy fashion.)

The next morning, I woke up and immediately checked my phone. There was another email from Corby Campbell. I opened the message.*

My English teachers probably mentioned writing voice . . . but for some reason, it felt like a new term to me! The term totally made sense as you said it though. I have been sick this weekend, so maybe my brain is just short-circuiting? Anyway, I'm glad you enjoy my writing voice (ahhhHA! My natural inclination is to put the word *style* here).

Organizing duct tape!? Explain yourself!! Random connection: My company just moved to a new office, and yesterday, a coworker couldn't find some tape, so I let him use the duct tape that I ALWAYS KEEP in my backpack haha. Yeah, I'm an Eagle Scout.

Also I'm glad you've enjoyed my songs. The recording quality is meh, but it's definitely more fun to create something knowing someone has enjoyed your creation. It's not creepy at all. Can girls be creepy? It feels like a guy thing in my mind. I know I'm always trying to improve my creepin'. I've got a practiced

* *I can text from my computer, so it's super easy to tab over and text while at work. In fact, I text faster at my computer than I do on my actual phone. Plus, jobs are stupid, and texting is fun. So yeah, I text a lot at work (or in this case, email). But I get stuff done, too, because I'm a boss! Metaphorically.*

creeper stare, even makes my close friends uncomfortable. Oh baby.

Yes, girls can be creepy. I'll bet that if Corby were aware of how much time I had spent researching him over the past week, he would find it creepy.* I was planning not to reveal that bit of information. But my evil plan to casually mention duct tape to a guy who I already knew liked duct tape had worked! The blog research was paying off! And this time, he had asked a question, so it wouldn't be weird if I responded! I had a few minutes before I had to leave for school, and I had already gone this far. Maybe I should be flirtatious? How does one act flirtatious in an email? This whole "acting interested" and "taking initiative" thing was already uncharacteristic. I felt like I was being dishonest.

> I rarely use duct tape to actually tape things. I use it for entertainment. Lately, I have been designing wallets. One summer, I even made a dress entirely out of duct tape. It was cool, but I never wore it anywhere. Duct tape is NOT comfortable.
>
> Girls can definitely be creepy. Except I don't have a creeper stare. However, you should probably become more aware of stalkers and stop talking to random girls who send you emails and listen to your voice while playing with dangerous weapons, such as duct tape. Just a thought.

There. An I-am-verbally-avoiding-you-but-I-actually-am-interested message. Isn't that how the flirting game worked? I didn't have any textbook example problems related to the technicalities of flirting.

I closed my laptop, packed it up, and embarked on the thirty-minute commute to school. Halfway through my drive, my phone

---

* *Fun fact: I never learned about the full extent of Tess's internet research about me until I read the first draft of this book.*

chirped. I glanced over at the passenger's seat. I already had an unread email message. From Corby Campbell.

I completed my morning quest to find a parking spot. It was in the back corner of a gigantic lot, so I had a walk ahead of me. I heaved my backpack over my shoulders and started reading the email while weaving between the endless rows of parked cars.

> Woah! That sounds ductastic! I think the fanciest thing I've ever done with duct tape is hand carve a piece of redwood into a sword shape and cover it with duct tape when I was like 11.
>
> Thanks for your advice! I'm going to politely reject it though. We must learn more about the stalkers! We should probably take them to dinner!* (Depending on where they live.) Or at least entertain some email correspondence for the month.

Hmm. The witty banter over faceless emails was proving to be very entertaining. Corby wrote emails exactly like he wrote blog posts. I approved. But he had proposed going to dinner. In person! After only three messages! What? Could I ignore that bit? The normally functioning part of my brain was never going to allow a message like, "Of course! Let's go to dinner! As soon as possible! I want to meet you in person!" No. Even the impostor piece of my brain would not write that way.

I made it to class right on time and spent twenty minutes copying notes before giving up and responding to Corby.

---

* *Starting this correspondence was forward for Tess. But inviting a cute girl to dinner was easy for me. Where I lived, I didn't think girls were looking for noncommittal hookups with a guy in a wheelchair, so I could assume anyone contacting me had genuine motives. I know a lot of people are afraid of commitment, but isn't the primary point of dates to find someone to commit to? Fun is great too, but secondary. You can continue having fun with someone after marriage, too, ya know.*

> You like living on the edge, don't you? You take stalkers to dinner? Even when you know that they are expert duct tapers and you just told them that you always have some in your backpack?
>
> I live in the super exotic land of Bountiful. We have strange and wondrous creatures, such as squirrels and deer.

Bountiful is a small city just north of Salt Lake City, Utah. Corby, according to his Facebook page, lived in Orem, Utah. Driving between the two would take about fifty minutes without traffic. This was farther than I wanted to drive for a date, but it wasn't ridiculous.

My next class was much more interesting. I was so intrigued that I checked my phone for new messages only once every five minutes instead of every two minutes. When a new Corby message popped up, I skimmed the slide, and during the least interesting bullet point, I inhaled the email.

> Heck yes, I live on the edge! However, it's less risky than you imply. Even if I bought you dinner and afterward you used my own duct tape to kidnap me, it'd probably be worth it. Unless the cute pictures you posted on the made-up account you're currently using are not really you, in which case, when I show up, I can run over your legs and drive away. No one will even think I'm at fault. You get away with everything in a wheelchair! You see? I've thought this through.
>
> Hmm, I have Friday night open if you do, and I was thinking it'd be tacky to ask you on a date this way, but it's *texting* that's tacky, right? This is email! Plus, I don't have your number. Plus plus, it wouldn't be a date; it would be me buying you dinner and learning about you. For science.

We got a ten-minute break halfway through class. I pulled out my laptop and quickly pounded out a response.

> Since when did wheelchairs become a weapon to rival duct tape? You have an unfair advantage.
>
> What? You want me to give up on my fantastically exciting Valentine's celebration plans? Where I watch the Olympics and eat ice cream all night . . . while editing papers . . . ? Okay!

I had been talking to Corby for less than twelve hours, and we were already planning to go out. On Valentine's Day. I am sure the giggly girls in high school would have found that fact significant, but Valentine's Day was just a normal Friday to me, and it just happened to be the first Friday that we were both available to go out with each other. It would be silly to pick another day just to avoid the potential romantic implications. I turned my full attention back to class. For twenty-three minutes. At which point, I got another email. Class was almost over, so I decided to exercise restraint and wait.

> It's really only power wheelchairs that rival duct tape, and my kind have only had good tech in the past decade or so, so it's not really publicized how powerful they are. We also like to keep it on the down-low so as not to have to share our power with very many people. So don't tell anyone about this discovery, or something bad may happen to you. Accidentally.*
>
> Huzzah! It's a da—! Er, I mean, a research-gathering appointment. You'll be representing the stalker population in this study. I plan to interview myself as the stalkee afterward and contrast the viewpoints. I will provide my phone number, although we can coordinate over emails if you prefer to keep your stalker anonymity. You can also wear a paper bag for any photos if you don't want to be recognized in my article. Unless you're sure people can identify you by your collar bones, in

* *This applies to you, too, dear reader. Watch yourself.*

> which case, I'll just put in a random picture for the article and pretend it was you.

This was certainly the most fun I had ever had in a written conversation. I responded:

> Those wheelchairs are pretty awesome. One day, you will be able to teleport to Lithuania in one if you feel like it.
>
> I guess you can have my number, seeing as you have already figured out my name and could get a real picture even if I did wear a paper bag.

I added my phone number to the bottom of the email and sent it. I then answered some normal emails—boring school messages that I had to answer in professional, nonsarcastic language. I had scarcely finished when Corby's next email showed up in my inbox. Goodness. He sure responded quickly.

> If ever I got a teleporting wheelchair, Lithuania wouldn't have even crossed my mind as an option! It's a good thing I have you in my . . . day . . . digitally . . .

My last class was about to start. I crammed everything into my backpack and typed out a reply during the first few minutes of class. I hadn't been a very attentive student today. But this extreme level of socialization combined with breaking my usual patterns of ultra-studious behavior gave me a rush. I felt giddy. And anxious.

> Hey, if you ever get a teleporting wheelchair, I will go with you to Lithuania or Liechtenstein or Venus . . . wherever.

What? What was I saying? I didn't want to go anywhere with anyone! Who had I become? Why was I trying to be so accommodating to this man's dreams?!

I closed the laptop and started paying attention to the lesson . . . until I got a text from an unknown number, and I knew it had to be Corby, based on what it said.

Look behind you.

That was it. I was done paying attention. But this was an optional class, so it could be argued that paying attention was technically optional as well.

T: Don't tell me that you have become such a professional stalker that you figured out my address!

C: Fine! I'll keep it a secret . . .

T: Fine! I will go look yours up!

C: I've actually never tried such a feat. It feels like a morbid curiosity haha. I'm turning off my phone for a couple hours, though, so if you find me, you'll have to wait a little before gloating.

Okay. So maybe I would pay attention.

## Chapter 7

# Invasion of Impostor Brain!

Class finally ended. I layered on three jackets and a pair of gloves and went outside to my car. I turned on the radio and practiced responsible driving by checking for new messages only at lights. Red ones. But there weren't any new messages.

I parked in the driveway and slipped in the front door. It was late, and my family had already gone to bed. I retreated to The Zone.

C: I am returned! Did you get anything useful done? Or find where I live? Or discover any new cat videos?

T: I attempted some homework but still have a few problems left. I decided that I don't need to figure out where you live . . . yet. And I'm not a huge cat video fan.

C: Do you have any pets? Or did you have any growing up?

T: No, my mom never wanted to take care of kids AND a pet, so we never had one, though one of my sisters has always wanted one.

C: You've never had a dog or cat!? Triple sad! My parents have had at least one of each my whole life. And I believe that God sent them here to teach us what unconditional love is like.

T: Hey, it wasn't my choice! I had an ant farm once for about a week. Does that count?

C: Only if those ants were excited to see you when you came home and cuddled with you at night . . . mmm . . . cuddling . . .*

T: Uh, no. I cuddle with . . . pillows . . . and . . . that is about it.

C: *Picture of Corby asleep on a bed with a black cat stretched out right up along Corby's side.

T: That does look nice . . .

Did it actually look nice? Objectively. But did I envy the position of that cat? No. Saying, "That does look nice," is what I imagined the typical I-like-physical-affection-type girl would say. The kind Corby was looking for. But I still didn't understand why I was trying so hard to fit that mold.

C: You are welcome to try being in the cat's position sometime and seeing if it's as good as it looks.

T: Oh, it looks good.

---

* *In retrospect, it's quite embarrassing how often I brought up cuddling or the like. I know I was a bit starved for physical attention, but that doesn't justify being a weirdo. Oh well. I guess I didn't mess up too badly.*

WHAT WAS I SAYING?!

T: Have you ever tried switching places to lay on the cat?

C: Yes, the cat gives you a look like, "Seriously?" But he bears it for a good 15 minutes before he wiggles out.

T: Now here is the real question, Do I beat out the cat?

I had lost all reason. I didn't know who I was anymore. Anonymity was very, very dangerous.

C: Yes, I would rather cuddle with you than with my cat. But my cat is TOTALLY suave!

T: You really like making risky assumptions about people you have never met. I could very well be the world's worst cuddler, and you would find yourself wishing for the cat.

Okay. That was a more typical message. It was still sort of flirty but not as blatant as the ones the impostor brain had sent a few minutes ago. Corby was out of luck. If he tried to chase me down, all I would have to do to avoid him was find a staircase. Or even a single stair. I really had to stop talking about cuddling; it was going to set the wrong expectations for our upcoming date.

C: While theoretically true, the emotional aspect of human relationships tends to be more fulfilling than cat relationships. Cat relationships are just much easier to form and maintain. If there's no emotional aspect to speak of, chances are I won't be cuddling in the first place, so it's kind of a moot point.

T: You think about cuddling a lot, don't you?

C: Actually, I made up all the points above on the spot. I used to think about cuddling a lot when I had the opportunity a lot. But now I'm a stingy old fart. Now the question is, Should I call you? Or go to sleep and answer that in the morning?

T: Well, I will be up for a while, so it is totally your call.

Ooh. An accidental pun. I enjoyed a brief moment of feeling clever.

My phone started to vibrate.

It was Corby.

So I answered it. And said hi.

We talked for three hours. It was 2:00 a.m. by the time we hung up. I had never talked to someone for that long before. And I had never enjoyed talking that much.

Corby told me that he was a computer-science major (which I already knew from his blog). And he asked about my actual major. I reluctantly told him that I was in engineering, and . . . he didn't seem to have a problem with it. In fact, he asked questions about it. He seemed to be genuinely interested in what I was working on. If he was faking, it was an impressive show.

This had been a most exciting day. I couldn't wait until Friday. It was a foreign feeling; I was never excited about dates.

I finally managed to finish my homework, which should have been done hours ago. I knit a few rows on my latest project, took a very hot shower, and went to bed at 3:30 a.m.

The next morning, when I woke up, there was an unread text from Corby. We continued to text all day. And it continued to be just as entertaining.

T: Dear Mr. Campbell, We regret to inform you that siestas are not allowed under current company policy. Therefore, we must ask you to wake up. NOW. Any comments, concerns, or suggestions should be directed to human resources. We value your opinion.

C: Just 5 more minutes . . .

T: There are no snooze buttons in this scenario!

C: I'm good at pushing people's buttons.

T: Well, in that case, go smack the person closest to you.

C: Other than myself? And are we talking physical proximity or emotional bond?

T: Go for the person closest to you. By the way, I'm not going to accept the blame for the consequences of this action.

C: Mission accomplished. I asked the victim coworker if she had any comments about the experience. She said, "Well done," and I said, "To me or my friend?" and she said, "Yes."

T: I can't believe you actually did it. I grant you five more minutes of nap time.

C: HUZZAH! I'll save it until I get desperate . . . I was starting to crash at 11:45, but lunch was the boost I needed. They often say that bad sleep decisions catch up with you TWO days later, though, so maybe I'm in for that.

T: Well maybe if you stay up late tonight, the effects will be squared and not hit until the weekend.

C: I miss you too, babycakes.*

Babycakes? Weird . . . I stared at the text for a moment, feeling mildly uncomfortable. No one had ever used a term of endearment in reference to me before.

T: Did you send that message to the right person?

C: Yes. The bigger problem isn't that I'm a little tired today, it's that I have to wait till Friday to . . . to meet you? We should have waited until Thursday night to have a chat so the suspense wouldn't kill me all week haha.

T: Well, I'm always up if you want to call again. Or I could mysteriously disappear for 2 days, and you can pretend that the late-night chatting was a crazy-realistic dream.

C: Weird question: How do you feel about being dirty? How about being sticky?

T: I can deal with dirty. Sticky is slightly more annoying. Why?

C: *shrug* Just cuz I'm planning on pushing you into a pile of honey on Friday. (To show I like you, of course. Elementary school style.) Okay, I dunno. Cuz it's a question that came to

---

* *Intentionally awkward here, by the way.* Babycakes *is not standard Corby vocabulary. I think it's fun to say the unexpected and catch people off guard.*

mind haha. I'm also fine being dirty, but I hate being sticky.

T: Well, first, I will tell the teacher that you pushed me. Then I will write an anonymous crush note to give to my friend, who will give it to her friend, who will give it to you. Elementary school style.

C: Hmm, we may need more mutual friends for this to work. PS the teacher is used to my shenanigans. It won't really get me in trouble. What is your favorite food?

T: I love eating fresh peaches and ice cream. On the porch. Right after the sun goes down. What do you like?

C: You. *bursts into giggles*

Corby and I kept up our text conversation for the rest of the day. After he was in bed, he called again. But this time, we talked for only forty minutes, so he went to sleep at eleven thirty. Still irresponsible, but not *excessively* irresponsible.

After Corby hung up, I was so full of nervous excitement that I stayed up for two more hours, attempting to revise my discussion section to match what was taught in that three-hour-long lab class that I had *definitely* paid attention to earlier in the afternoon.

## *Chapter 8*

# Impostor Brain Hijacks a Date

*Valentine's Day*

After talking on the phone for several hours and sending several hundred texts in less than a week, I was finally going to meet Corby in person.

I rushed home after class was over and headed straight to the basement. I had an assignment due at midnight, so I had to finish it before Corby got to my house. I would have finished it the night before, but I had been talking on the phone with Corby. I felt like I was having an out-of-body experience. I pounded on the keyboard, only stopping to text Corby. Obviously. Texting Corby was most essential.

When Corby mentioned that he would be driving in rush hour, I offered to meet him halfway. Although I made it sound like I was trying to save him some driving time, my real motive for my offer was so that he wouldn't have to come to my house. If he came to the house, he would have to meet my family, and I hadn't told anyone about him yet.

> C: It would make us closer to South Jordan if we want to play games at my parents' after dinner, but a potentially misguided chivalrous bone in me screams, "No! You ALWAYS pick

the girl up!" so I'm not really sure what to say to that :P

T: It isn't misguided. It is attractive. However, there is an annoying lack of things to do up here, and I would still find you chivalrous even if you didn't drive up. It is your call.

C: Well, I'm thinking I'll drive all the way this time. If I'm lucky enough to do things with you often, maybe I'll let you help with part of the drive in the future :P Also, I keep second-guessing that decision.

T: Well, why don't you think about it for a few more moments? Either way we will get to see each other.

C: Logically, it totally doesn't seem like the right thing to do, but for some reason, I feel more comfortable about the idea of you coming down part of the way* (assuming it's no big deal to borrow the car tonight). Does that sound all right to you? We could meet at my parents' house, and we could go get food from there. Or I can meet you anywhere between?

Corby lived in Orem with some roommates, but his parents kept a bedroom ready for him in South Jordan, which was halfway between us. He frequently stayed there on weekends or when he was sick, since it was easier to let his mom help him than impose on his roommates.

T: The car is no trouble at all. As soon as I finish editing this report, I can

---

* *This was a* massive *debate for me, and in retrospect, it was obviously inspired.*

T: leave. And your parents' house sounds better than the back parking lot of a random 7-Eleven, though not nearly as adventurous.

C: We can always end up in a 7-Eleven parking lot anyway . . . OH! GAS STATION HOT CHOC—. . . er, sorry about the caps. I get excited . . .

T: Excitement is GOOD!!

C: Your PERSONALITY is good!!!!!!!1!!!!!one!!!!

T: ThaNk yOU! ! !!

C: *mental vomit*

T: That was sporadic excitement.

C: I should stop texting you so you can finish your paper editing, huh? haha

T: I only have three paragraphs left, and once I finish, I will submit it and get out of here.

C: The second-to-last paragraph is missing a comma.

T: Aha! You're right!

C: *looks at the word *you're* and heart melts all over again*

T: *blushes while finishing up the conclusion of the paper*

C: Haha I'm truly excited to meet you tonight :D

T: So am I. :)

I hammered out three more paragraphs, skimmed the assignment to verify that I had written complete sentences, and hit the Submit button. I slammed my laptop shut and yanked the lightbulb string. I felt like my hands weren't attached to my arms. I ran up the twenty-eight stairs to my bedroom, only stumbling once, and selected a plain, black long-sleeve T-shirt and jeans. I then added a black scarf. Good enough.

I proceeded back down fourteen stairs and entered the kitchen. I had strategically selected this moment. Mom would be busy making dinner and would hopefully be too distracted to think up any questions so I could escape. It was my fault she always had questions; I was rarely home at normal hours when she could ask any.

I tried to keep a neutral face. If I appeared excited in any way, she would *definitely* have questions. I was never excited for dates.

"Hey, Mom, I am going out on a date tonight. I won't be here for dinner."

Oops. I think I smiled a bit.

Yep. She noticed something. I was bad at acting.

"Are you going out with whoever you have been talking to on the phone all week?" Mom innocently asked.

Huh. Apparently, she could hear me through the floor. The Zone didn't seem as secluded as it had five minutes ago.

"Uh, yeah? But I have to go!" I backed away from the kitchen and ran out to the car. I checked the directions on my phone and pulled away from the house, hoping that nervous excitement didn't count as impaired driving. I felt like my senses were sharper than usual. I gripped the wheel and glanced in the rearview mirror far more often than I usually did as I inched down the freeway in rush-hour traffic.

I followed the GPS instructions to the end of a cul-de-sac. There was a minivan decorated with decals parked in front of one of the houses. The decals showed a man in a wheelchair rolling down a slope into the mouth of an alligator. I had found the right place! I pulled my car up to the curb and put it in park.

I studied the house. The front door was made of frosted glass. I could see the silhouette of a power wheelchair and the outline of a head behind the glass. Corby was clearly waiting for me. I was hoping to have a minute to calm down, but if I just sat there, Corby would wonder what I was doing. I tried to breathe. I couldn't tell if I was nervous or excited, but I was on the verge of bursting into panicked tears. What was I doing here? I needed to get moving. I climbed out of the car, locked the door behind me, and started up the pathway.

As I was walking up the porch steps, the door suddenly swung open. Corby was sitting in the doorway, his arms thrown wide, with a huge grin on his face.

He yelled, "You look like your picture!"

He looked up at me, clearly expecting a hug. I bent over and awkwardly put my arms around his shoulders. Corby reached his arms up and briefly rested his closed fists on my elbows. Then I backed up while experiencing a moment of panic.

What was I supposed to say now? I couldn't think of anything! Thankfully, Corby suddenly sped off down a hallway to the left, yelling at me to follow him. I rushed down the carpeted hall. Corby's chair was faster than I'd expected.

He turned into a doorway. It was obviously his parents' bedroom. I entered the room to find Corby pointing* at a black cat curled up on the corner of the bed.

"This is Gambit. Go pet him. Isn't he soft?" Corby said.

I had heard about Gambit many times already. I had never owned a pet, and I didn't particularly like animals under normal circumstances, but this was an unusual circumstance. At this particular moment, I was very grateful for this particular cat. I had been instructed to pet this cat. This was a concrete task that required no thought, and it would keep my hands busy so I would stop twisting the bottom of my scarf into a knot. I slid onto the edge of the bed, and since it was a

* *"Pointing" for me is really a general gesture in a vague direction with an entire fist, and only if the object in question is within the operable range of my arm muscles. I can't precisely point with a finger because my fingers don't work. But usually, I get my "point" across. Ah! A pun! Tee hee . . .*

waterbed, as I sat down, the waves rippled through the mattress and disturbed Gambit's slumber. He cracked one eye open and scrutinized me. I started to rub him. Corby delightedly watched our interaction.

Gambit was soft. I had no idea if he was more or less soft than other cats, but a statement of opinion was expected, so I delivered my brilliant observation. "Yeah. Wow, he is really soft."*

Corby listed the virtues of each pet cat he had ever owned while I petted Gambit longer than necessary. I surreptitiously brushed my eyes just in case a stray panic tear escaped. I was slowly getting a grip, but I needed to say more. A generic greeting and one statement about the quality of cat fur would not cut it.

After Corby finished his speech about cats, I stood and brushed cat hair off my hands. Corby swung his chair around and sped off down the hall again. I followed him past the front door and into an open-concept family room, dining room, and kitchen. We turned into a tiny hallway.

Corby precariously leaned forward to grab a long fabric strap tied to a door handle. I watched him as he wiggled his limp thumb around the fabric, trying not to lose his balance and face-plant into his own lap. When he had managed a partial grip, he smashed his fist into the door handle while simultaneously backing up and pulling on the fabric strap, swinging his feet out of the way so the door could open.

As soon as the door slammed into the wall, Corby swung his feet forward so the door couldn't close, then he rattled his way out onto a small wooden landing in the garage. I slowly followed. The maneuver was clearly well practiced and quite impressive, but based on the corner protectors and scuff marks on the door, I suspected that it sometimes didn't go quite right.

He rolled his chair onto a platform elevator while I went down the steps. Once I arrived in the middle of the garage, I watched as he held down a switch and was very slowly and *very* noisily lowered to the

---

* *But seriously, he was softer than other cats. I can vouch for this as someone who* has *pet many cats.*

garage floor. Considering the total distance traveled was only about three feet, it took a long time, and the elapsed time felt even longer as Corby decided to just look at me and smile while I tried not to awkwardly fidget.* I didn't know what to do with my face. Smile? Blank stare? Would it be weird to examine the items on the garage shelves as a distraction? I needed another cat to pet.

After Corby disembarked from the elevator platform, we headed down the driveway toward the van. Corby used his thumb to hook a key ring out of a pocket hanging off his chair, then he bit down on a button, making the side door slowly glide open. I figured this was his way of opening the door for me, so I approached the door. As soon as the door opened all the way, there was a popping sound, and a ramp started to inch out from under the floor. The timing was unfortunate, as I was just about to step into the van. It was too late to stop, so I launched myself into the air, jumping over the half-extended ramp and landing in the middle of the van floor like an uncoordinated superhero.

Great. Real smooth. Clearly, Corby had opened the door for himself, not me. Why would he have opened the side door for me when I needed to get in the front passenger seat? I should have just opened the door myself.

If I had possessed my normal capacity for logical reasoning, I would have walked back down the ramp and gotten in the car the normal way. Instead, I attempted to cover my blunder by yelling that the van was "so cool" and wiggling my way through a tiny gap between the passenger seat and a joystick sticking up out of the van floor so that I could sit down.

I'm sure I looked ridiculous. But Corby didn't say anything. He rolled up the ramp into the van and turned into the gap where the driver's seat should have been. There was a loud clunk as the chair

---

* *Shouting over the noise is ineffective. For such a small contraption, it's impressively loud. Looking and smiling is the only valid option!*

*Bonus fact: My neighborhood/church ward raised the $4,000 to buy this elevator when I first broke my neck, and serviceable people like that are the best.*

locked into a mechanism on the floor. Corby reached under the steering wheel with his left arm, slowly pulled himself forward, and used his right fist to get the key into the ignition and turn the car on. As soon as the car started, he pushed on the steering wheel with his left arm, and his torso fell back against his wheelchair.

He slid his right fist over the joystick that had hampered my attempts to sit down and pushed it forward to brake the car. He then used his left fist to push a button on a panel mounted on the door. A clicking noise accompanied the button push as the car shifted into Drive. Corby then slid his left fist over a handle sticking out of the steering wheel and slowly backed out of the driveway.

Once we were moving and Corby wasn't looking directly at me, I regained my power of speech. The drive took about thirty minutes in rush-hour traffic. It felt like we were talking on the phone again, except I was sitting next to Corby in a minivan. The driving experience was the same as if we were in a "normal" car, although Corby drove like an eighty-year-old woman, turning, accelerating, and braking slower than everyone else. He apologized for his geriatric tendencies and explained that because he didn't have any working core muscles, if he whipped around corners, the momentum would tip his torso sideways and make it impossible for him to steer properly.

Because it was Valentine's Day, all the restaurant parking lots were crowded. Black Bear Diner was no exception. The accessible parking spaces with ramp cutouts were taken,* so Corby drove around to the very back of the restaurant and found a regular parking spot where his ramp could pull out onto a sidewalk. He was obviously accustomed to not always finding wheelchair parking.

---

* *Those spaces next to accessible parking spots that are covered in diagonal lines are so that people in wheelchairs can get out of their cars with a ramp or so that their caregivers have a spot to assemble a manual wheelchair and transfer the person out of the car and into the chair. Those spots are not for motorcycles, or "I just need to run in and pick up one thing." It is incredible how many people I have talked to who have no clue what those areas are for.*

He used the steering wheel to lean himself forward so he could hit two buttons on the dashboard: One started the side door/ramp-opening sequence, and the other released his wheelchair from the locking mechanism on the floor.

I got out of the car in the conventional manner this time, opening the door and stepping out. It was smooth and sophisticated. I watched the ramp pull fully out, the end clanging as it dropped onto the sidewalk.

Corby rolled out, then bit on his key ring again. The ramp slowly disappeared back under the floor, there was a click, and the door slowly closed itself. Corby bit on a second button to lock the car door. He then leaned sideways and set the keys back in the little pouch hanging on the chair. It was a good thing we weren't in a hurry. Getting in and out of the car took a minute.

He swung his chair to face me and opened his arms with a cute little grin and asked, "Would you like a ride?"*

I was very, very grateful that I had foreknowledge of this possibility of physical contact. I knew Corby loved it when girls rode on his lap, both from pictures he had posted and because he had mentioned it multiple times in his texts and phone calls. I had even visualized this moment—although I hadn't thought it would come up quite so soon. Was it appropriate to sit on someone's lap less than an hour after meeting them in person? That seemed wrong. But we already knew each other so well! How was I supposed to reject that hopeful offer?

After assessing that both sitting on Corby's lap and rejecting the offer to sit on Corby's lap would be awkward, I chose to lap-sit. "Lap-sit" was less intimate sounding than "permacuddle," though I knew that was what he would call it. I needed the practice, and I knew it would make him happy.

---

* *I didn't always offer a ride on first dates. We had just conversed so much that it really did feel like we had already established an advanced bond.*

Although I had anticipated sitting on Corby's lap, I hadn't considered the logistics of how it would work. How was one supposed to go about mounting the knee of a wheelchair user? I had no experience sitting on someone's lap even without the obstacles of foot and arm rests. Trying not to imagine what it looked like from behind, I stood in front of Corby with my feet wide apart and sort of shuffled backward. When I could grab his knees with my hands, I sat down, collapsing back against his chest. He immediately wrapped his arms around me in a hug. I didn't want to seem too stiff, so I lightly rested my arms over his.

I was sitting on a man's lap in the middle of a parking lot. This was definitely the closest, most intimate thing I had ever, ever done with a male in my entire life. Ever. I had done it voluntarily. And I didn't completely hate it. In fact, if I didn't think too hard about what I was doing, it was kind of okay. I knew that Corby was happy, and that made me feel good inside.

This strange new impostor part of my personality was growing alarmingly powerful.

After a moment, Corby adjusted the speed settings on his chair and started driving down the sidewalk. I quickly lifted my feet off the pavement, but I didn't know where to put them. Was it okay to put them on top of Corby's feet? I was pretty sure that would count as playing footsies, and I was pretty sure that implied some sort of romantic flirting. I didn't want to do that with anyone, even if they couldn't feel what was happening. Also, I didn't want to hurt his feet. But I didn't want to get my feet tangled up in the front wheels. I decided that I would just let my legs dangle and hold my feet off the ground.

But what should I do with my head? I didn't want to lay it on his shoulder. That was a bit too cuddly. So I tried to tilt it at an angle that wouldn't block his line of sight.

This evening had already required a lot more decisions than I'd anticipated.

Corby kept a firm hold around my waist with one arm as we sped around the building, our heads just high enough to be seen through the windows. As we rushed past, I saw a few diners' heads snap to the side to look. As soon as we got to the doors, I slid off Corby's lap and held the door open. A waitress took us to a table, and Corby told her which chair to remove before he did a fifteen-point turn to get into the right position. I sat in the chair across from him.

Once we were settled, he started into some very normal first-date questions.

"Do you take long showers or short ones? It takes me forever to warm up after a shower, so I kinda hate them now . . ."

Ah, a question that I could answer; I adored showers. "Long ones usually. But it takes extra long if I have to dry my hair afterward."

"Ahh, hair—yeah, sorry about that. I know as a guy, I personally love when girls have long hair. But I also recognize it's a huge time chunk to maintain. If I were a girl, I'd probably go short hair for the convenience factor. I'm glad everyone doesn't think like me."

"My hair used to be almost down to my waist in high school."

"WHAAAAAT? I can't picture that!"

"I donated about fourteen inches my junior year, and I'm thinking about growing it out again."

"I think it would look good long. Oh, except hair is *expensive*! Have you ever seen how much it costs to get extensions? Yikes!"

Corby's only sister was a cosmetologist, so he probably knew more about the price of hair extensions than I did.

At this point, the waitress arrived with our food. Corby asked if I could help him tear his pot roast into smaller pieces, but he didn't need any help beyond that. I pulled the top crust off my pot pie and hoped it would cool quickly, then I stabbed my salad and took a bite as Corby continued our gripping conversation about hair.

"I had a guy friend with blond eyebrows, and he hated it. As a result, the first thing he'd notice in a girl was her eyebrows. I don't think I ever notice anything about a girls' eyebrows."

"I bet you would notice if someone didn't have any."

We continued our conversation in this fashion until we both finished eating. I scraped his leftovers into a Styrofoam container and held it while he paid at the front counter. He had the cashier place the receipt on his arm rest, then held the pen against his chest with his chin so he could weave it through his limp fingers. He then used the other hand to steady the pen while he drew a wiggly line that contained some vague *C* shapes. He kind of looked like an uncoordinated kindergartener learning how to write, but it got the job done.

Immediately after exiting the doors, he turned around and threw his arms open again. I climbed back onto his lap—this time I had to juggle a Styrofoam container of leftover pot roast—and we sped past the windows again, startling a new set of diners behind the windows. When we got to the van, Corby held me for a long moment, obviously not wanting to let go. I felt like my brain was no longer attached properly. I was voluntarily sitting on a guy's lap for the second time in less than an hour.

Based on our text conversation from earlier about meeting in a gas station parking lot, Corby drove us to 7-Eleven and insisted that we get gas station hot chocolate because I had never had the pleasure. He instructed me on the proper creamer-to-chocolate ratio and advised me not to taste it for a while since it was too hot to sample—a rule that he immediately broke and then regretted.

Since he couldn't hold a cup and drive at the same time, I put both cups in the cup holders, and we talked all the way to his parents' house. When we got back, we sat in the driveway and sipped the now-perfect-temperature hot chocolate. It was far superior to the cheap powdered mix I had consumed up to this point.

After we finished, we went inside, Corby ascending the obnoxiously loud platform elevator. The house was a lot busier than it had been earlier. Corby's youngest brother, Mason, was sitting at a card table set up in the middle of the living room. He had giant headphones on and was watching a TV show while simultaneously doing homework. He sort of gave me a half wave, then turned his attention back to the table in front of him.

Corby's mom, Ronda, was at the kitchen table, setting up a board game. Two other adults were with her: Corby's oldest brother, Ryan, and Ryan's wife, Charie. They had a two-year-old son, who was repetitively crawling up and sliding down the basement staircase on his belly. Ronda moved some chairs away from the side of the table to make a spot for Corby, and we sat down to play with them.

Just before we started the game, Corby's dad, Scott, got home from work. He asked if he could interrupt for a minute so he could give Ronda a Valentine's gift. Ronda stood, and Scott handed her a CD of one of her favorite singers. He formally told her how much he loved her, and Ronda giggled while hugging him. I was fascinated by this exchange, amazed that they would be so open in front of a random girl their son had just met.

Scott put some headphones on and sat on the couch behind Mason. The rest of us started playing a game called Lords of Waterdeep. It was unlike anything I had ever played before. There were multiple decks of cards and a bunch of colored tokens, and you had to make strategic decisions. I tried my best to keep up.

About a third of the way into the game, Scott got off the couch to make little snack plates. First, he brought over a plate of cucumber slices, silently going around the table offering them to everyone. After the cucumbers were gone, he retreated back to the couch. Ten minutes later, he got up and mutely passed around a bag of dried mangoes and again returned to the couch. He repeated the entire procedure a third time with a plate of cheese cubes, wordlessly offering the plate to me first.

"Oh, no thank you. I don't really like cheese."

The table went silent. Corby and his family were all staring at me. I had inadvertently offended a table full of cheese lovers.*

For the fourth pass, Scott made a pitcher of Kool-Aid and distributed cups to everyone. He had done all this while still listening to his audiobook and not saying a word. Clearly, his board-game participation only extended to regular snack distribution. If we had all been born 200 years ago, Scott would have been a fantastic butler.

Corby had a cutting board on his lap so he could spread out his own cards. When he needed to move something on the board, he asked me or Ronda. He was very good at giving instructions.

---

* *Super offended. Still a pain point to this day.*

After he won the first game, we played a second game called Puerto Rico. This game was a little more complicated than the last one, but I did okay. It turns out that my dating profile assumption wasn't a lie—I did like strategic board games! Corby was absolutely delighted that I could mostly follow along.*

After that game was over, Ryan and Charie captured their son and headed off. At this point, it was almost eleven. Despite the late hour, Corby led me into a small sitting room next to the front door, which was completely filled by a white baby grand piano, and had me pull a stack of sheet music out of the piano bench. I sat down and started sight reading while Corby sang. He had a gorgeous voice and sounded even better in person than he did on those recordings on his website.

In the middle of one of the songs, I felt Corby's hand on my back. He was making really light, intentional brushing motions. It took a minute before I realized that he was trying to pull a hair off my shirt, but because his fingers didn't work, he couldn't just grab the hair in one quick motion. He had to brush at it until he could make a big enough loop to slide a limp finger underneath and slowly tease it off. I found his touch very distracting and made more mistakes until he stopped.** I hoped he wouldn't spot any more hairs.

Corby and Ronda, who had been listening from the kitchen while doing the dishes, were both complimentary of my playing, even though I kept making mistakes. Corby procured endless amounts of sheet music from the stack on his lap. We didn't stop until after midnight. Ronda and Scott had both disappeared and the rest of the house was dark and silent.

---

* *Board games are an activity I can fully participate in, so although I liked them pre-breakneck, I have leaned into them further since. As such, I had taught many a person game rules over the years, and it's no idle comment to say Tess's comprehension was way above average.*

** *This was still less distracting than when Gambit decided he wanted attention* now *and stood up on Tess's shoulder mid-song. "Meow?" "I said, 'MEOW!!'"*

It was late. I had to leave. I clicked the piano lamp off, and Corby backed out of the piano room to the front door. I bent over and gave Corby a long hug in the last remaining pool of light before I went out to my car.

It had been a fantastic date.

# Chapter 9

# Stairs Are Stupid

*Three days later*

Throughout the rest of the weekend, I continued to text Corby. Monday was Presidents' Day, and I didn't have class, so Corby decided to leave work early so we could go out to lunch and spend the afternoon together. He drove up to Bountiful this time and decided to take me to Texas Roadhouse because I had never been there before. The wheelchair parking at the front of the restaurant was available, and I watched as Corby rolled down the ramp and onto the sidewalk. I opened the restaurant door for him, but he asked, "Hey, could you help me empty my pee bag?" and zoomed off down the sidewalk toward the corner of the parking lot without waiting for an answer.

The pee bag? That thing on his leg that I had seen in his Facebook pictures? I let go of the door and hustled after him, catching up just after he got his feet tucked into a bush. I crouched at the side of his chair and raised Corby's pant leg by a few inches. There was a translucent bag full of pee held on to Corby's calf with Velcro straps.

"Do you see that green lever? You are going to open that, but before you start, make sure the end of the hose is pointing at the ground."

I examined the bag. I could see the green lever . . . and I could see the hose. The hose was pointing at the ground. I squatted next to the chair and twisted the lever by 90 degrees. A thick stream of urine immediately started pouring onto the bark chips. It splattered a little, and I shuffled backward so I wouldn't get splashed,* and Corby started telling me a story.

"One time, I had someone at church do this. He turned the lever and then told me that nothing was happening. I leaned forward to look, and my right shoe was slowly getting darker. He hadn't noticed that the end of the hose was tucked into my shoe! Now I tell everyone to make sure it is pointing at the ground. I had my mom wash that shoe, but it was never the same color again."

I silently listened, trying not to breathe. It felt like the bag had been emptying for ages, and it did not smell pleasant. How much could this thing hold? I tried not to look. Corby was technically going to the bathroom, which demanded some level of privacy. What would happen if someone else walked past us? They would see a crippled man parked with his toes sticking into a bush, a woman crouching next to him on the sidewalk, the unmistakable sound of liquid pouring in front of them. Maybe they would assume that we were . . . emptying a water bottle into an ant hill?**

When the bag was empty, I twisted the lever closed and moved out of the way so Corby could pull his chair out of the bush. When he did, he left behind a nasty puddle. I logically knew that I hadn't touched anything contaminated. However, I *had* just participated in a joint bathroom experience and habitually felt like I should wash my hands. Unfortunately, the bush was not equipped with a hand-washing station.

Corby had sped back to the restaurant door like this was not a big deal, so I opened the door for him, and we were led to a table. Loud music was playing from a speaker right over our table, and my brain

---

* *I've been asked if I had prepped Tess on how to do this in advance, and the answer is nope! There's not much to teach, so I just don't overthink it. I ask people when I need help in this way or other ways. I'm sure I've weirded people out a time or two, but I like to think that if I don't make it a big deal, other people won't either, and then we can move on to enjoying each other's personalities.*

** *Surely a thing people still do, right? No? Oh. This is awkward.*

started whirring. Conceptually, the idea of a leg bag had seemed okay. Peeing was a natural bodily function, and the bag was just a tool to make it easier. I knew that touching that tiny green lever was perfectly safe, but I felt dirty. Did I want to keep going out with someone who couldn't go to the bathroom by himself? Did I want to water shrubbery with urine every time I saw Corby? I certainly did *not* want to sit on his lap right now.

After we finished eating, we got back into the van, and Corby wanted to make plans.

"What sorts of things are there to do in Bountiful?"

Ice skating? Required legs. Hiking? Also required legs. It was too cold to visit any parks, and there were no museums. Bountiful was not a good place for wheelchair dates. I would have suggested that we go back to my house to sing at our piano or watch a show there, but my house had two stairs up to the front door. Corby's chair couldn't get inside.

I had woken up with an uncharacteristically happy internal balloon. I was ready to have another amazing date with Corby! But the balloon now had a puncture. Air was rapidly hissing out, like pee escaping a leg bag. Soon there would only be a sad shrivel. The impostor version of Tess had run away. I was back to my usual, practical self. How could I have been crazy enough to think that a relationship with a disabled man was viable? He couldn't even get into my house! I wanted to go home, hide in the shower, and have a good cry.

Corby could tell something was wrong. We had been sitting in silence in a parking lot for several minutes.

"Why don't we go to that Michaels?" he suggested.

"What would we do in there?"

"I dunno. Walk around, look at stuff?"*

"All right, I guess."

Corby tried to find wheelchair parking, but it was all taken. We went to the back of the parking lot and got out of the van.

---

* *Yes, despite the fact I can't walk, I do often find myself saying stuff like, "Walk with me." But it doesn't stop me from teasing people if* they *say it.*

"Do you want to ride in my lap?" he asked.

"Uh . . . I want to try the back this time!" I replied, trying to sound excited. Really, I just didn't want to touch him. I had seen pictures of people riding on the back of his chair, and it seemed less intimate.

Corby looked sad, but I didn't change my mind. I placed my toes on the small anti-tipper wheels, then Corby turned his chair up to max speed and took off across the parking lot. I let out an involuntary giggle. Riding on the back of the chair at max speed was rather exhilarating! But it was bittersweet. This was the one and only time I would get to experience this because I wouldn't be going out with Corby again.

We wandered around the craft store. This didn't seem like a standard date activity, and I decided Corby must be faking an interest in crafts just to connect with my favorite hobbies. I gave him a tour of the yarn section. It was the aisle I was most familiar with because of all the knitting I did.

In the wood-crafting section, I showed him some cheap 3D wood puzzle kits. The pieces came in flat sheets, and you could punch each piece out, slide them together, and paint it after it was assembled. Corby really liked one of the sets, a large pagoda. I liked it too. He decided to buy it, and I lagged behind as he paid, thinking about how fun it would be if we could get inside my house so we could put it together. But we couldn't. I realized that I knew exactly zero people, besides Corby, who had wheelchair-accessible houses. Every house in my neighborhood had stairs of some kind.

We got back into the van.

"Do you want to go to my parents' house? We could build the pagoda there."

"It would be silly to drive all the way down to South Jordan just to bring me back here. Besides, you have that thing in Orem tonight. There wouldn't be enough time."

"What if you drove down to South Jordan in your car?"

"Then what was the point of you driving up here? I should have just met you there in the first place. Besides, I should probably get some homework done."

Corby sadly stopped trying to come up with new ideas. We drove back to my house in awkward silence. This relationship was over. Not that it had been close to being an official relationship. But it had had more potential than anything else I had experienced.

I trudged down to The Zone and collapsed in a heap in the middle of my carpet island. Why had this happened? Why had I met Corby and liked him so much just to have it fall apart so quickly? I felt like we had started off so strong, on the same level. But now, I was standing at the top of a metaphorical mental staircase, looking down at Corby, who was stuck at the bottom. And he couldn't follow me.

I opened my laptop and started looking for blogs. Surely some other woman on this planet had dated or married a quadriplegic and written about it. What did they do on dates? Was a relationship even possible?

I found a blog. And it didn't help my dismal mood. The woman had married a quadriplegic with the same injury level as Corby, and she said she loved her husband, but almost every single article was full of complaints. She was his primary caregiver, and she frequently wrote about being tired and sore from lifting him and then going to work all day, then coming home and taking care of him some more. She wrote about battling to get home healthcare covered by their insurance but then not liking the caregivers who were assigned to come help. She wrote about wanting to go out with friends or go to the beach but not being able to because the venues were not wheelchair accessible, so she went to these fun places by herself and reminisced about the freedom she'd had before getting married.

There were a few positive lines buried in the complaints, but the negative commentary far outweighed the positive. I did not want a life like the one this woman was describing. It wasn't worth it!

But was Corby worth it? I had loved talking with him, and our first date had been magical. Did I want to give that up so quickly? Would I just be cruelly leading him on if I kept going? I had spent hours researching quadriplegia before contacting him so that I could avoid this *exact* situation! But here I was, surrounded by little wads of soggy tissues. And it had been only a week.

A few hours later, Corby sent me a picture of the first part of the pagoda. One of his roommates had helped him start it. We should have been able to build that pagoda together. I loved those sets!

The next day, Corby continued to text me as he had for the last week. I responded, but not in a flirty way. Imposter brain was gone. And after reading that depressing blog the day before, I didn't want to talk to Corby.

I went upstairs to take a shower at 10:00 p.m., right when I knew Corby would try to call, and I "accidentally" left my phone in the basement. It was a long shower, during which I continued to stew over everything I had read. Afterward, I sat on the bathroom rug to dry my hair while reading a book, the pages held open with a brush. I ran the dryer until my hair was completely dry and ridiculously fluffy, then I sat up tall enough to see over the edge of the counter, where I peered through the fluff at my reflection in the mirror. I looked like a mutant broccoli. The effect was particularly grotesque when paired with tired, puffy eyes.

When I finally went back downstairs, I discovered my timing had been successful. There was a missed call from Corby and a text asking why I hadn't answered. Knowing he would be asleep by now, I texted back and said that I had been in the shower. This was not a made-up excuse. It was the honest, preconceived truth!

# USEFUL

## Catheters

In this chapter, I will provide some information about how Corby pees. If you don't care, go ahead and skip the next couple of pages.

The bladder has a ring of muscle at the base that pinches the bladder opening closed and holds in the pee. "Normal" people can choose when to relax this muscle, therefore choosing when and where they urinate. People with certain spinal cord injuries do not have this choice. That ring of muscle no longer communicates with the brain, so they lose control of when and where they pee. They must use a catheter.

A catheter is a tube. One end of the tube is sealed and has a rounded tip. Just below the tip there are a couple of small holes. When a catheter is inserted into the bladder, the pee enters the holes, travels down the tube, and exits at the other end.

Every spinal cord injury (SCI) patient has their own catheter program.

Some people do "intermittent catheterization." This means that a new catheter is inserted up the urethra and into the bladder once every few hours. They usually hold the end of the catheter over the toilet. After they are done, they pull the catheter out and throw it away. This method is supposedly the one that has the least risk for urinary tract infections (UTIs) since the catheter is inserted for only a few minutes rather than being left in and becoming a freeway for bacteria directly into the bladder. However, it can get rather expensive since each catheter can be used only once, and inserting a catheter requires working fingers.

Everyone who doesn't do intermittent catheterization uses a Foley Catheter. These catheters have balloons on the end. Once the catheter is inserted into the bladder, the balloon is inflated with some water so the catheter can't sneak back out, and it is left in for hours or days or even weeks. The end of the catheter is attached to a bag, and that bag must be emptied a few times a day. Most people strap this bag to their leg, but some hang it on the side of their chair. (If you ever go to a hospital to see someone who is not supposed to get out of bed, you will usually see a urine bag hanging on the side of the bed. They are using one of these balloon catheters.)

Many people insert these sorts of balloon catheters up the urethra. But some have a "suprapubic catheter." Instead of using the urethra to access the bladder, a surgeon punches a hole through the stomach wall and into the bladder, sort of like a giant ear piercing. The catheter is inserted through this hole into the bladder, and the balloon is inflated to keep the catheter in place. It works exactly like the other catheters; it is just inserted in a different place that is easier to access. This is the type of catheter Corby uses. When he needs a catheter change, I don't have to move him to a bed and take his pants off. We can access the catheter by lifting up his shirt.

Unfortunately, suprapubic catheters are the most prone to infection. Instead of being used for a few minutes, the catheter is inserted and left for up to six weeks. (We usually change Corby's catheters every two weeks.) Because they are left in for so long, bacteria have a huge amount of time to sneak up the catheter and invade the bladder. Corby has struggled with UTIs for years. He has gotten so many that his UTIs have become resistant to antibiotics. We are mostly in control now, but to prevent UTIs, he takes various supplements every day, he uses a fancier style of catheter with two balloons, I flush it at least once a day, and I give him a weekly ozone treatment. The thing we found that helps the most is a drink called "Urinary Tract Complete." The ingredient list looks like a witch mixed every homeopathic remedy mentioned on the internet into a disgusting potion. But it works!

Catheters may sound inconvenient and uncomfortable, but before these bladder routines were discovered, most SCI patients died within weeks because of kidney infections. We are very grateful for catheters and leg bags!

*Chapter 10*

# On a Scale from 1 to 10 . . .

*March*

I was sitting in an empty conference room with my lab partner, Matt, as we tried to interpret some results from an experiment we were conducting. My phone was sitting on my laptop in the space between the screen and the keyboard so I could see the screen light up. In addition to a nightly phone call, Corby had started sending good morning texts every day. I knew that I would be getting a message soon.

Sure enough, the screen lit up. I felt my face smile. Matt was sitting on the opposite side of the conference table. He glanced up over the top of his screen but didn't say anything. I tapped out a reply and put the phone down. A minute later, I got a response. I tried to fight back, but my face muscles betrayed me again. I felt Matt studying my expression. We had been silently staring at discouraging data all morning; smiling did not fit the mood in the room. As I thought about it, I wasn't sure if Matt knew that I owned a cell phone. Up until a month ago, my phone had lived at the bottom of my bag.

Corby sent a third message. I was only able to convince half my mouth to remain studious. The resulting expression was worse than smiling.

Matt couldn't take it anymore. "Who are you texting, and why do you keep smiling at your phone? Did you meet someone?!"

"Uh . . . sort of?"

"You 'sort of' met someone?"

I started talking in a rush. "I met a guy online, and I really like him, but he is paralyzed and in a wheelchair, and I don't know if I can deal with it!"

Matt was beaming. He looked proud of me for finally doing something that wasn't just school. "That's amazing! I'm so happy for you! And you can totally handle it; you should definitely go out again!"

Matt didn't seem to think the wheelchair was much of an obstacle. Easy for him to say. He was already married to a perfectly normal human. I had seen pictures. She was standing up. I'll bet *they* could have found all sorts of stuff to do in Bountiful.

I decided to ignore Matt's opinion. Despite his nonchalant attitude, the wheelchair *was* a big deal. I couldn't just go out again. I already felt like I was leading Corby on. I had been coming up with dumb excuses for why I couldn't go out since that disaster of a date, yet I still answered all his calls and texts. I couldn't help it. Talking with Corby broke up my otherwise boring evenings. It was nice sharing things about my day with someone who really seemed to care.

In our text conversations, Corby started asking me to rate things on a scale from 1–10, things like "How much do you like spicy food?" or "How competitive are you?" I started to suspect he had a list of these things saved on his computer.*

Today, he asked another one.

C: How would you rate yourself 1–10 on how romantic you are/like things?

T: Like a 1. Or maybe a 2. Maybe. I haven't really had the opportunity to find out though. I guess I might be an 11.

---

* *He did. He still has it!*

I felt like I *should* be a one or a two, but I did like watching old mushy movies, like *Pillow Talk*. My grandma had a lot of them in her DVD collection. Did watching movies like that indicate that I was a romantic? At least a little bit? I also liked imagining dancing with a future husband in the kitchen, another romantic notion. Maybe I liked the *idea* of romance but didn't know how to handle it if it showed up? I didn't have a lot of experience with this kind of thing. And I wasn't going to tell Corby any of these thoughts.

C: It doesn't mean you don't know for sure. Would you like to have a guy like the ones in the old movies you watch?

T: I don't know. Which guy?

C: Well, that's the question! I haven't seen most of these movies, remember? If you were to date a guy who was like a character in one of the old movies you watch, which character would you want him to be like?

I didn't have any favorite male actors, old or modern. I guess if I had to pick a meaningful characteristic of old male characters, it was their confidence in . . . well, everything. They just took charge of the situation, no matter what it was, and went for it. They saw a woman in trouble, and they just jumped in and handled it. They weren't always right, but it didn't matter. Like in *Pillow Talk*, when Rock Hudson just jumped in and picked up that silly drunk kid when he passed out on the dance floor, thereby getting Doris Day out of a very awkward situation. He didn't ask for permission; he just helped out. I knew a bunch of women who would have an issue with that sort of attitude now, but I needed someone who would just do things sometimes, because if they asked permission, I would reflexively refuse.

But I wasn't about to explain all this to Corby. Why did it matter what I liked in old movie characters? Was he going to try to force himself into that role? What if he tried to change to fit what I said, and I didn't end up liking it at all? If he told me what he liked in old female leads, I would start molding my own behavior, whether consciously or not. I knew this because I already had evidence. Corby had mentioned, like three times, over text that he liked long hair on girls. He wasn't harping on it; it just naturally came up in conversation. I was pretty sure I liked short hair better, but I had stopped trimming my hair anyway.

I decided not to answer the question.*

Late that night, I noticed that I had a voice mail but no missed calls. The voice mail was, of course, from Corby.

T: My phone must be going crazy. I had no missed calls. It never rang, even though it was charged, yet I had a new voice mail. I have no idea how that works, but whatever.

The next morning, I read this message.

C: Doh! You hadn't responded to my text in five hours either, so I thought something might be wrong with your phone. Whoops. I even tried twice!

T: Humph. Well, at least texting seems to still work. It must be the phone.

I wasn't about to reveal that I had deliberately not responded five hours ago and risk restarting that confusing conversation about romantic tendencies.

C: Next time, I'll text, too, just in case. It was also wise for me to go to sleep, though, so maybe it was a blessing haha.

---

* *I like to think that throughout our dating, I could tell the difference between when Tess really didn't have an opinion and when she just wasn't willing to share. At times, I would consciously try to press her to stretch; other times, I let it go.*

T: So maybe your lack of sleep is divinely causing my stuff to pretend like it's broken?

C: OR! You subconsciously knew you would finally be willing to share on an emotional level, so your brain subconsciously telekinetically sabotaged your phone to keep your defenses up.

T: Oh, are you in favor of that now?

C: Me? In favor of sharing on an emotional level? Always! Well, maybe not while I'm playing a video game. But that just makes for another argument in favor of playing less video games, not the other way around.

T: Well, whether you are playing anything or not, I highly doubt that I will crack anytime soon.

C: Which still confuses me. You were open our first 10 days or so of talking. What did I do to make you so closed? :(

T: Nothing. This happens with everyone.

C: You make it sound like it's outside your control :P

It *probably* wasn't out of my control, but I didn't know. I just knew that I had never been able to sustain a relationship with anyone—male or female or even my own family members. Once we passed the surface-level stuff and they wanted to know about my feelings and opinions, I reflexively shut them out and ran away. I'd thought it would be different with Corby, but the only thing that was different was that I was still talking to Corby about the surface-level stuff every day instead of *completely* avoiding him.

Maybe if the wheelchair weren't a thing, it would be different? But if Corby hadn't been in a wheelchair, I would have never contacted him at all. I would have just assumed I'd have no chance with someone like him. I had assumed that guys in wheelchairs would be more willing to settle for girls with communication problems and messed up ideas about relationships. I had already been working on these things a bit, but Corby wanted me to work on them even more.

C: Why not try with me? What do you have to lose?

T: I sort of think that I would be a mess for three days afterward.

C: I'd be there for you those days too. But I won't press you further today (without your permission anyway :P). Have you made any decisions on accepting/declining school offers?

I had been accepted by two different graduate school programs—one at the college I was already attending and one in Georgia. I was trying to decide which one to accept. I had submitted my applications in October, long before I'd met Corby. His existence was making my decision harder. Paradoxically, even though I didn't want to go out with him, it still felt like there might be some potential, so I was leaning toward staying in Utah. Also, I had completely drained my savings account to pay for my undergrad, so I didn't have enough money to move across the country. Since I had never lived on my own before, the only thing that I personally owned was a laptop and a bunch of old textbooks.

T: I haven't made any final decisions. If I could take the Utah professor and stick him in GA, I would definitely be moving to Atlanta.

C: Huh, well, putting my personal bias aside, I'm not sure what I'd recommend. Probably in favor of out of state, really, just for the important learning experience of being away from home. If bias is allowed, my primary recommendation is "in my arms."

T: Well, there are opportunities for out-of-state internships. And seeing how I will be all of 25 when I finish, I would probably do a postdoc out of state. Also, you are the biggest flirt ever.

C: *deep shameless bow* It's not like it works; might as well have fun :P

## Chapter 11

# A Movie-Worthy Kiss

*April*

Corby got a new job. He was offered a position at Vivint Smart Home as a software engineer. He was pretty pumped about it. Observe.

> C: VIVINT JUST CALLED TO OFFER ME THE JOB!!

See? Pumped.

That same night, we went to see Blue Man Group with CJ (Corby's brother) and Megan (CJ's almost fiancée). I had seen Corby only once in the last month, using my busy school schedule as an excuse not to go on dates. The week before this, we had gone to a comedy show with a huge group of Corby's friends. That had been okay. Being with Corby was tolerable when there was a concrete plan—something to watch or do that had been decided in advance and was reliably wheelchair accessible. That way we weren't just sitting in parking lots while I thought about all the things Corby *couldn't* do.

Blue Man Group was literally a group of bald men who painted themselves blue, played giant percussion instruments made from PVC pipe, splashed a lot of paint while they hit things, and did some silent comedy skits. They didn't talk for the entire performance. Or smile. They communicated exclusively through body language and eye widening, which was quite noticeable because their eyes were stark white compared to the thick, blue paint layer. The performance was on campus, so I met Corby at the theater. CJ and Megan had already gone to their nonwheelchair seats.

The performance was amazing. The music was fun, the blue men were somehow able to communicate effectively with nothing but eyelid muscles (a skill I was deeply envious of), and Corby didn't try anything sneaky, like hand holding. I had never held hands with anyone before, and I wasn't about to start now. He just brushed my arm affectionately a couple of times, which I found annoying but acceptable. At the end of the performance, a ton of paper streamers fell from the ceiling. Due to the piles of paper streamers and the crowd, Corby was stuck in his gap. While the rest of the audience slowly filtered up the aisles, I avoided any serious conversation by scooping up armfuls of paper streamers and burying Corby up to his neck. It was a glorious use of time. (For the next two weeks, Corby kept finding bits of paper streamers caught in various bits of his chair.)

Eventually, we made it out into the lobby. We found CJ and Megan and paused to take a picture with the ever unsmiling group of blue men. Their shiny-face lacquer was much less pristine up close, and their wide-eyed stares were rather disconcerting, but they didn't attack us while being photographed.

Corby's van was parked up a small hill, so he sped ahead to get out of the crowd, and I ran to catch up. When we got to the sidewalk, he slowed down, and we chatted a bit. I turned around to see if Megan and CJ were still following us, just in time to witness something I had seen only in movies: They had just been walking along, holding hands, but just as I turned, CJ pulled Megan in close and kissed her, positioned perfectly in the pool of light under a streetlamp in the center of a dark sidewalk. And it wasn't just any old peck; it was a serious kiss.

I had been feeling pretty good about being with Corby just a minute ago. We had enjoyed a great show and had happily talked about his new job. It had felt like an ordinary date with a guy I liked and had been texting all day. But watching CJ, who looked so similar to Corby, grab a girl and kiss her *standing up* . . . well, my doubts about

Corby wiggled themselves back into my brain. I had never been kissed before, but the only way I had pictured it was with a guy who could stand up. A guy who could reach out with a functional hand and lace his fingers through mine, not a limp gimp hand stuck in a permanent fist. A guy I could walk side by side with on the sidewalk while holding hands. I had never tried to hold hands with Corby, and I didn't see how it would even work. I was on a sidewalk with Corby at that *very moment*, and I was walking slightly behind his chair because I couldn't comfortably fit next to him on the sidewalk without getting my feet in the way of the wheels. Did I want to marry someone I couldn't walk next to on the sidewalk? Did the ability to occupy the same sidewalk square really matter on a list of qualities in a potential husband? Logically, it didn't really seem like it should be a requirement. But it felt pretty important.*

I shouldn't have turned around. Megan and CJ were adults. They would have found the parking lot without me checking to see if they had managed to find the sidewalk on their own. I'd risked the sighting of a happy, practically engaged couple, who both had fully functional limbs. Gosh.

---

* *The obvious solution nowadays is, of course, the permacuddle. But as you've seen, I'm already being too overbearing about physical touch.*

## Chapter 12

# Celebratory Ponchos

*Also April*

The week leading up to graduation, I was super sick. I spent the entire ceremony cursing graduation gown designers for not including pockets in their expensive celebratory ponchos. The only reason I wasn't constantly coughing was copious amounts of cough drops. Throughout the speeches, I tried to fish cough drops out of one side of my bra, unwrap them quietly, and then push the wrappers into the other side. This procedure was complicated by the massive and highly impractical poncho sleeves that flapped around and made rustling noises.

I eventually shuffled across the stage to receive my placeholder diploma folder, which felt silly since I was going to be back at that exact same school in three months (I had accepted the Utah grad school offer), so I wasn't sure what monumental endpoint I was celebrating. Afterward, I went home, choked down some eggs, got into my pajamas (releasing all the cough-drop wrappers from their bra prison) and collapsed for the rest of the weekend.

A few days after graduation, I was visiting Kate, my best (and only) friend, who had just gotten engaged. I was going to be a bridesmaid. There were eight people in the wedding party, and she wanted to have a meeting to discuss . . . mysterious wedding things? I'm not sure why she had the meeting. The only thing I learned was that we would have to buy matching outfits that hadn't been picked out yet. I wasn't sure why I had driven forty-five minutes for that terribly uninteresting piece of information, so I spent most of the meeting thinking about how Corby's apartment was only one exit away and how I wanted to stop by and see him in person. Between graduation, final presentations, and getting sick, I had wiggled my way out of three weeks of in-person dates, which made Corby sad, so visiting his apartment seemed like a good way to show him that I did care about him.

Since Kate had gotten engaged, I hadn't seen her very much. Despite calling her my best friend, I didn't voluntarily tell her anything. She didn't know I had a fake boyfriend who had been calling me every night for nearly three months, and since she always got way too excited every time I simply talked to a male, I decided to keep Corby a secret and let her continue describing her ridiculous bridesmaid-dress dreams.

I texted Corby to "accidentally" let him know that I was nearby, and of course, he immediately suggested I come over, even though he was already in bed. This sneaky approach made the visit sound like his idea, so I wouldn't appear too eager.*

I drove to Corby's apartment complex, and because I didn't have a key card, I waited outside while Corby called a few neighboring apartments to find a helpful person with functional legs. It was still kind of cold, so I was happy when some random guy appeared and used his immense residential authority to push on the door handle and let me in.

I walked down the hall and let myself into the dark kitchen. Corby started cheering from the back bedroom. He was lying on his side in the dark, his face glowing in the light from his phone screen. I went in and gave him an awkward hug, trying not to push him onto his back.

This was the first time I had seen Corby out of his chair, and he took advantage of the opportunity to make me sit in it so I could personally experience the luxuriousness of the FDA-approved padding.

---

* *Like I'm really worried that the attractive girl who has been avoiding me for weeks is too eager.*

It felt strangely intimate sitting in Corby's chair; after all, it was essentially part of his body. After a moment, I slid down and sat in the middle of the floor instead. I told him about the meeting I had just attended, complaining about the overblown nature of weddings. Corby had his own experiences to share, as he had been sitting in on similar meetings to plan CJ's upcoming wedding. And of course, Corby wanted to know what ideas I had for my future wedding. I didn't want to answer these types of questions, so I distracted him by asking if he had any ideas first. Corby, being Corby, had already thought about what he wanted for his own reception and was eager to share.

"My siblings think I should have a gravy fondue fountain at my wedding, with pot roast and potato chunks to dip in it. Honestly, it sounds like the greatest idea of all time!" he said.

"You could dip roasted carrots and onions too. And maybe some really delicious rolls? What would the cake be?" I replied.

"Uh . . . not a gravy product? I *love* angel food cake. Do they make large ones? It never occurred to me until now."

I couldn't help but feel like a daring rulebreaker as I listened to Corby's voice, coming from the dark bed, move on to describe his summer plans to go to Lake Powell. I had always been instructed never, ever, under *any* circumstances, to go into a boy's bedroom. But here I was, sitting on Corby's bedroom floor. In the *dark*. And he was stripped down to his underclothing! Sure, the situation was nothing close to what those responsible adults had been warning against. I would have to be *extremely* cooperative for anything . . . interesting to happen. But still, it felt pretty reckless. And for the first time since our first date, I didn't feel worse after spending time with him. I had crept down a single step on the flight of stairs between us. Maybe some progress had been made? I drove home, happily imagining what it would be like if Corby asked me to be his date at Lake Powell, just like those other girls in the pictures on his blog.

## *Chapter 13*

# Cheese and Bedsheets

*Yep, still April!*

I saw a graph today that backs up your opinion about hating cheese. Turns out that per capita, consumption of cheese correlates with the number of people who died by becoming tangled in their bedsheets."

We were having a typical late-night phone call. Corby often found weird things on the internet and told me about them when he called at night. On this particular afternoon, he had found a website that calculated statistical correlations between ridiculous and completely unrelated events. In this case, the aforementioned fact about cheese and death by bedsheet, which apparently happened to several hundred people annually.

Corby followed up his interesting fact with a typical Corby question. "Do you have a preferred way to die?"

This seemed like a sarcastic question, so I answered it in kind. "Nope. As long as it is slow, drawn out, and painful."

"Don't forget alone! Since there's nothing good about marriage and, therefore, nothing good about children, by extension."

Crap. Corby was going to try to turn this entertaining conversation into something serious.* He had cleverly repurposed his

* *Not premeditated, just on my mind with embarrassing frequency.*

graph about cheese and bedsheets into a tool to probe my feelings about relationships.

Corby was getting more and more frustrated. He had started asking me if we could be an official couple, seeing as how he called me basically every night. On all nonphysical counts, we were sure acting like a couple. But I didn't want to be in an official relationship. It seemed so formal and restrictive. Wouldn't Corby expect me to kiss him? Or at least hold his hand? Wasn't that the main qualifier for being someone's girlfriend? I was not on board with this idea yet. But I didn't know why, and I was trying not to analyze it too closely. Other than the fact that most of Corby's muscles didn't work, he was amazing. I had even given up going swing dancing, trying to get used to avoiding leg-dependent activities. I had been trying so hard . . . so why couldn't I just give in and say yes?

I was decent at holding conversations about light topics, but when it came to personal feelings, I was . . . reluctant.* Whenever Corby tried to ask me about things like relationships with my family or relationships with him or relationships in general, the conversation became pretty one-sided.

He would ask, "Tess, can you just give me one concrete reason why you can't date me?" Or, "Why did you build up so many walls after our first date?" Or, "Why do you have such a hard time touching people?" Or, "Why are you so scared of relationships?"

And after a long, uncomfortable pause, I would come back with the articulate, enlightening answer of, "Because," or, "I dunno." I strategically selected these short answers because I was trying to hide the fact that I was crying, and I could usually only manage two syllables at a time in a normal-sounding voice.

These one-sided conversations would last for *ages*. The current record was five hours—Corby hadn't hung up until 3:00 a.m., and for four of those hours, I had been curled up under the table in The Zone, holding my breath to repress sobs while rocking back and forth.

---

* *A hilarious understatement.*

I knew Corby was frustrated. I was frustrated too. Why did these simple questions provoke such a strong emotional response? And why couldn't I come up with answers? After these conversations, I would feel drained for a couple of days, while Corby would keep trying to get answers over text.

Corby had apparently concluded that my "because"s and "I dunno"s meant that I couldn't find anything good about starting my own family. In one of our recent phone conversations, Corby asked me to list just *one* thing about marriage or even just being in a relationship that sounded nice, and I had tried so hard not to explode that I hadn't answered the question. I'd silently wiped snot off my face for about a minute while holding my breath, and when I couldn't stand it anymore, I'd whispered a strangled, "I dunno."

I'd thought of a few reasons why a relationship seemed okay, but if I had listed them, Corby would have wanted to analyze my responses, and I would have never been able to get off the phone and blow my nose properly.

I understood why Corby was making assumptions. But I was still annoyed that he was interpreting my opinions without having all the facts. I felt like I needed to defend myself. "I never said any of that!"

Corby scoffed. "Okay. But you're hard-pressed coming up with anything good about marriage and need a long time of uninterrupted thought to be able to come up with even one reason. Does that not accurately describe our conversation?"

"The conversation, yes. But I can think of more than one reason. I just have a feeling that you are going to get a whole lot of additional interrogation material if I attempt to explain the reasons in the way I normally think about them."

This was more information than I had revealed in a good while. Corby was very excited. He loved it when I said anything other than, "Because."

"OHHHHhhhhh!!! So what you really meant was, 'Yeah, I can think of reasons. But I need time to find a way to phrase them that will keep you emotionally distant from me'?"

"Not necessarily emotionally distant. I just *know* that you are going to have a ginormous list of questions about these reasons, and I honestly can't think of any way to verbally explain some of them. How about I just write this list in my novel?"

"Are you writing me a novel!?"

"No. Just my journal. And it isn't for anyone to read."*

"Oh, Tess, if you could push a button and you knew with 100 percent certainty that it would magically convey to my brain the reasoning for these walls and insecurities of yours correctly, would you press it?"

"Probably not. It sounds rather invasive, don't you think? And not at all nice for you. But it would be nice if someone could explain myself to me in a way that I could understand."

"I'm trying. But it's pretty difficult to do when you purposely hide yourself or refuse to answer questions that might lead me to ask you about you."

"How am I supposed to explain something I don't understand?"

"By trying and not hiding."

I was sick and tired of trying. I already felt like I was trying harder than I ever had before—I had never talked this much before in my entire life! I hadn't expected that men would be this interested in feelings. I avoided feelings. And these types of conversations were not helping me feel good about having feelings.

---

* *Turns out it* was *meant for reading! I hope you're enjoying it.*

# USEFUL

## Stuff About Tess

Dear Reader: Based on feedback from beta readers, around this point in the book people started wondering if I even liked Corby. I did. I promise. It turns out there was a bigger factor at play that I was completely unaware of at the time. This chapter belongs later in the story timeline, but I've moved it earlier to provide context for my frustrating approach to dating. Therefore, welcome to the first and only useful chapter about Tess!

Out of the entire book, this is the chapter I am most reluctant to have people read. I haven't told very many people about this stuff, and when I have, it doesn't always turn out well. Some people argue the diagnosis, some try to discount it, and some people go too far the other direction and try to make all sorts of special accommodations. So if you know me in real life, please don't make a big deal about this. I am the same person I was before you read this.

In a few chapters, you will meet Jennifer, a therapist. Jennifer was the first counselor to ever suggest that I had either a sensory processing disorder or autism . . . perhaps both. This happened in 2015. As I write this, it is 2025. I have now seen several additional counselors and therapists. All of them have also said that I have a sensory disorder and that I might be on the autism spectrum. While I definitely have a sensory disorder, I am still not totally convinced about the autism angle. There are a lot of symptoms associated with autism, but I experience only a few of them. If I do have autism, I am the high-functioning, high-masking sort. So if it helps you to visualize me as mildly autistic as you read the rest of this book, go for it. However, it is also possible that I have something other than autism—the symptoms overlap with several other disorders. It is also possible that I just picked up some quirky behaviors from my environment.

The only way to know for sure is to get an official diagnosis, but I have consciously decided not to do that. I don't need an official label to know that I struggle with processing both sensory input and emotional reactions—to an extreme. The presence or absence of a label doesn't change who I really am. I have worked on improving these things independent of a diagnosis.

This chapter will dive into just those two specific challenges and how they impacted my relationship with Corby.

There is a lot of variation in sensory disorders. Some people seek out sensory input. Their brains underreact to stimuli, so they want a lot of noise and light and touch—abnormally high amounts that often disturb those they live with.

I, on the other hand, am intensely sensory avoidant—to an abnormal extreme. One of my therapists gave me a long questionnaire that confirmed this. If Corby is not home, I close all the blinds and turn on as few lights as possible. I don't wear certain fabrics. I use unscented cleaners and soaps. I avoid touching anyone other than Corby. Lots of motion in my visual field is exhausting and painful. When I go grocery shopping, I avoid aisles with lots of scents or colors.

I struggle the most with contrast in stimuli. For example, the moderately loud volume of voices in a restaurant is okay. But if a waiter starts crashing plates onto a cart, my brain starts to implode. Same with lights. If the light level in a room is constant, I do okay. But if anything starts flashing . . . well, it is not good. The bigger the contrast, the worse it is. I choose not to drive at night for this reason. I know that a lot of people find oncoming headlights uncomfortable, but in my case, headlights and electric billboards turn me into an unsafe driver. Even worse is when it is sunny outside, and I drive down a street with big trees or buildings; the sudden and repeated switches between sun and shade are awful.

Corby tells other people that I experience life the way everyone else experiences the first thirty seconds of a movie in a theater, when the bright screen and massive speakers assault your senses. You adjust to a new environment after a few minutes; I don't. I'm not sure if this analogy is accurate or not; I don't think I have ever experienced "normal" senses. But it is a logical assumption.

When I try to describe a sensory disorder, I prefer drawing little line graphs. The graph represents how you are handling sensory input. If you are at a family party and your adorable niece belts out a piercingly loud screech, no one likes it. Your sensory line heads up in a slope as you experience the unpleasant input. Maybe you get a little bit tense. After the terrible screech is over, you recover, and your line gradually returns to zero, and you relax.

My line takes forever to return to zero.

Let's say that it would take an hour for me to get back to zero after the screech instead of just a minute or two. Well, just eight minutes later, someone drops a handful of forks while unloading the dishwasher, and there is a loud clattering sound. Your line goes up and back down again. But my line hasn't gone back down from before, so it just goes up more. By the time I have been at a party for an hour, my line has made a picture of one-half of an Aztec temple, ascending in rough stair shapes.

Your line might be a little higher than average as you head home, but by the next morning, it is back at zero. Again, my line takes forever to return to zero. Usually, this means that I will be mostly useless for at least a day. Sometimes two or three days. The last time I saw a movie in a theater, I didn't feel "normal" again for three months. It took three months for my sensory line to return to a manageable level and for me to become a fully functional human again. I haven't set foot in a movie theater since.

While I wait for my line to come down, I don't just feel tired or emotionally depleted like an introvert might after going to a party. There are observable physical responses. When my line reaches a mysterious and undefined point, I will feel like I have the flu the next day. I have a thermometer that I regularly use to take my temperature because I legitimately feel sick. But my temperature is always normal because I don't actually have a fever. The feeling is just a reaction to the sensory input. Sometimes I stagger sideways and bang into door frames because I can't walk straight. Sometimes I drop everything that I try to pick up, like my muscles aren't responding properly. I almost always feel sore because my muscles get tight every time there is an unexpected noise (massage therapists are always commenting on how rock solid my muscles are, but not in a good way). If I have to go to multiple sensory-heavy events without recovering in between, the effects compound until I am a completely useless shell. The physical symptoms are so pronounced that for several years, we thought I had a terrible disease. We went to endless specialists, attempting to diagnose why I was so tired and in so much pain all the time. I have been tested for MS, lupus, thyroid diseases, various infections . . . The list is quite long. But do I have any of these things? Nope! All tests come back negative. My body just thinks that light, sound, smell, and touch are big, scary monsters and depletes all its resources trying to run away. Hilarious.

I usually don't notice any of these physical reactions happening in the moment. The negative effects don't hit for several hours (this is extra unusual—none of the therapists or doctors I saw had ever seen a reaction this delayed before, which is why we thought it was something else for so long). However, when the line climbs too high, the reactions begin right away, which means that I literally crumple wherever I happen to be. There are a few memorable times when I have bolted from someone's loud house, sprinted a block, and collapsed behind an electrical box, shaking. Or times when I have climbed onto Corby's lap so he could get me away from fireworks or motorcycles when my legs have stopped responding. If a fire alarm starts chirping in the middle of the night, I involuntarily curl up in a rigid fetal position, whimpering and shivering.

After a decade of hanging around me, Corby is actually better at recognizing this point than I am. He will suddenly drag me out to the van with no warning and no explanation. And I usually start crying and shaking a few minutes into the drive as my body starts to respond. He has become my mechanical service dog, sniffing out potential sensory danger and pulling me away from it.

Based on this book, you are probably under the impression that I cry all the time. This impression is inaccurate. Before I met Corby, I didn't cry very often. Did I cry because I was confused about Corby? Yes. But I think the bigger contributor to the constant tears was actually sensory based. Until I met Corby, I didn't experience a lot of sensory input. I have always adapted my lifestyle to avoid sensory stimuli without consciously realizing it. I never shared meaningful physical contact with a male subject until Corby came along. I gravitated toward hobbies I could do quietly in complete solitude: knitting, origami, sewing, etc. In high school, I would sit outside the doors of the "mean" teachers to eat my lunch because I knew those hallways would be empty and quiet. At home, I avoided spending time upstairs with my family, instead choosing to disappear to The Zone and do my own thing. I never thought about why I did that. But The Zone was safe because it was darker and quieter than the rest of the house.

So why wasn't it caught earlier? Because I hid in corners and did my own thing, I was absolutely no trouble at all. I was an amazing student, dutifully churning out perfect homework assignments. The adults in my life loved these behaviors and praised me for them. I never connected the dots until therapist Jennifer got me on the sensory track . . . and I only went to Jennifer after meeting Corby. Being in Corby's life exposed me to a lot of sensory experiences for the first time, and it was overwhelming. He wanted hugs. He wanted to do things with his friends and family. He took me to restaurants and plays and family vacations.

For the rest of the book, pay attention to the pattern. If we go on a quiet date with little physical interaction (like when I sat on his bedroom floor and talked to him in the dark), I think I can handle a relationship. But when I spend time with Corby in loud environments or with other people, I lose it and don't want to see Corby ever again. After a few days of recovery time, I miss Corby and want to see him again. That was the sensory line graph in action; I would build an Aztec temple over the course of an evening with Corby, then I would leave, collapse in my car, and interpret the negative sensory effects as negative feelings about Corby himself. But after being alone for a few days, the line would return to zero, I would feel capable again, and then I would wonder why I was struggling so much. The realization that the negative sensory experience of being with Corby was different from the way I felt about Corby was a major step in our dating story. As you read the rest of the book, it should be obvious how much physical stimuli clouded my judgment. Our first date was a glaring exception to this pattern, which is why we are pretty sure a host of angels was present, preventing the usual reactions from happening. Corby needed a glimpse of who I could be in the future, or else he wouldn't have stuck around as long as he did.

But, Tess . . . now you are married to Corby! Who is a ball of sensory input! Believe me, I know. Unfortunately, getting married ensured that my sensory line will never be at zero for the rest of my life. It isn't Corby specifically; any man I married would have caused that line to permanently increase. It is impossible to live with someone without experiencing some sensory input from them. But I choose to accept the physical consequences that come with being married to Corby. The rewards are definitely worth the physical discomfort. Just because I have this problem doesn't mean I can hide forever. And just because this is a "disorder" doesn't mean I can't get better at dealing with it. I choose to work on overcoming these challenges, and Corby helps me with that.

But, Tess, you spent a whole chapter talking about how much you loved dancing! And that has noise and touch! I know. I still miss dancing intensely. Dancing is the only instance I can think of where I liked the noise and touch. When dancing, I knew what to do with the noise and touch.

But, Tess! I have seen you before, and you look normal! I know. I spent twenty-one years not realizing that I struggled with these things. I knew how "normal" people were supposed to behave, so I copied them, not realizing what I was doing. I am still very good at behaving normally on the outside. One occupational therapist said that my coping mechanisms were "astonishingly well developed." I can't hide from sensory input, so I do my best to accommodate the inconvenient response while still living a meaningful life.

But, Tess . . . you seem to be overdramatizing your response. It is just light! It is just sound! Don't you think this is silly? Yes, I do think it is silly! But I can't deny the effect that these things have. I stopped telling people about the sensory disorder for a few years after a handful of people told me, "It is just sound. Get over it." That is like looking at Corby and saying, "It is just a little bruise on your spinal cord. Get up and walk." Corby can't walk. And I can't not respond to physical stimuli. I have tried, and I will continue to try, but it is likely some brain abnormality that cannot be changed. I have seen several therapists about it, but none of them have been able to provide any effective strategies. I have more tools than I did a decade ago, but for now, most of them involve avoiding the worst triggers in the first place, or simply acknowledging that my behavior is being heavily influenced by the environment.

My other nemesis is emotions—both happy and sad. I hate experiencing any emotion, and I sometimes have trouble interpreting the emotions that other people are expressing. Emotion has nuances, and I like clean, black-and-white groups. Corby wanting me to explain how I felt all the time was like trying to speak Russian, because I had never really thought about my own feelings before.

While I haven't been able to improve my reactions to sensory stuff, I have managed to improve a lot when it comes to emotional stuff. Did it take a lot of work? Yes. From the day we met, Corby forced me to process a bunch of emotions that I would rather avoid. It was a grueling bootcamp. Even today, he is still my emotional coach. He encourages me to express my feelings about all sorts of topics. After we leave a social event, he checks to see if I correctly interpreted the emotions expressed so I don't misinterpret what was said. He gives me little signals during group conversations if my responses need adjustments.

I still prefer being an efficient, emotionless robot, so sometimes Corby needs to explain the motives and behaviors of other humans, but with Corby's help, I am now much better at interpersonal communication. In fact, I changed so much during the first two years of our relationship that people who knew me pre-Corby and ran into me post-Corby would often stare at me uncomprehendingly. I was basically a different person. It was quite amusing.

## *Chapter 14*

# The Two-Stair Ascent

*May*

Every year for Mother's Day, Corby and his siblings all make a few scrapbook pages with pictures from the previous year as a gift to Ronda. It is a great tradition. No one needs to stress out about finding the perfect gift, and Ronda always has an up-to-date scrapbook without having to put in the effort!

Corby had asked if I would help him make his pages this year. Scrapbooking is a crafty activity and, therefore, something I knew how to do. My sister Rylee had several large boxes of scrapbook supplies she was willing to share. But scrapbooking is an indoor activity; therefore, Corby would have to come *inside* my parents' house. You remember—that house with the two stairs? The one that ruined our second date and triggered a huge wave of confusion? But it was time. Corby was coming in.

(Many people assume that it is easy to lift power wheelchairs up stairs. It is not. Corby's power wheelchair weighs more than 400 lb. It takes at least four strapping men to lift it. Therefore, when Corby wants to visit someone's inaccessible house, the best method is to put him in a manual wheelchair, or carry him all the way inside and put him on a couch.)

Corby pulled up in front of my parents' house and rolled out onto the lawn. Corby had a specially fitted, cushy manual chair. This chair did not fold; it had to be assembled. I got all the pieces out of the trunk and constructed it on the lawn. While I worked, he chatted with two of my sisters, who had been eavesdropping often enough during our nightly phone conversations to be familiar with Corby. They had even started drawing stick-figure Corbys in stick wheelchairs, having various adventures, on my basement whiteboard.*

After all the pieces were clicked into place, I dug some thick, rusty metal plates out of the trunk. Ronda had found these plates several years before and loaded them into the back of Corby's van, thinking they could be used as makeshift wheelchair ramps if necessary. Well, that day had arrived. I heaved the first plate out of the van, staggered across the lawn, and gingerly leaned it against the bottom step. I repeated the process with the second plate. At some point in the plates' history, a tremendous force had bowed them, so they didn't lie flush with the edge of the stair. Instead, after they clanged against the concrete, they rocked back and forth, making ominous rumbles.

The next big event was moving Corby from the power chair to the manual chair. I unbuckled his seat belt, put my left arm behind his back, and scooped my right arm under his knees. He threw one of his arms around my neck and the other around my shoulder. The transfer was technically successful in that I did not drop Corby, but I'm sure it looked ridiculous. I knocked Corby's dangling feet against the chair about a dozen times, trying to locate the cushion. Once I set him down, I had to rush to the back of the chair and pull Corby up by his armpits to prevent him from sliding onto the lawn. I buckled him in as fast as possible.

Now, lest you think I am some sort of body builder who can lift fully grown men, I will take this opportunity to tell you that Corby is extremely scrawny. He weighs only about 100 pounds. Do not be impressed.**

---

* *These pictures were often shared with me via text. They were delightful.*

** *The hospital taught me a fancy way to transfer that's better for my helper's back if they do it right, or there are assistive accessories, like a slide board, that can help. However, it felt like these special tools, with just my instruction, were harder on people's bodies than just picking*

Next, I pushed Corby's power chair back into the van for safekeeping. The chair was so heavy that I had to lean my entire weight against the handles to get it moving.

All the preparations had been completed. It was time. Corby's life was in my very incapable hands. My sisters watched from the lawn, waiting to witness any catastrophes. The incline was steep, and the wheels were nearly flat; it was going to be a rough ride. I lined the chair up, got some momentum going across the bumpy lawn, resolutely rammed the chair into the plates, and hoped the chair wouldn't tip sideways. The plates extended about an inch above the step, so when the chair got to the top of the plates, the weight of the chair lifted the bottom of the plates off the ground. When the chair dropped onto the cement, the plates crashed back down, making a very loud clang. But we had made it halfway! Corby was now sitting on a tiny patio, barely big enough for the chair. I twisted the chair sideways so I could get the ramps up to the second step. One by one, I lifted them into place, squeezing around the chair.*

I twisted Corby's chair around to face the door. The back wheels were barely gripping the edge of the first step, and I had to tip the chair backward to swing Corby's feet over the sides of the plates. I lined the wheels up and then bumped Corby into the house, making another loud clang, the noise amplified in the confines of the porch. But Corby had made it! We had survived the terrifying fourteen-inch ascent!

I slowly followed Corby as he made his way back to the kitchen. My mom greeted him and then proceeded to herd my five interested siblings into the computer room. My siblings ranged in age from

---

*me up with one arm under my knees and one arm behind my back. This only works because I'm super skinny; it's definitely something I'm grateful for. Asking for help with transfers is just another thing I do when I need it, and it is fine if people refuse if they don't feel comfortable trying it.*

* *Fun fact: if we'd had one of her parents help, we probably could have gotten me in way easier by not using ramps. I don't know why we did it this way for as long as we did.*

eighteen to just five years old, and I never brought dates to the house, so Corby was a major attraction.

I thought I was done lifting Corby, at least for a few hours, but all the transfers had made him more lightheaded than usual, and he needed to get onto the couch so he could recline.* So we got to do another transfer! The couch was a much bigger target though, and it didn't matter that he tipped over sideways as I dragged him over the armrest.

Corby wanted to watch an old movie so he could familiarize himself with my favorite eras. I chose *Charade*, with Audrey Hepburn and Cary Grant. Compared to the other movies I had seen, it was one of the scariest. I inserted the DVD and sat on the couch section next to Corby's couch section. But he wanted to snuggle, or at least have some form of physical contact. He spent the duration of the opening credits slowly urging me over the cushion line until we were sitting right next to each other, with our shoulders touching. I wanted to retreat, but I forced myself to stay. I needed to practice.

Halfway into the movie, I leaned forward to grab the remote, and Corby seized the opportunity to fling his arm around my shoulders. He had to fling it since his muscles didn't let him slowly stretch his arm up and over the back of a couch. He had to defy gravity and aim well. He almost hit me in the face. I sort of stiffly leaned into his bony shoulder, and his arm sort of flopped down my back. It was not comfortable at all, but I didn't want to annoy Corby by shifting around a bunch. I turned into a statue until the movie was over.

After lifting his floppy body several times and then enduring this scrawny snuggle, Corby seemed so weak and incapable. But I pushed those thoughts away. Logically, I knew I was just scared of snuggling. I had to keep going.

Corby didn't let go after the movie ended. He gave me a skeptical look. "Is that seriously the scariest movie you have seen?"

"Uh . . . yeah?"

---

* *This was not a cuddle trap! In my power chair, I can recline a little at all times, and it makes all the difference. In my manual chair, I'm stuck fully upright and become lightheaded much more easily.*

He started laughing, and I couldn't figure out why. It was a murder mystery. They had found a body in a bathtub! I guess it didn't seem as scary when watching it upstairs in the middle of the afternoon, but at midnight in The Zone, it had seemed pretty creepy. (Corby has since introduced me to movies that are actually scary. In comparison, *Charade* is admittedly rather corny. But I still like it.)

Corby reluctantly let me get him off the couch and back into his chair. (Prying a paralyzed person out of the depths of a couch is not an easy task. Even if the person is super skinny.) I was aware that my mom was not-so-discreetly observing this interaction from the kitchen, and I wanted to look like I knew what I was doing. I failed. I half lifted, half dragged Corby over the couch arm and got his torso leaned against the side of the chair. His legs trailed behind, ensuring that I had something to trip over. I couldn't manage to get a decent hold on the twitching legs, so I tugged on Corby's pants, twisting them horribly. After the wrestling match was over, I was mostly victorious. Corby had made it into the chair. His clothes were all crumpled, and he was sort of tipped to one side, but he was buckled in!

Once he was up and sitting next to the table, my siblings were released into the dining room. Rylee opened her scrapbook paper boxes, and we spread everything across the table. Ivy (the five-year-old) had a grand old time trying to convince us to use cute stickers of kittens and butterflies. Rylee, Eric, and Kyle went through the rest of the stickers and suggested farfetched ways to make Corby's pictures work with stickers that said things like "Grandma time" or "Baby on Board." And Mom asked Corby questions about his family over the kitchen counter while she made dinner. I was glad Corby was so laid-back. He didn't seem to mind the family involvement. He just kept talking to everyone while I cut the photos apart.

Among Corby's photos from the past year, there was a picture of me—the one we had taken at the Blue Man performance. It felt weird gluing my picture onto a scrapbook page that was going to be given to Ronda. It made our relationship seem more serious, and I wasn't sure I wanted to be in a relationship at all, especially after today.

After dinner was over, the giant front-porch adventure had to be revisited so Corby could get home. This time, I slid Corby's chair down the steep, shaky ramps while I used every arm muscle I possessed to resist gravity. I unlocked the van and heaved the ramps back into the trunk one at a time, only smashing a few fingers. I got Corby into his power chair and took the manual chair apart. I was grateful to hide my face in the trunk while I wedged the pieces inside. It had been a long day, even harder than I had thought it would be.

I just wanted Corby to leave.

After he drove off, I took a very long, hot shower and contemplated what had just happened. On one hand, Corby got along with my family really well. We had proved that it was *technically* possible for Corby to visit my house. *However.* If we were going to do that workout routine every time he wanted to come inside, I was not on board. The effort was not worth it for any visit lasting less than six and a half hours. If it had been winter, I wasn't sure I would have been able to balance frozen iron slabs against an icy porch and push the wheelchair inside without slipping.

If we got married, would we ever be able to easily drop by and visit my family? And not just my family. I thought about the houses I regularly visited, and every single one of them had stairs! By the end of my shower, I concluded that if I chose Corby, I would be choosing to never visit anyone ever again. This conclusion was extreme, but those heavy ramps had dealt my fragile optimism a decent blow. And lifting Corby had been harder than I had expected. How much of his care would I need to take on if we were living together? Would I even be physically capable of doing it?

The future was bleak. My brain constructed a few stairs at the top of my mental staircase, and I backed away from Corby even further. Today, he was sitting in a manual chair, his cute little hopeful face staring up at me. I couldn't make eye contact with him, even though it was imaginary Corby, so I just stared down at the imaginary carpet and tried to convince my brain to stop imagining things so I could go to sleep.

## Chapter 15

# And I Would Drive 300 Miles, and I Did Drive 300 More

*June*

I was avoiding Corby. I had seen him only once since our ramp adventure, and that had been three weeks ago. He still texted me every day, but he had skipped a couple of our nightly phone calls, and I knew he had taken a few other girls out on dates. I was simultaneously relieved and distressed. I really liked Corby some days, and other days, I didn't want to message him or talk to him. I couldn't figure out why.

Corby's family vacation to Lake Powell was in a week. He had asked multiple times if I wanted to go, but I kept saying that I wasn't sure if I could make it. It seemed strange to go on a family vacation with a guy I wasn't dating. And I didn't know if I could spend a solid week with Corby without going crazy. But . . . I didn't want Corby to be lonely, vacationing with his married and engaged siblings. He thought a week-long vacation would help me decide if I wanted a serious relationship or not.

Getting out of the basement did sound lovely. My summer job hadn't started yet, and Corby knew it, so he kept asking. And I kept coming up with weak excuses.

In the meantime, my family took a summer trip to Las Vegas. Confusing thoughts about Corby occupied my mind for the entire seven-hour drive. When we arrived at the hotel, I volunteered to take the couch bed. Although it was incredibly uncomfortable, it was in a separate room from everyone else.

The pool made up for the serious shortcomings of the couch bed—it was the best pool I'd ever seen, with a super-long lazy river that I could float down while wedged in an inner tube. We went to the pool every day. As I floated in endless circles by myself, I tried not to think about how such an activity would be impossible with Corby. Well, not impossible but much more difficult. Going around a lazy river would be much less lazy if I were trying to keep a limp quadriplegic from falling through his inner tube and drowning. And I didn't even want to contemplate how much work it would be to get a wet, slippery Corby out of a pool. I decided yet again that dating Corby was a bad idea. I wanted more of this lazy river in my future.

But wasn't Corby more important than a pool?

On Friday, Corby sent me a text.

C: . . . Tess?

T: . . . Hmmm?

C: Do you have 15 private minutes I could call sometime today? Before 5:00?

T: Ooh, you must have a date tonight! We are about to go to some pinball museum. There should be a few minutes in between that and another trip to that lovely pool, but I don't know when that will be.

C: I do have a date. Call me when you can :D. If I don't answer, I'll call you back within a few minutes.

T: Why is this particular call so important?

C: Seeecreet. Wow, that word looks weird when stretched out.

T: A secret? What topic of secret?

C: I can text you about it if you insist. I just thought it'd be easier to discuss with real-time response. You prefer written, though, huh?

T: Maybe if I knew what the subject was I would be able to tell you.

C: You'll possibly be annoyed with the topic.

T: Well, what is it?

C: Haha, ok. Is there a chance we can get you to Powell? Are you willing to look for solutions rather than just the issues? Or is it just my wishful thinking, and it's still not something you think worth pursuing? I wanted it to be a phone call cuz your knee-jerk response seems to be coming up with a few excuses that I can easily shoot down first. Think about it. I will call you later tonight.

I needed to make a decision. I started making a list in my head. It didn't take long; there were only two options: 1) Go on a week-long boating trip with a guy I didn't even want to talk to sometimes—a phenomenon that I could not figure out. 2) Sit in a boring basement and go to campus for a meeting.

Ugh. The basement and campus did not sound appealing *at all*. This decision should be so easy! So why was it so difficult?

Late that night, I was sitting on the tiny hotel balcony by myself, staring out at all the lights in Las Vegas. My phone started buzzing, signifying an incoming call.

"How was the pinball museum?" Corby asked.

"Better than I thought it would be. There were a bunch of old arcade machines, so we each got a stack of nickels and tried them all. Eric loved it. How was the date?"

"Fine, I guess. I probably won't take her out again."

"That bad, huh?"

"It doesn't matter. Can we talk about Powell?"

"I guess."

"I just wanted to make something clear: You know that if you go to Powell with me, I'm not expecting a relationship, right?"

Just hearing him say that sentence so directly made me realize just *how* worried I was about that very issue. Going to Powell suddenly became more appealing.

"I guess so. But won't your family think it is weird if you just bring a random girl?"

"My family won't think anything of it! I have brought three other girls before who were just friends. CJ brought a nongirlfriend once. All my brothers have brought friends-who-were-girls before, and no one has ever said anything. They just want to have fun, and we always bring extras. In fact, this year, it will be smaller than usual since two of my sisters-in-law are staying home with their newborns."

Corby kept talking about his family and how they would love to have me there. Especially his mom. He reassured me that it was not too late to join and that he really did want me to come.

"What else is worrying you? You can tell me anything. It's easier to talk about things than hide them."

I silently stared out at the lights, trying not to cry. I made a mental note to do an internet search on whether there was some sort of tear duct removal surgery. I still didn't understand why simply talking to another human about my opinions had this effect on me. Corby loved it when I said anything personal, and he was one of the least judgmental people I had ever met. I needed to practice.

I covered the bottom of the phone and took a deep breath, trying to steady my voice before talking. I got up from my chair and started pacing the tiny balcony like a caged animal. "I am worried about how much you like physical touch. I just really have a hard time when you brush my arm and try to give me back scratches."

There. I successfully said something meaningful and potentially dangerous! I covered the bottom of the phone again to hide my ragged, frantic breathing. I crouched down in a tiny ball, pressing up against the corner of the railing, and put all my mental effort into not dropping the phone. My muscles didn't seem to want to obey.

"Oh, Tess. If that is the only reason holding you back, I will do my best to limit it. I can hang out with girls without touching them, you know. Physical touch is just my primary love language, so I don't always realize I'm doing it. If I promise to keep it to two hugs a day, will you come?"

I couldn't talk. My muscles were quivering as I tried not to sob. Why did he have to be so patient and perceptive? Why couldn't I compose my thoughts enough to form sentences?

Corby had been on the phone with me enough that he knew I wasn't going to respond. "Hey, it's late. Why don't you think about it and tell me what you're going to do tomorrow? Just know that I would really, really love to have you come with me. And if you come, it doesn't mean you have to be my girlfriend or anything, mmmk?"

"Okay," I whispered.

"Sleep well! It's your last night on the couch bed!"

I stayed huddled in the corner of the balcony for a few more minutes. After recovering control of my leg muscles, I went inside, closing the sliding door as quietly as I could. I found some tissues and slumped onto the couch. It wasn't worth pulling out the terrible mattress; the couch would work tonight. I punched my pillow into the corner and lay down, knowing that I probably wouldn't get much sleep. The next day, we drove home. Corby, of course, texted me for the duration of the journey. And I responded. Of course.

C: Meet at my parents place tomorrow by 2?

T: . . . I guess so . . .

C: YEEEES!!!!

T: I have a feeling that I just caused a commotion.

C: INDEED.

I strategically waited until we were almost home to tell my mom I was leaving the next day to go on a family vacation with Not-Boyfriend. She was a little shocked that I had agreed to such a thing, but she took the news surprisingly well.

I felt pretty good about my decision, until I walked upstairs and looked at my lovely, glorious mattress. Why had I said yes!? I was so tired, and I didn't know what the sleeping accommodations would be like on a boat. Was I doing the right thing? I hoped that even if I were miserable, I would be able to fake it well enough not to ruin everyone's trip.

The next morning, I got up and went to church. As soon as that was over, I rushed home, changed into normal clothes, threw some stuff in a duffel bag, and left.

The car was boiling hot. I was a bundle of excited nerves because I was doing something incredibly reckless. It was either going to be a great week or a terrible week. I wanted to go on this magical trip that I had read about months ago on Corby's blog, before I had even met him. I wanted to go with Corby and make him happy. But I didn't want to go with Corby. What was I doing?!

I pulled up in front of his parents' house to find major packing activity going on—people scurrying out the front door and the garage with boxes and coolers, loading them into a boat, a trailer, and trunks of various cars. Corby was sitting on the driveway, waiting for me to appear. He pointed at a spot on the street where he wanted me to park my car.

"You're here! I'm so excited you're coming!"

He opened his arms for a hug. I gave him a brief squeeze and then asked where I should put my things. I occupied my shaking hands by loading my bag into the trunk of Corby's van. Then we went to the gas station for a pre-vacation fill-up.

It was good to get away from the activity for a minute. Corby was obviously elated that I was going with him. I hoped I could live up to his expectations, at least the nongirlfriend ones—but I carefully steered all conversation away from serious topics. That would be dangerous.*

We went back to the house, where the packing was almost done. Corby's parents came over and told me how excited they were that I was coming, then rushed off to pack more. Corby started pointing out who everyone was as they scurried around like industrious ants. Altogether, there would be six kids and fourteen adults. It was a lot to keep track of.

We drove to St. George on exactly the same route I had traveled the day before. The first night, we stayed at a relative's house. The amount of noise and commotion generated by twenty excited people who had been cooped up in cars for six hours was tremendous, and it was a relief to finally go to bed, even though I had to share a luxurious couch bed mattress with Megan. I felt like I had been hit by a truck. I stayed up late into the night, staring at the blinking red light on the DVD player, trying to figure out how I had gotten here.

---

* *I also knew to avoid serious topics, seeing as I had convinced Tess to come only by assuring her it was nothing serious. Tee hee.*

## Chapter 16

# Stars and Squirt Bottles

*Lake Powell*

"Tess . . . can we date?"

I was studying a hand of cards for a board game we were playing. I put the cards down, grabbed a spray bottle on the counter next to me, and squirted Corby in the face like he was a naughty pet that needed to be trained. He scrunched up his face and turned his head so I could get the whole thing wet, then smirked with satisfaction.

Quadriplegics can't sweat, so when Corby was on a hot boat, someone had to regularly spray his torso so he wouldn't overheat. Over the past three days of being on the lake, Corby had taken advantage of my antidating reflex by asking for a relationship every time he needed a spray. I could see Corby's mom and sister smile at each other in the kitchenette. They wisely didn't say anything, but they were deeply amused by Corby's strategy.

The first day on the lake had been absolutely exhausting. I wasn't sure if I would be able to last an entire week. The boat was small, loud, and hot. It was hard spending literally all day with Corby, with nowhere to escape, and although sleeping on a dark, quiet deck helped a little, I felt like I had made a mistake.

But now? On day three? I was cautiously starting to enjoy myself. Corby's brothers had the same laid-back personality that he did and were quite easy to talk to. And Corby kept gently pushing me to do activities that he couldn't do, like go for tube rides on the speedboat. I had never been on a boat before, but it was quite fun! And the night before, Corby had asked his brothers to carry him up to the deck early. We laid on our backs, watching the stars slowly appear as the sun went down. We talked, just like we did every night on the phone, but the Powell scenery was *much* better than The Zone.

As the week went on, I started to feel less tied to Corby and did more stuff with other members of the family. I learned how to jump into the lake every few hours to cool off. I washed my hair with Angie using lake water. It probably didn't clean my hair much, but it felt nice. I helped wash the dishes and cook dinner. I played a video game with Ryan for an hour. I talked with Adam, taught Josh how to sew after the button on his only pair of swim trunks popped off, and helped Ronda make breakfast.

On Monday, I had wanted to go home. Now, I wanted this vacation to last longer. I loved tucking myself into a corner of the back deck with a book, dangling my legs into the water. It was lovely. I could have stayed there all summer, reading in the sun. I leaned back, looking around at the perfect view. The sunset was gorgeous.

Corby was true to his promise not to be so touchy. It was strange how much easier it was to sit next to him for hours on end, playing game after game, without worrying about him reaching over to brush my shoulders or hands. Why would something so small make such a huge difference? I didn't understand. I loved talking to him in the dark. We spent hours under the stars, chatting with each other and anyone else who happened to come to the top deck.

On the last night, Scott took some of us on a lake tour on the speedboat. Corby came for that one. He sat in the deepest seat so he could hold himself up against the armrests. I sat with Josh and Mason on the back bench. Scott drove up several canyons, looking for potential docking sites for future Lake Powell trips, and it was hard to listen to their discussions. I wasn't going to be there next year! Right?

The next morning, we docked, loaded the steaming hot cars, and drove away. I was leaving a magical place behind with little prospect of ever returning. I wished we could jump back a week and do it all again. The biggest regret I had about the trip was that Corby had never gotten in the water. He had pictures and videos on Facebook from every previous Powell trip of a "sacrificial drowning of a vamplegic,"* where the family came up with a different way of throwing Corby into the water every time. Often, his companion of the year was waiting in the water to help roll him over and hold him up so he could breathe. But we had played so many board games during the last week that he had never asked to jump in, so I didn't get to participate in this tradition. The time had passed way too fast.

Corby dropped me off at his parents' house so I could get my car. He had to get back to his apartment so his nurse could give him his first shower in over a week. I quickly got all my stuff out of his van and said a hurried farewell.

I stayed around for a couple more hours to help wash and wax the outside of the boat. When I finally left, I was fighting back tears. This time, they weren't nervous tears. The tears were because I knew I was never going to do that again, unless something crazy happened and I ended up marrying Corby. Why couldn't I have met one of the other single Campbell men before I had met Corby? That way, I could have married into the family and become a part of these awesome traditions but wouldn't have to deal with the wheelchair! It was an interesting thought, but I knew it was ridiculous. Out of all of them, Corby was and always would be the best match for my personality. And marrying someone just to gain access to a houseboat for one week a year was not a healthy long-term strategy.

I sat on my mental staircase, holding a spray bottle, staring down at a shirtless Corby in swim trunks. He was still staring up at me. I squirted him in the face to make him stop. But he just smirked.

---

* *My chair sparkles in the sun, which is a vampire thing to do, so my technical medical classification is "vamplegic."*

## USEFUL

### Secondary Conditions of SCI

Imagine that SCI is an iceberg, like the famous one the *Titanic* hit.

Usually, only the tip of an iceberg is visible, while the majority of its mass remains submerged beneath the water. In this analogy, the tip of the SCI iceberg is "inability to walk." That is the thing everyone can see. When people think of quadriplegia or paraplegia, the first thing they picture is a wheelchair. But that is just the tip of the iceberg. And there is a whole lot of stuff underneath that few people are aware of.

Here are some of the other factors hiding beneath the surface:

1) Spasticity. If you hang around Corby, you'll notice that sometimes he'll shift around in his chair a bit, and his legs will suddenly start to shake. The shaking is not voluntary. People with SCI and other types of nervous system conditions often have muscle spasms. The brain tries to send messages to the muscles, but those messages don't make it. And when muscles try to send messages to the brain, those messages get lost too. The spinal cord tries to make up for the lack of brain response, but the nerves in the spinal cord are not as . . . sophisticated? . . . as the ones in the brain. The muscles will suddenly stiffen or jerk. Usually, this isn't a problem. In fact, sometimes it is helpful if the spasms make you aware that something is painful and needs to be fixed. But sometimes it can be annoying. Like when you are trying to sleep, and suddenly, your husband's legs start shaking uncontrollably and messing up all the blankets.
2) Loss of sexual function. See USEFUL—The Honeymoon.
3) Loss of bladder and bowel function. See USEFUL—Catheters.
4) Pressure sores. When you sit in one position all day, the tiny blood vessels underneath the skin are compressed. If too many blood vessels in one place are compressed for too long, the surrounding tissue doesn't get enough oxygen and starts to die. This creates a pressure sore. A "sore" doesn't sound *that* bad, but if it is big enough or gets infected, it can be fatal. Luckily, Corby

weighs only about 100 lb., so his risk of pressure sores is not as high as for others. But he has gotten pressure sores on his shoulder, tail bone, and feet. They are certainly something to look out for. I am always wary when buying new shoes for Corby, and every few days, I examine his backside for angry-looking spots. If I find one, we need to relieve all pressure until the sore is healed, or else it could become serious.

5) Temperature regulation. Corby has lost the ability to sweat and shiver. When he gets cold, he stays cold . . . for hours. We don't go outside when it is too hot, and we don't go outside when it is too cold. If we have to go outside in the heat, we take a spray bottle and make sure Corby doesn't overheat. Sometimes we don't spray him often enough, and then he is sick for a few days. Not fun. If we go outside in anything colder than 55 degrees, Corby dresses up like an eskimo, complete with a battery-operated heated vest. It makes outdoor activities a bit more complicated than they would usually be—things like summer barbecues or Christmas caroling. We keep our house set at about 74 degrees, but even at this temperature, Corby sometimes wears a blanket and jacket.* He wears a scarf every day; since he can don a scarf himself, it is a way that he can control his temperature independently.
6) Loss of breathing capacity. Breathing, coughing, and sneezing use muscles in the chest and stomach. People with injuries above C3 can't breathe independently. Corby, with a C5/6 level injury, can breathe on his own but has reduced lung capacity. He wasn't able to sing at all for over a year after breaking his neck, but he slowly regained most of that ability. The fact that he can still sing as strongly as he can is miraculous. But his coughs and sneezes are not impressive. A newborn is better at sneezing than Corby is. Watching him try to cough after swallowing wrong is agonizing.

---

* *Sometimes I regulate fine, but it feels like if my body is uncomfortable for any reason, the first system it redirects power from is temperature regulation. I like to assume my body is successfully fighting off a small cold I don't know about, and that's why I'm wearing a jacket indoors and still feel chilly.*

And when Corby has a cold, he can't really cough anything up. For this reason, pneumonia is one of the highest causes of death among quadriplegics.

7) Lightheadedness. This is one Corby struggles with a ton. There are many mornings when he gets out of bed and immediately reclines so he can rest his head on the wall. There are times when we pull over to the side of the road because he is too lightheaded to keep driving. After dinner, he usually leans on the wall for a few minutes. This has gotten better over time. For the first couple of years post-injury, he couldn't sit up at all for longer than a few minutes. The pictures taken during that time are of a lying-down Corby or a Corby bent in half. One of the main reasons he doesn't use a manual chair is that he needs the recline function on the power chair.
8) Psychological effects. Most SCI patients struggle mentally post-injury. Corby is a weirdo and didn't really struggle at all. His mental struggles came years later, after coming to the realization that he might not ever find a girl who would marry him. When Corby was first injured, the nurses started giving him antidepressants as a matter of routine, assuring him that he would need them sooner or later. A few weeks later, he finally convinced the nurses that he was fine, and the doctors stopped prescribing them. This is certainly not the case for everyone. Every few months, someone reaches out to Corby, saying that some acquaintance of theirs just broke their neck. Corby is always open to giving support and advice, but more often than not, the person is in a sort of shut-down mode. They are not open to any feedback and don't want help. This can go on for months or years, and it is hard to know what to do or say.
9) Chronic pain. A lot of people with SCI struggle with constant pain or tingling in the paralyzed parts of their bodies. Corby doesn't struggle with this, but it sounds exhausting.

As explained before, all injuries are different. Corby struggles with lightheadedness. Other quads with his same injury level don't. Many people with Corby's injury level are able to use manual wheelchairs. Corby can't. Some struggle with pressure sores more than average.

The big takeaway from this chapter is that the inability to move the legs is one of the easier aspects of being paralyzed because it can be mitigated with a wheelchair. The issues listed in this chapter are a *way* bigger deal. If Corby (and many other paralyzed people) could choose one thing to fix, it wouldn't be the legs. They would choose to regain the ability to poop on their own. Being able to go to the bathroom independently is far more liberating than being able to stand up. More on that in a future chapter.

## Chapter 17

# Scandalous Sandal Contact

*July*

Corby still insisted that we go out every week. An event that I tried weekly to wiggle out of, but an event that Corby was so persistent in planning that it still ended up happening anyway.*

The Fourth of July was coming up. My mom's family always got together for a barbecue, then went to a park to watch fireworks. It was one of my favorite traditions. I didn't know what possessed me, but I invited Corby to come along since he didn't have any plans and was trying to set up his usual weekly date anyway. Rylee, Eric, and Kyle drove with us in Corby's van to my grandma's house, and they had a grand old time sitting in the back, with endless amounts of leg room,** watching Corby drive with only his hands.

---

* *I'd like it known that I felt particularly inspired to keep asking Tess out, despite her consistent attempts to wiggle out of it. If anyone else told me they kept trying to go out with a girl every week who always backed out, I'd tell them to stop being a creep and knock it off. This felt different and like it was the right thing to do.*

** *Fun fact: In addition to tons of open space in front of you because there is no middle bench, the floor is also lowered enough that even my tall friends can swing their legs like a kid, and their feet don't touch the ground.*

Corby went around the house to the backyard and parked under a tree. My aunts and uncles didn't seem to know what to do. They had never even heard of Corby. I hadn't told many people about him because the situation was a bit complicated to explain. And although Corby had slowly started getting me to talk more, I wasn't the type to just inform my extended family of significant life developments unless directly asked.

Corby was in fine form the whole evening, making so many jokes that my cousins were rolling around on the grass, laughing. I contributed by kicking a plate of whip cream into Kyle's face. He was angry, but the opportunity was too good to pass up.*

My grandma thought Corby was fascinating. Her first impression came as she was walking out the back door just as I dumped a cup of ice water over the top of Corby's head. Her face was priceless. She thought I was playing a very rude prank, but I was just making sure Corby didn't overheat.

For part of the evening, I sat on a chair next to Corby. I decided to try to make some sort of small effort to show him I did care about him and that I was trying to make progress, so I decided I would use his knee as a footrest. I was wearing shoes. Corby was wearing pants. I reached out a single foot and lightly rested the sole of my sandal on his kneecap. No skin contact was made, and Corby couldn't feel my foot anyway. I didn't think much of it, even though it was easily the most casual contact I had ever made with a boy before—if you didn't count the nonsensical time I lost my head and rode on Corby's lap on our first date. The family looked askance at this physical gesture, tiny as it was. I ignored their expressions and left my foot where it was.

After dinner, we went to the park for fireworks. Yet again, my family was shocked as I stood on the back of Corby's chair, and we bumped across the grass. In the past six months, I had changed quite a bit. I set up a lawn chair, and we sat next to each other and watched the fireworks far off in the distance—they were being launched from a park over a mile away from where we were sitting.

---

* *This shot was legendary, by the way.*

About halfway through, Corby quietly leaned toward me and asked, "Tess, can I hold your hand?"

Shoot. Using Corby's knee as a footrest had gotten Corby excited and hopeful. Even though it had been a great day, I still couldn't do it. I resolutely stared ahead at the fireworks and gave a brief head shake. I didn't think Corby was surprised, but I could tell he was disappointed.

A few nights later, he pushed into uncomfortable-question territory, asking where our relationship was, why I still didn't want to date him, why I had such a hard time touching people, why I wouldn't share anything personal with him. We stayed up until 4:00 a.m. It wasn't much of a conversation—I cried the entire time, and there were a lot of long silences.

The next weekend, my family went on a very rare camping trip with my mom's siblings. I set up a camp chair away from everyone else and tried to read. I was so tired and confused I couldn't get myself to interact with other humans. Besides, this was the first opportunity I had to think about Corby without Corby being able to call or text me every few minutes. We didn't have cell reception, and the break from my phone was lovely.

I would have gone hiking, but my dad and the boys left without asking if anyone else wanted to go. That was frustrating because I really liked hiking. But after a while, I decided it was for the best. If I was supposed to be with Corby, I would have to get used to never going hiking. I might as well start now. Just like I had with dancing. I would also need to get used to never going camping.

This trip was not helping with that plan. I loved camping. I had somehow ended up in my own tiny tent, so I could leave the flaps open all night and stare at the stars without making anyone mad for letting all the cold air in. Staring at the stars reminded me of Powell with Corby. Which made me think about Corby, which I didn't really want to do, but I couldn't stop. I tried to force myself to forget about camping and hiking and dancing and all those other things. They didn't matter in the long run. Not really.

*Chapter 18*

# White Giddy Blur

*August*

C: Hmm, woulda been a good morning for sleeping in.

T: Well, why didn't you?

C: Because no one would be around to get me out of bed haha. Wheelchair problems!

T: Roommate problems, more like.

C: Roommates are a common solution, and the one I mostly leverage at this phase of my life. But certainly not the only solution any more than potatoes are the only solution for hunger. And if I were hungry, I wouldn't say "potato problems."

T: Depends on the time. You would if you happened to be living in the 1845 Great Irish Potato Famine.

C: I actually originally planned to be born in Ireland in the 1820s, but 1810 rolled around, and I saw the imminent famine, and I was like,

"No potatoes? No way!" and rescheduled my birth. It being this late in the millennia, all the good families were booked through 1986.

T: You seriously have the best comebacks ever.

CJ and Megan were getting married. Megan's family lived in Georgia, so the whole Campbell family was preparing to fly across the country for the wedding. The night before they left, I went over to Corby's parents' house. We ate dinner while they discussed what they still needed to pack and what time they needed to wake up and leave. Ronda was in charge of bringing the wedding dress and all the suits in her luggage, so all the fancy outfits were hanging in their plastic wrappings from the handles of the top kitchen cabinets.

After we finished eating, Ronda suddenly interrupted. "You and Megan are about the same size . . . You should try the dress on!"

I was wary. Trying on another bride's dress seemed immoral.

Ronda insisted as she started unpacking the dress. It *was* beautiful. And since Ronda noticed my break in protestations, she herded me back to her bedroom.

Corby stayed out in the living room and started yelling about how he wanted to see it and that I'd better not hide from him like he knew I wanted to.

After I got it on, I carefully speed-walked out into the living room, around Corby's chair, and straight back into the bedroom. I was terrified of breaking the zipper or ripping the hem. Megan had to wear this for her wedding in two days!

Meanwhile, Ronda had run down to the basement to examine her store of wedding dresses from past family weddings. She shuffled through them and brought up a different wedding dress that had been neglected for a few years. She tied me into the corset. This dress was safer. Its glorious moment had passed, and it didn't matter if I tripped in it. I spent a few minutes skipping around the house, giggling all the while.* This dress was particularly poofy. It was great fun. Corby was trying to take pictures on his phone, but between his gimp hands and my running, he ended up with nothing but white blurs.

Once I was back in my straightforward jeans and T-shirt, I watched Ronda give Corby a spiffy prewedding haircut. Then we played a board game, and I went home.

I really enjoyed myself that evening. Why wouldn't my brain let me date that boy already? And why was I fine after *this* date? I didn't get it. Right now, I was at the bottom of my mental staircase, wearing a poofy wedding dress, wanting to date Corby. But in a few hours, I knew I would be back at the top. I was constantly running up and down that stupid staircase. And it was exhausting.

The Campbell family embarked on their grand adventure the next morning. The wedding went great; the rest of the trip was kind of a disaster. One of their connecting flights was canceled due to inclement weather. After analyzing the situation, Corby, his parents, and the rest of the people at the airport decided they should all find a hotel and stay the night in Denver.

This procedure probably went fine for the rest of the "normal" airport travelers. But Corby wasn't normal. The family frantically made calls to all hotels in the area, trying to find one that had a) a wheelchair-accessible room that didn't already have a sleeping occupant and b) a van that could transport a power wheelchair. Luckily, a nearby traveler overheard the phone calls and gave them his hotel reservation—for an accessible room *and* a van!

Corby got off the phone to head out but then texted a few minutes later—the ramp on the van was broken. They spent thirty minutes borrowing tools from other vans so they could manually crank the ramp. The van that picked them up the next day to bring them back to the airport *also* had a broken ramp. But they finally made it home, only forty hours behind schedule.

---

* *Tess looked uncharacteristically giddy while wearing the dress. I was very surprised.*

Because Corby was sitting at boring airports for hours on end, he called and talked to me while I worked on projects. I got to hear most of these shenanigans happening in the background. Was this how all trips with Corby turned out? Were vacations worth it if he had to deal with this stuff? I wasn't sure I could handle this many arrangements on my own. This was yet another argument in favor of not marrying Corby. And if I knew I couldn't marry him, then what was the point of dating him?

Because I liked him too much, that was why.

# USEFUL

## Airplanes and Travel

Corby and I don't travel very much. Reasons:

1) Bowel care. Don't worry, you will get to read the chapter on bowel care eventually. The short version is that Corby has to poop at very specific times, even while on vacation, and it takes over an hour to do. Scheduling bowel care into travel is quite tricky.
2) Issues with accessibility. Even when a van or hotel room is labeled as "accessible," it doesn't mean that it is. Most people don't think through whether something is truly accessible or not, likewise with a wheelchair van. Often, a "wheelchair-accessible van" means "I have a big enough trunk for your chair." But whatever vehicle Corby uses must have a ramp/lift for a 400 lb. power chair. And if he can't stay in his chair for the drive, he needs someone who can transfer him to the car seat. That person is not me. Lifting Corby into a tall van would not go well.
3) The amount of stuff we need to take with us is ridiculous.* We need to be prepared for all possible scenarios—pillows, medications, catheter kits, multiple changes of clothing for different temperatures, chair chargers—everything must come with us, even if it is just for one night.
4) Airplanes. Corby cannot stay in his wheelchair on the plane—he has to be transferred to a regular seat that doesn't have the padding he needs to support his torso. The chair has to be taken apart and loaded like baggage, and we just have to hope all the wheelchair pieces make it to the destination unharmed. This is the biggest reason we don't fly. I'm not sure what would happen if they didn't arrive or broke en route. It takes *at least* six months (but usually around a year) to order a new power wheelchair. You

---

* *Tess and I seem to place a lot less intrinsic value in travel than the average person. Many people in wheelchairs travel all the time because the prep and planning seem worth it to them.*

> can't just run to a store and pick up a new one. I once read an article that claimed seven wheelchairs were damaged/lost every day by airlines. I don't know if that statistic is accurate, but the only two times Corby has needed to travel by plane post-breakneck, the airline workers weren't allowed to touch him or his chair (that specific airline's policy),* and when he got off the plane, his chair had sustained minor damage. The mere idea of Corby being chairless for six months squelches any desire I have to go anywhere by plane. (Also, airplanes are super loud and destroy me for about a week). It would be much more appealing if a regular plane seat could be moved out of the way so Corby could stay in his chair on the plane. But this hasn't happened yet.

So far, we have gone places that we can reach by van and have stayed for a maximum of three days. Our favorite place to go is the Utah Shakespeare Festival in Cedar City. Lots of old people go to this festival, so it is a reliable wheelchair-friendly zone. We leave on Friday right after bowel care is over and come back on Sunday so we are home in time for Monday bowel care. The only times we have not followed this pattern were family trips with Corby's parents and our honeymoon. Ronda is an angel and drove to Cedar City halfway through our honeymoon to do bowel care on one of the mornings so that we could stay longer than a couple of days. It was a little awkward to have my new mother-in-law show up in our hotel room, but we appreciated it. Thanks, Ronda!

---

* *I've heard airlines are a bit better than this now. Whatever the case, with this airline at the time, the workers told us they weren't allowed to touch my chair, and they seemed sheepish about it. We had a wonderful picture of three workers all standing around my mom while she deconstructed the chair. They were doing their best to try to help, even though they weren't allowed to help.*

## *Chapter 19*

# A Stupid Argument About a Song That Doesn't Matter

*September*

Traffic was worse than I'd ever seen it. I inched past a series of accidents, the biggest being a six-car pileup. One of Corby's friends was in a community theater production of *Thoroughly Modern Millie*, and Corby wanted to support her. I had agreed to accompany him last minute, so I hadn't been able to leave early enough to beat rush hour. I got to Orem forty-five minutes late. We rushed through the Arby's drive-thru and hurried to the theater, arriving with only a few minutes to spare.

The play was good. But Corby wanted some sort of physical contact. He was a typical male subject who continually asked me to hold his hand. I was still opposed to this concept. Also, low theater seats and tall power wheelchairs make normal physical contact quite difficult. The only thing he could reach was the back of my neck and the top of my left shoulder. I felt like a dog sitting next to a human. Except that dogs seem to like it when humans awkwardly tap the back of their necks. I was not a dog, and Corby's hand was driving me *nuts*.

I really wanted to enjoy the play, but I could feel his pulse through his thumb, and I was compulsively counting Corby's heart rate.

I didn't want to hurt him by shrugging his hand away, but the only friendly alternative was to reach up and hold his hand like I was a normal person. And that would imply way more affection than I felt for him at that moment. Between crazy traffic and thumb pulses, I was on edge.

I stood up the second intermission was announced and leaned on the front row of seats. Thankfully, Corby didn't try to talk about hand holding. Instead, we talked about our favorite musicals. Included in that list was *Hello, Dolly*, and I made an off-hand remark that one of my favorite songs from a musical was in that play. I was referring to "It Only Takes a Moment," but Corby thought I was referring to the title song "Hello, Dolly."

I said, "Oh yeah, I guess that is the song," but the ever-perceptive Corby sniffed out yet another avoidance of discussion.

Unlike myself, Corby *was* a dog. He wanted to know what song I was *really* thinking of, but I refused to tell him and tried to divert the conversation to a new topic so he would forget about my question avoidance.

He temporarily allowed that tactic, but he was definitely bugged. He didn't touch me for the beginning of the second half of the play. (I was hoping that it would last, but it didn't.)

When we were driving home, he brought up the favorite musical song again. When I kept avoiding the question, we got into an argument. Like, Corby was actually yelling. I didn't know he could do that. He yelled about how he couldn't understand why I wouldn't tell him something so basic as a song title, but he probably was letting out a lot of pent-up anger from other things as well—I had also been refusing to tell him what movies and foods I liked. I was basically refusing to have opinions, and Corby's patience had finally run out.

The reason I enjoyed the song "It Only Takes a Moment" is the casting choice, not the song itself. Well, the song itself is okay, I guess. But it was one of the only times in musical history that I could think of that one of the main characters did not actually sing well. Which was very unusual in a musical. As much as I liked musicals, it bugged me when a derpy character sang in a sophisticated, pristine tenor, then went back to being all derpy again. But this particular character talked like a low-level feed store clerk, acted like a low-level feed store clerk, and sang like a low-level feed store clerk. I appreciated the continuity.

As for the lyrics, they didn't describe me whatsoever. The idea of me having a favorite song about falling in love in a single moment was ludicrous. I could not relate to that at all. But I liked the *idea* of knowing if I liked someone in an instant. I was tired of being so confused about liking Corby, even after 45,000 moments.

So why couldn't I just give Corby this song title the first time he asked? I didn't know. Probably because the boy overanalyzed every single item I expressed a liking for, picking it apart and trying to glean every last bit of information he could out of it. The way he seized onto the phrase "I like" was alarming. And without the somewhat extensive explanation above, the only thing he would be able to analyze was the lyrics, which would only serve to artificially imply that I was secretly a hopeless romantic. Which was more true than I wanted to admit.

Corby had never even seen *Hello, Dolly*, so this explanation wouldn't have made much sense. And trying to discuss my opinions about the lyrics would have encouraged Corby to initiate a huge discussion about my deeper feelings about attraction and falling in love and why wouldn't I be his girlfriend yet, and I was sick and tired of *discussing* things all the time!

So now I was sitting in Corby's van, listening to him yell at me for never telling him anything and not trusting him. It was scary. I was sure that when we got back to my car, he was going to throw me out and tell me he never wanted to see me again.

I really wanted to be the kind of person who would talk more. The kind of person he was obviously hoping to find. I was trying so hard. I had talked to him and confided in him far, far more than anybody else I had ever met. But it still wasn't enough.

The next morning, Corby sent a bunch of apology texts. And within a few days, our regular texting pattern resumed. Everything was mostly fine again. Except that I felt even more pressure to do even better at the whole “communication” thing. Which meant that I would have to share more about myself in the future, going against every natural instinct and habit I had carefully cultivated in reaction to . . . something. I still hadn’t figured out why I was so messed up.

## Chapter 20

# A Really Annoying Letter

*Later in September*

Okay. So everything was *not* actually fine after that argument. If I had known the trouble it would cause, I wouldn't have started it. Which was a silly thing to think because I didn't start it on purpose. I just habitually tried to avoid sharing any information about myself, a strategy that was no longer working as well as it used to.

A week after the argument, I hauled Corby into my house so we could watch *The Music Man*, my favorite musical. (I was getting faster at getting him inside). He obviously wanted to cuddle. I obviously did not. I sat close enough that our shoulders were touching but at an angle that would prevent him from getting his arm around my shoulders.

About halfway through, Corby's legs started twitching, so I swung my legs on top of his thighs to make them stop. Personally, I thought that calf-to-thigh-while-wearing-pants contact should count as snuggling, but I kept forgetting that Corby couldn't feel such contact. At the end of the movie, we had a rather long, twisted, sitting-next-to-each-other hug. Hugs were easier when both people could stand up.

I dragged Corby down the sketchy ramps, put him back in his chair, and we went for a drive. Neither of us had much to say.

Corby finally broke the silence. "So, on Sunday, I wrote a letter to you. Care to guess what's in it?"

Oh no. A letter? My heart sank. Corby had finally come to his senses and decided to move on. I was shocked that it had taken this long. I naturally didn't want to talk about it, so I followed my usual avoidance protocol and didn't say anything.

After Corby dropped me off, I unsuccessfully attempted to fall asleep. I gave up and grabbed my phone when a thunderstorm blew in and discovered that Corby had emailed me the letter at 4:00 a.m. What was he still doing up at 4:00 a.m.?! I glared at the notification. This email, whether I read it or not, had made any chance of sleep impossible. I opened it, deciding it would be better to get it over with.

> I have a lot to say, and I thought it might be overwhelming if I did this all verbally, so I decided to write you a letter.
>
> Almost none of this will be a surprise to you because we've discussed most of it in one format or another over our association, but I know you don't believe a lot of it, so it's probably worth reiterating. Plus, I hope I can be clearer here than I've managed to be so far.
>
> First of all, I really do appreciate you. I miss it when we go long periods without talking. I enjoy spending time with you. Friends have commented that they can tell I really like you. I love your quick wit and your intellectual way of describing things. You are beautiful, and I love that you don't try to prove me wrong when I tell you so. I love your consistency, how we text little bits throughout the day and spend time talking almost every night. I love how the wheelchair isn't a big deal to you, and you've still been willing to spend as much time with me as you have, despite it. These are not common traits. I even have a statistically-valid-sized data set of dating experiences to back it up.

What I struggle with is your seeming unwillingness to be vulnerable. It manifests in lots of ways. Your unwillingness to even let me touch your hands. Your insistence that you are fully to blame for anything that happens. Your unwillingness to believe me even when I make a promise. But most important to me, the communication walls that you keep. Not only do all these things bother me, but you also aren't even willing to help me understand why.

I feel like I've been understanding so far. I ask about your past and your feelings all the time. I try to apply enough pressure that you know I'm serious about it, but I also generally allow you to say no in the end because I understand it's personal, and being vulnerable is hard. However, Friday sent me through a loop. Maybe I don't understand the big picture at all here, and I'm entirely open to the possibility that I'm looking at this completely wrong, so feel free to correct me. But when you absolutely refused to even tell me the name of a song you thought of, I was hurt and angry. As I see it, I wasn't asking you to be vulnerable. I wasn't asking you for commitment. I wasn't asking for a favor. It seemed to me the simplest of requests. A type of thing you'd have told me a hundred times over the past six months in our talks and texts. When you refused, I was totally taken aback.

When I ask you to tell me things like this, you often use the phrase "I can't." And maybe I'm being insensitive, but I don't believe it. I don't know if you're using *can't* in the context of "and never will be able to" or just "I haven't figured out how," but you've been able to effectively manipulate your mouth to articulate all sorts of words before, and sharing things like a song name is just more words. The thought that really haunted me was, "If she's not willing to share things like the name of a song, how will we ever communicate about things of actual significance?" I have done absolutely everything I can think of to be a safe place for you to share things, and it doesn't appear like it's enough.

The reason I'm writing this letter is because I've discovered where to draw my line. Not being able to communicate about things that seem so insignificant to me is not something I'm willing to be patient with indefinitely. I feel like we either need to take a step forward or a step backward. I truly have seen you making an effort and growing in just the six months I've known you. I've tried to thank you and honor you for those efforts as best as I know how. This letter might not seem like I'm honoring the efforts, but I feel like it's the best thing I can do for both of us right now. I hope it doesn't undo some of the progress you've made. But I'm not willing to stay in this in-between zone.

Step forward:

Commitment: Either we are a couple, and I can refer to you as my girlfriend, or we're not. Where we are now is far enough along that if I went on a date with another girl and we held hands during a movie, I'd feel like I was cheating on you.

Touch: It doesn't have to be this specifically, but consistently allowing something like letting me hold your hand or riding in my lap. I know you've let me put my arm around you, but I'm sorry, that isn't enough for me; it's something I could do with my sister or roommates. If we are to take a step forward, there would need to be times where you'll share with me physical tokens of commitment. I'm not asking you to kiss me. Particularly after my yelling on Friday, I don't feel like I'd have enough trust to merit you taking such a step with me just yet. But I'd love it if you actually liked physical contact and reached out to me sometimes—at a minimum, I'd need to know it's something you're encouraging me to do because you want me to know I'm appreciated.

Acknowledgment of my responsibility: This one I've probably explained the least, although we've argued about it a few times. But I'll try to explain here. It seems like when things go wrong in your life, almost regardless of circumstance, you immediately take all the blame and beat yourself up about it. I'm not saying this to criticize you but to share how your taking all the blame affects me (outside of how sad it is to see you or anyone tear themselves down). I don't think I always do everything right. I plan to make mistakes. But I want to grow from them. I need someone who will help me see my side of a problem so I can learn and grow too.

There are times with you when I feel like I'm just repeatedly sticking my finger in an electrical socket, but when I try to learn from it, you won't help me understand why. Since you're important to me and I don't want to give up, I don't really have any other options than to stick my finger in again to see if I can learn why. This hasn't felt like a particularly effective technique. By not even admitting that I have responsibility in my blunders, you aren't strengthening me; you're actively discouraging me from growing.

Communication: I imagine this will be the hardest one for you, but there has to be much less "I can't" when it comes to communication.

Option two!

Although it's not my preference, I believe it's entirely possible for me to be just friends with you. Obviously, I wouldn't see or talk to you nearly as often as we do now. But as aforementioned thus far, it has never been my intent to be just friends with you. I would need time to change. And my experience shows me that the easiest and quickest way for me to do that is to break off all contact for a few months.

Note that if you choose to take this step, it doesn't mean you're deciding once and for all that we will *never* date. You never know what the future holds. But I will not be the one to initiate such a thing. If we do take a step back and later you change your mind, *you* will have to make a consistent effort to get the message to me. Indirect implications wouldn't cut it. I'd need clear communication.

I care about you a lot, Tess. I wasn't hurt or angry when I wrote this. My objective was to identify and articulate my thoughts, feelings, and needs, and I feel like I've done a decent job. I want the best for both of us. I'd still love to help you grow and to be a part of your life, but not at the expense of my own growth. I sure like you, though, and I'm still open to working on our relationship, contingent upon the stuff above (or whatever we conclude after further discussion).

Good <whatever time of day you read this>

Love,
Corby Campbell

*How*? How was Corby able to articulate his thoughts so clearly and then send them to me with the intent that I would actually *read* them? Why did he sign his letter with the word *love*? Did he use that term because it was a generally acceptable way to finish a letter, or did he actually think that he loved me? Why had he included his last name? And why was physical contact so blasted important to everyone?! Was mutually activating nerve endings really that crucial to forming significant relationships? Was I an unfeeling android who would never be capable of understanding how humans were supposed to feel and act?

I threw my phone off the side of my bed and flipped the pillow over to the dry side. I sat on top of my mental staircase, angrily glaring at the mental Corby sitting at the bottom. I stewed over the letter for two hours, trying to figure out why the idea of dating Corby was so terrifying. I finally fell asleep at 6:30 a.m.

I was awakened a couple of hours later when the Saturday morning vacuuming began. I trudged down the twenty-eight steps to The Zone. My mind was racing so fast I couldn't even cross-stitch. This had never happened before. I paced in endless circles—around the tower of boxes, past the water heater, through the food-storage shelves, around the unused exercise equipment, through the tiny space that had the *potential* to become a bathroom, and back to the small square of carpet that used to be my safe space. It sure didn't feel safe now. A decision had to be made, but both options felt terrible.

Corby had the worst timing ever. He had decided to send his letter two days before I started grad school. So two days later, I arrived on campus, exhausted.

I was assigned an office the size of a coat closet, just big enough for a table and a garbage can, and I had to push my chair against the far wall to open the door. Whoever had designed this office space had not anticipated that the occupant might want to pace in circles. Still, it had a door. I had never had my own door for my workspace before. It was delightful to have the power to shut everyone out and not worry about being interrupted.

The door was the only good part about grad school. I was aiming for a degree in cognitive psychology. I wanted to understand how humans interacted with technology so I could return to engineering ready to design medical devices that would be less confusing for users. Problem: I had taken a grand total of one psychology course in my life. All the other students had graduated in psychology and understood when the professors mentioned landmark studies and various research methods. I sat in the corner and scribbled notes that made no sense. Making decisions about what to do with Corby was the last thing I needed.

On Friday, I went with Corby to his sister's house for a barbecue. He was so lightheaded that he reclined against the wall while I sat silently on the couch. After the barbecue, we drove separately to Corby's apartment. None of his roommates were home, and he needed help getting in bed.

After all of Corby's limbs were situated on their designated pillows, I turned off the lights and lay in the middle of the floor. I felt empty inside. I knew that this was the last time I was going to see him. I couldn't keep dragging this relationship out if it was hurting Corby so much. And under the threat of losing him, I figured that I might as well take this opportunity to practice talking like a human. For the first time in our entire relationship, I forced myself to answer all his questions, even the personal ones where I had to state opinions instead of facts. I didn't try to avoid them or give the shortest answer possible. Thankfully, Corby didn't try to discuss our relationship. Somehow, it was easier talking into the darkness, listening to Corby's voice come from the shadow on the bed.

Eventually, it was time to leave because he was having a hard time keeping up his end of the conversation without nodding off. I rolled him onto his back, gave him a long hug, and gently tucked the covers around his neck. I went over to the corner and picked up my bag, which contained one of Corby's favorite book series.* I had intentionally brought them with me that night, knowing this would be the last time I would be in this apartment. I silently slid the books back into their spot on the shelf and left the bedroom, closing the door behind me. The corner of my heart cracked. Corby had been the best friend I had ever had, but I couldn't be the person he needed. I was just wasting his time. He needed to move on and find someone who could communicate like a normal person and hold hands on a normal-person timeline.

---

* Mistborn *by Brandon Sanderson.*

I already hated that person. Why couldn't I be a normal person?! Why did I have such a hard time with things other people seemed to do naturally?

When I got home, I typed out a letter.

> Dearest Corbinealious Brycetholomue Campbelliticus Maximus Danger the III,
>
> After a week of literally running around in circles, here are the two options written as succinctly as possible.
>
> 1) Date Corby. Seriously. As in, I would have a "boyfriend." This would naturally require that I accept the title of "girlfriend." A very odd concept indeed.
>
> 2) "Break up" with Corby. (Technically, I suppose breaking up is not possible given the current status of our relationship, but that is what it feels like.)
>
> Neither of these options is even remotely appealing, making this a ridiculously difficult decision. It is like being asked to choose between swiss and parmesan cheese. Both of which are disgusting, by the way. I wish this could be a decision between swiss cheese and cheesecake—quite an easy decision, see? But it isn't. Choosing from two options that are basically different flavors of being miserable? Not fun at all.
>
> I wish that Option One could work. I really, really do. If anything, contemplating never seeing you again has made me realize how much I actually like you. I have never been this close to anyone in my entire life. Until now, I didn't realize how nice it is to talk about something that happened at school and have the other person immediately know exactly what you are talking about because they are already familiar with the names and places and what it is you are working on and why it is such a big deal. I love being able to text you about totally random things and how

I can use big words, and you still know what I am talking about. Even though I find it rather exasperating at times, I love your persistence. If you had taken me seriously, we would have gone on two dates. We would never have done any puzzles or played with Legos or gone to Powell, which is the best week I have had in years. I wish that we could go back.

But in spite of all that, I still can't manage Option One. A tiny bit of me wants to and is already insanely jealous of any girl you are going to take out in the future. But realistically, with my current mental state, I can't handle the physical touch and communication aspects of a relationship that you expect. If I had to choose one word to describe my attitude toward Option One, it is *resigned*. Not *excited*, or *happy*, or even *scared*. But *resigned*. Doing something that you don't necessarily want to do. This is the word that I generally use to describe writing lab reports. And that isn't how it is supposed to be. You deserve someone who isn't forcing herself to be yours. But right now, that is how it would feel. I would be acting. I already have been, to some extent. It seems the longer I know you, the harder it becomes to talk to you or touch you, and I am not exactly sure why. When I picture us in a relationship, the imagined scenarios don't involve touch. I know you think I am just scared and that I would realize it isn't that big a deal if I just try it, but it isn't that simple. I have struggled with physical touch for years. This problem is not going to go away simply by declaring myself your girlfriend and grabbing your hand. I think that would make me resent you rather than like you more, and I am pretty sure that isn't your goal.

I guess what I am saying is that I choose Option Two. I wish I could still be able to talk to you, less often than we have been, of course, but based on what you wrote, I'm guessing that isn't an option. I really hate the idea of not talking at all for several months, but if that is how it has to be, I understand.

I care about you, too, Corby. I wish I could choose Option One and be excited about it. I can't believe I'm giving you up. But I can't move forward. At least not right now. I hope that changes in the future. I am definitely going to focus on it more now than I ever have before.

Hopefully, that all made some sort of sense. Thanks for everything. Even if we never see each other again, you will always be one of the best friends I will ever have.

Tess

The next morning, I got the following response from Corby:

Thank you so much for writing this. I tried to spend time yesterday thinking about what I should do if I didn't hear from you, and I was drawing a blank haha. Thank you for honoring the boundaries I set and, uh, eating the cheese?

This isn't the focus of my response, but I do want to point out that you're still welcome to go back on your decision. Your communication with me has improved to acceptable levels since I triggered this path. It hasn't been a cakewalk, but in the end, you've discussed things with me that you refused to before. I certainly haven't stopped overnight wanting you in my life. (Weird sentence structure, but "wanting you in my life overnight" can mean something else.)

Thanks for talking about some of the things you like about me. They were good to hear. Thank you for usually following up the things you "can't" do with an

The actual first-dance dress.
Look how excited she looks! :/

High-school Corby with
working legs and jazz hands!

The infamous zone! Its full name, dubbed by a sister, was "The Tessie Time Zone," and they liked to draw adventures and messages on the whiteboard.

Corby always knew Tess could snuggle because this tree got snuggled in her dating profile.

This was the first picture Tess saw on Corby's dating profile. Is this headshot from high school? Yes. Should he have picked a different one by this time? Probably. But Corby still thinks he looks hot here.

These guys had a better creeper stare than Corby did.

Corby loved when Tess wore this "May the Fourth Be with You" hood and saved this photo in his phone.

This is how Corby drives his van. He stays in his chair, which locks in behind the steering wheel. Then he can accelerate, brake, and blinker with his right hand.

Corby's logo. He keeps this alligator to scare off vermin.

Every year at Lake Powell, the fam found a new way to throw Corby into the water. They called it "the sacrificial drowning of a vamplegic." Vamplegic because his chair sparkled in the sun like a *Twilight* vampire.

Tess and Corby appreciating nature.

The beginning of "Platypus!"

Snuggles from behind are great snuggles.

This is a selfie taken the day Tess helped fix Corby's video-game controller.

Gotta look hoity-toity for a '20s-themed murder party.

If you don't find this adorable, we can't be friends.

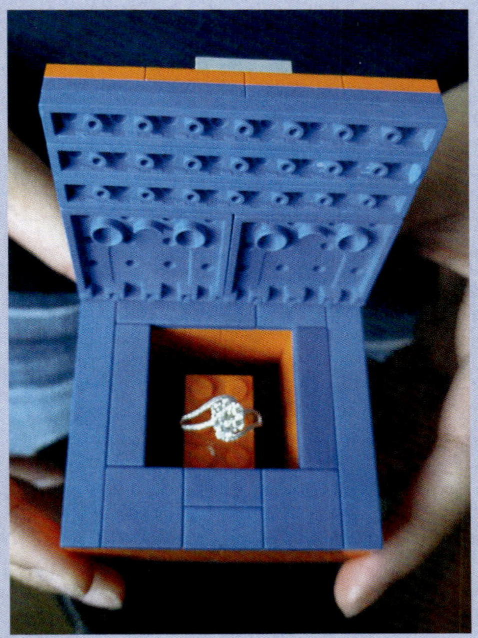

The ring box Corby made to propose.
He made the box out of their wedding colors,
blue (for Corby) and orange (for Tess).

Engaged. Huh. I guess that happened!

The face Corby made every time he remembered they were getting married.

The rice krispy wedding cake.

These photos are from Tess and Corby's bridals, taken at the Draper Utah Temple. Corby loves the passion in this photo.

Dancing at the wedding.

"at least right now" type of statement. I understand that whether either of us logically thinks you should feel certain ways or not, it doesn't change that, at this point in time, it *is* how you feel. It's a huge burden lifted to see you at least taking the first step by essentially saying, "But maybe I'll be able to change." Please don't lose that spark.

If I had my full body function restored today, I'd still want to date you. If I'd never broken my neck, I'd be an entirely different person. It would have been way easier for me to continue to be as selfish as I was, and maybe *that* Corby wouldn't have been interested. But now I am the person I am today, and I recognize the qualities you have are the important ones I want, with the exception of the disconnects we've discussed already that I still believe we can work through. I know you don't believe me. But I just wanted to say it again.

Any communication, if you're having a really hard day or a great victory, would be fine. It's really only the regular nightly calls and the consistent text small talk that I think I'd better go without for now. Although it doesn't feel like I need to at this moment. I guess I'll start trying to ask other girls out and see how it goes.

I feel like there should be some concluding paragraph, but it implies a finality that I don't feel right now.

I sure like you, Tess.

I didn't hear from Corby for several days. I felt like I had two lives: the summer life with Corby and the normal school life, where I didn't talk to anyone. The summer life was already starting to feel like a dream. In a way, it was kind of nice not talking to Corby. It was easier to pay attention in class when I wasn't constantly checking my phone for Corby messages, and I didn't have to make time to drive all the way down to Orem. I wondered what I had been so distraught about. Clearly, I was designed for a secluded academic life!

I stared out my office closet window. It was dark outside. I could see my laptop screen reflected in the glass because I hadn't bothered to turn the lights on, letting the office slowly get dark around me. I couldn't stand to read any more psychology articles that I didn't understand.

Who was I kidding? I did miss Corby. Well, I missed talking to someone, at least. That was Corby's fault. I had never missed talking before. Corby had somehow trained me to talk. I crept down a few steps on my mental staircase. But no one was at the bottom to see it.

## Chapter 21

# The Conception of Platypus

*The very end of September*

Corby's cut-off resolution did not last long. After a week of silence, he started texting me again. And after a few weeks of just-friends texting, he came up with a new rule. He decided that he could see me in person again as long as he went on a date with a different girl during the same week. That way, he was not putting all his relationship eggs in the very reluctant and potentially dangerous Tess basket. I thought it was a very odd rule. If I were Corby, I would have stomped on the Tess basket ages ago. But I was glad he was still around. Our relationship went back to how it had been before—constant texting and going out every week. But we weren't dating.

C: I've been on the other end of the spectrum of physical touch being a problem. But this is new.

T: What is new?

C: I've never been so close to dating someone and had lack of touch be the issue getting in the way.

T: This is a good thing because I am broadening your horizons!

C: Uh, sure?

T: You don't seem to agree.

C: Um, not exactly. I don't disagree that it's broadening; it's just not useful-seeming broadening when I prefer dating-broadening.

T: I have no idea what any of that meant. Therefore, platypus.

C: Definitely platypus.

T: Oh good, we agree.

C: I agree you have no idea what any of that meant?

T: No, we agree on platypus. Whatever that means.

C: Platypus works, I guess.

Corby invited me last minute to accompany him to dinner with a group of his friends. They had a coupon to Spaghetti Factory. I drove down and met Corby at his apartment. It had been only a month since I'd left for the "last time." All his friends, including the newlywed CJ and Megan, were nice and didn't ask any awkward questions about my attendance. Halfway through dinner, a balloon guy came around and offered to twist something up for each couple. He was good. He made a buffalo, an alien hat, and a somewhat functional bow and arrow set. When it was our turn, we requested a platypus, in reference to our conversation earlier in the day. After thinking for a moment, balloon dude whipped up an unmistakable platypus. His skills were impressive.

We were still using the word *platypus* in random conversation the next night.

C: Platypus.

T: Pelican.

C: Good night.

T: I thought that was what platypus meant. Night.

C: Does that mean by saying *pelican* you refused to say good night?

T: No. "Good night, Tess" and "Night, Corby" are both three syllables, but they aren't exactly the same. Therefore, "platypus" and "pelican"—both are 3 syllable words starting with *p*, referring to large-billed mammals.

C: Man, that makes so much sense I don't even get it.

T: That is the point of a secret language.

C: A three-syllable animal seems to arbitrarily match up with any three syllable phrase. For all I know, you could have meant, "Yes, let's date," or, "Hold me, Corb."

Because of balloon-animal dude and these text messages, over the next few months the word *platypus* somehow changed from an inside joke to a code that meant "I really like you." Or maybe even "I love you." But since neither of us directly said what it meant, we weren't really telling each other that we loved each other. That would have been dangerous, as we were NOT DATING.

*Chapter 22*

# Not-Boyfriend Needs Food

*October*

I was sitting in The Zone, working on the tenth draft of a frustrating research statement. It had a strict word limit, and I was struggling to convey the methodology succinctly. I had tentatively planned to spend the evening with Corby, but he had to work late. I reread the introduction of my paper for the thirty-seventh time and only managed to delete one word.

I felt reckless. I picked up my phone and texted Corby.

T: Do you still have a lot to do? I could bring you food . . .

What was I doing? Who drives forty-five minutes to bring food to her not-boyfriend who is working late?

Corby was, of course, enthusiastic about the idea.

C: I do need food. I'd love to see you, if you want to come. I could take breaks and cry a little. Actually, I'm a little hyper at this point. But I could easily be here till 10 PM, and I'm going to hang around for a long time unless my bosses kick me out.

My mind, being its typical confusing self, had flipped in the last thirty seconds. I now felt weird about driving down to bring Corby food. I tried to back out.

T: Well, I want to get out of this basement and have an excuse to stop reading this statement for the 1,000th time. But I would definitely count as a distraction in this situation, and you will probably want to collapse after you finally finish. I don't think my coming down would help you much.

C: I'd want to collapse with you far more than I'd want to collapse alone. Feel free to come down and do homework here, with the known risk that I may have to mostly ignore you for three hours. But I may get kicked home in an hour *shrug.*

I glared at the message. Corby was far too flexible and accommodating, as usual. I turned back to my paper. I reread the methods section, rewording a single phrase to eliminate *two* words. Why had teachers in high school trained us to write so much fluff to meet giant word counts when grad school restricted us to almost no words at all?*

Somewhere on the other side of the basement, someone started playing loud, annoying music. I suspected it was one of my sisters. It didn't sound like it was going to stop anytime soon, which meant driving forty-five minutes to visit Not-Boyfriend was becoming a more attractive alternative with each passing minute.

I highlighted an entire paragraph, intending to delete all of it, but then my laptop froze. It was a sign! I was supposed to drive down to deliver dinner to Not-Boyfriend!

My mom had made a creamy broccoli cheese soup for dinner. I told her where I was going, and she immediately filled a bowl. She

---

* *Because.*

was overly supportive of this random plan of driving one and a half hours roundtrip to deliver soup to Not-Boyfriend.

I arrived at the parking lot and texted Corby. I had forgotten to tell him that I was coming, so my presence was a surprise. He came down the elevator and let me in with his fancy key card. I opened the containers of food and put them on his desk where he could reach them, then sat at a nearby desk to knit for an hour while he wrote code.

We didn't leave the office until 9:00 p.m. Since Corby's roommates were not around to put him in bed (they were all distracted by girls who were okay with being girlfriends), I followed him in my car to his apartment, thirty minutes farther south. When I was halfway done with the bed routine, Corby insisted that we watch a show. He used a remote control to sit the bed up and asked me to put his laptop on his legs. I then had to sit next to him. It was super awkward. He was only wearing half his clothes, and I was worried I would accidentally sit on his pee hose and pull it wrong.

After sitting directly next to him in his bed and smelling the faint odor coming from the pee bag for an hour, I decided for the fifty-seventh time that I should stop seeing Corby. I just couldn't envision this working out.

My resolve was strong.

At least, my resolve not to write research papers was strong.

I met Corby at his parents' house the very next night to play board games with some of his friends. After the other people left, I played the piano while Corby sang. Then he wanted to watch another show. I don't think he cared very much about what we watched; I think he just wanted an excuse to sit on the couch with me.

I had come prepared in case I might need an activity to distract from the potential of physical contact; I knit for the first episode. Corby tolerated it, though I could tell he wasn't happy. Before the second episode started, he asked me to put the knitting down and pulled my shoulder until I tipped over and my head was in his lap. He lightly tickled my back, and I froze. It wasn't *entirely* unpleasant. Corby let autoplay run two more episodes. Every time I tried to sit up, he pushed me back down onto his lap. I could feel my brain checking out, like it couldn't handle what was going on. I was technically still watching the show, but I wasn't comprehending it. All I could perceive was the sensations. I could feel Corby's femur pressing into my face—there wasn't much muscle to cover it—and the back of my head was brushing up against his stomach, so I could feel him breathing. All in all, the experience was extremely disconcerting.*

After the fourth episode in a row was finally over, Corby turned the TV off. I tried to sit up, but before I could escape, he got one of his arms under mine and pulled me onto his lap. He wrapped his arms around me and gave me a giant hug.

Hugging him felt different without a wheelchair in the way. There were no arm rests or wheelchair cushions getting in the way. When sitting on his lap, I could actually *hug* him with a normal-person-level-of-hugging contact. I guess I had expected that a Corby hug would be weak and helpless compared to the normal hugs I had experienced. But it wasn't. When sitting on his lap, I was in bicep range. He was able to exert some actual pressure.** I was shocked. It was warm and . . . safe? Since he was wearing a bulky jacket, his arms almost seemed normal-person sized. I stayed there for quite some time, trying not to think about what was happening.

When I stood up, Corby gave me a look. A very sentimental, meaningful, intense look. I didn't know what he was trying to convey, but it was uncomfortable. I had glimpsed this look before, whenever I'd left his van or apartment, but today, it was particularly powerful. I wanted to bolt, but I stayed long enough to drag Corby back into his chair.

I said good night and ran. Confusing and muddled thoughts plagued my car ride and shower. I simultaneously liked Corby more and less, and I didn't know what to do about it. I kept sitting on my mental staircase. But now mental Corby was intensely staring up at me. I wanted to mentally hide.

---

* *Whoops! I did often think that if she just tried physical touch, she'd see that it's not so scary. But maybe I shouldn't have pushed for it this hard?*

** *I don't exclusively exert emotional pressure!*

A week later, Corby drove up to my house. He was planning on coming inside and hanging out for a while, but his catheter decided to plug right before he arrived. Which meant violent leg twitching, overheating, and all-around general discomfort.

Both Corby and his mom had catheter kits in their cars for such emergencies, but his mom wasn't here, so instead of coming inside, he got back in his van, I got in my car, and I followed him down to South Jordan to a rental house his mom was renovating. There was plenty of space inside the van for cath change maneuvers, so the two of them stayed in there, while I chose to lean on the side of my car.

Corby's bladder must have been particularly full. Ronda kept squirting syringes full of urine* out the ramp and onto the sidewalk, trying to prevent it from . . . I didn't know what, but I assumed getting all over Corby's clothes. None of my other dates with male subjects had been interrupted by requisite visits to their mom so they could pee on the sidewalk by proxy from the inside of a minivan.

Once Corby was fixed, we went back to his parents' house, and I put him on the couch. He wanted to watch more shows. I was woefully behind on homework, so I pulled out a stack of academic articles and read a few while he watched the next episode. He didn't like that very much. He wanted me to cuddle with him like I had the last time. Every time I made any sort of progress, it became the new minimum expectation. Consequently, I did not want to make progress. I wanted to stop trying.

The next day, he texted me a potential insight.

> C: So, I took out a girl who is also the oldest of a bunch of kids, and she realized recently that she's a little touch averse because she also has little siblings all over her all the time. I was like, "Hey! I know someone else like that!" although she doesn't have your sensory hypersensitivity.

---

* *This was a particularly rare cath change, by the way—a real adventure. See the chapter about catheters for a more regular explanation.*

T: I don't think the little siblings were the primary cause though. How did you figure out that she was touch adverse on the first date?

C: Haha ahh listen to those little jealous questions. We didn't hold hands during the movie or anything. It came up somehow while talking on the drive home. If I remember the train of thought correctly, it's because she asked if I liked being fourth of six, so I asked her what the pros and cons are of being the oldest, and that's what she mentioned.

T: That isn't a jealous question. It just seems so bizarre to me that someone could attempt enough physical contact on the first date to figure that out.

C: Cuddling on the first date is okay in my book. Just kissing is not. It's not a first-date expectation, mind you, but it's acceptable if it happens. Isn't it bizarre to you that physical contact would be attempted ever?

T: Not really ever, but attempting anything beyond a brief hug on the first date just seems wrong.

C: You sat on my lap.

T: Yes, I know.

# USEFUL

## Finances

Being in a wheelchair is expensive. And Corby is in a very, very blessed position, where it doesn't affect us as much as it does everyone else. I will explain this later.

Let's start with the regular expenses. These are the averages as of 2025.

Corby takes several medications for the various side effects of being in a wheelchair. Insurance covers most of the prescription meds. We pay out of pocket for the nonprescription ones.

The catheter we use now costs about $14. Corby uses two to three per month. Drain bags are about $20 per month. That is approximately $600 per year for Corby to pee. And this figure is on the low end. People who do intermittent catheterization (use one every time they pee) spend over $2,000 per year on catheters.

Bowel-care supplies—gloves, paper towels, wipes, and suppositories—come to roughly $500 per year.

Between medical supplies and medications, we spend an average of $300 per month.

A new power wheelchair costs about $50,000. Insurance covers 80 percent of that cost once every five years. We save $75 per month in preparation for that expense.

Corby's van has all sorts of custom modifications. He can't just go somewhere and buy a wheelchair-accessible van that fits his particular chair and injury level. Instead, we buy a normal van and then pay a modification fee. By the time it is finished, it costs around $100,000. We save $600 per month in preparation for a downpayment and usually continue to pay around that much each month for five years to pay it off.

The last major expense is caregivers. I could technically attempt to take care of all Corby's needs on my own; however, Corby was warned by other wheelchair couples that using your spouse as your sole caregiver either leads to serious back problems or divorce. Neither of those sounds pleasant, so we rely on caregivers to help me take care of Corby. As mentioned before, Corby does not qualify for home healthcare. We tried to find an independent service to come do bowel care and morning/night transfers, but these services either 1) do not serve people without Medicaid, 2) are ridiculously expensive without Medicaid, or 3) can't come to your house until 9:00 a.m., which is difficult when bowel care and a shower take two hours, and you have a nine-to-five job.

We have found one company that will help Corby without requiring Medicaid. We use them on an as-needed basis for $120 per hour.

Currently, most of the people who come help are our neighbors and don't want to be paid. They just like opportunities to serve. In fact, we have so many volunteers to help that most of the people come only once a week! This neighborhood is the best. If they didn't come help and if I weren't able to step in, it would cost $720+ per week for Corby to poop. Hilarious.

So, all told, if we didn't live in magical neighborhoods with friendly people who want to help just for the sake of helping, we would spend about $3,600 per month on wheelchair expenses. This figure does not include doctors' appointments or medical equipment.

Corby has had these expenses since he was eighteen. For us, these items are set numbers in an excel spreadsheet that we will always budget for.

Corby happens to have a job he can 1) perform perfectly fine from a wheelchair and 2) generate enough income to comfortably provide both living expenses *and* medical expenses.

A couple of points to think about here:

1) How many people with SCI cannot work after their injury? Depending on the level of injury and their education or training, it may be impossible to find a job that pays enough to cover everything.
2) You cannot qualify for Medicaid if you make over $2,313 per month. I have read articles detailing the effects of this ridiculously low limit. There are wheelchair couples who choose not to get married because if they do, their combined income will be too high to qualify for medical assistance but too low to cover

> their living expenses and medical care. There are people in wheelchairs who are perfectly capable of working, but if they do, they will make too much money to qualify for home health care. People with disabilities who cannot make enough to pay for medical and living expenses have to choose not to work. This is a terrible reality. People are sitting at home, forced to contribute nothing, just because of an arbitrary limit.

Corby is also in an unusual position because his family happened to be able to support him financially when he first got injured. Their house already had a decent layout for a wheelchair. They were able to get a lift in the garage to get him into the house and afford a used wheelchair-accessible van so they could chauffeur Corby around until he recovered enough to get a van that he could drive himself. Not everyone can do that at the time of injury. But because he was in that sort of environment, he had the resources he needed to continue to grow and succeed.

The moral of this chapter is that wheelchair life is expensive. We are incredibly blessed to be able to afford it. I know that not everyone can say the same thing.*

---

* *The idea of another wheelchair user reading this and seeing how easy we have it, comparatively, makes us feel deeply guilty. Honestly, I feel like our setup is the best anyone could ask for, so unless your circumstances are just as good, they are probably worse. Sorry if that's the case.*

## *Chapter 23*

# Spam Emails and Indecent Exposure

*Mid-October*

I glanced at the clock. I had forty minutes before I needed to leave for Orem; Corby and I were planning on going to a devotional tonight. But first, I had to entertain a group of senior citizens.

One of my church assignments was to plan monthly activities at a local care center. This month, I created a PowerPoint to simulate a 1980s game show called *Concentration*. It was essentially a matching game, and as the matches were taken away, a little word puzzle would be revealed. The plan seemed well thought out. The slides worked, the chairs were set up facing the right direction, and some old people had shuffled in and parked their walkers.

The plan went awry almost immediately. An old man stood up and started reading one of those spam emails full of dubiously funny jokes. He read each one very, very slowly, pausing in between each one to give the residents time to wheeze and chuckle. Ordinarily, I wouldn't have minded, but tonight, these jokes meant that I would be leaving late. And I hated being late.

The second downside of this impromptu performance was that it gave my computer enough time to freeze for no good reason. I calmly restarted my computer, which prompted Windows to run an update—an incredibly large update with an estimated completion time of ten minutes. I peeked over the top of my computer. Spam man had sat down, and twenty-five care center citizens were blearily staring at me in complete silence. I suddenly wished I had my own set of spam emails to read to them. In fact, why had I bothered to make a fancy PowerPoint if a spam email was just as entertaining?

I frantically looked over at my sister Rylee, who had come to help. We awkwardly stood up and stalled by sharing our favorite parts about the past week. It was the longest ten minutes ever. I didn't need to look at the clock again to know I was going to be very late meeting Corby.

Once my computer decided to cooperate, the activity went great, almost as good as the spam email reading! Rylee and I packed up and rushed outside. I had been planning on dropping her off at home, but now she was going to come with me. She was delighted; she thought Corby was hilarious.

We met Corby at his apartment, but there was no chance of making it to the devotional on time. Instead, we leisurely went to the gas station to obtain hot chocolate and took the drinks back to Corby's apartment. Apparently, we had rushed all the way down to Orem just to sit and chat.

Corby asked me to help him get into bed since none of his roommates were home. I lifted Corby out of his chair and onto the mattress. Then I proceeded to pull his clothes off. *All* his clothes. I had pushed him onto his side, facing away from me, to pull just his pants down, but the rest came with it. Turns out, our evening would have an unexpected show! I grabbed a blanket and covered him before I could see much, but since I had let go so abruptly, Corby reached down and felt around his waist. His eyes got wide. We both busted out laughing. Rylee had no idea what was going on because my hips had blocked most of her view, and she had missed the big reveal. I'm sure she thought we had temporarily gone insane.

After I had mostly calmed down, I spent ten solid minutes trying to separate the pants from the underwear without looking and then pulling the underwear up straight without touching anything . . . *interesting*. It didn't help that I kept breaking out in bouts of laughter. This was a date activity I had never expected: pulling a man's underwear off in front of my little sister.

## Chapter 24

# Smash Bros. Is Paramount

*Late October*

*Super Smash Bros. Ultimate* was being released tomorrow. Was I excited? No. But Corby was. He had been counting down the days for months. However, his gigantic, lap-sized game controller with huge buttons and joysticks didn't work. He had been trying to fix it for several weeks but had been unsuccessful . . . and he had almost run out of time.

There was one tiny ray of hope left. He had called a bunch of obscure electronics stores, and one of them said they had the part he needed. So I got recruited to go on an electrical-part scavenger hunt. The disassembled controller was precariously perched on the passenger seat, and I didn't want to move it, so I climbed into the back of the van. Corby was not happy about that, but the desire to play *Smash Bros.* was too powerful for him to complain. He kept looking at me in the rearview mirror every three minutes, like we were in a sappy chick flick. It was disconcerting.

The store was tiny and cluttered. Corby showed a picture of the piece to the guy at the front counter. The guy thought for a minute and scrawled out a list of possible bin numbers on a smudged sticky note.

Corby followed me down the center aisle, moving slowly to avoid knocking anything off the overflowing shelves. I grabbed promising-looking items from the bins and took them back to Corby to see if the part number and picture matched. They had what he needed! Corby was elated.

We went back to my house, and I dragged Corby up the scary metal slabs, then carefully brought the controller pieces to the kitchen table. I poked around in the basement until I found my dad's soldering iron. Had I ever soldered? No. But I watched a short YouTube video on the basics of soldering, and I was much more confident about my ability to handle hot metal than I was about navigating emotional minefields or holding hands.

I sorted through wires until I found the broken piece, then melted the connections. Corby sat nearby, providing emotional support, making suggestions from his own YouTube browsing, and chatting with whatever sibling wandered by. We worked on it for several hours. When my dad got back from work, I had him check the connections to make sure the controller wouldn't blow up if we plugged it in. He took a couple of minutes to clean up a few things, but he said that it "wasn't bad." High praise indeed.

The moment of truth arrived. We plugged in the controller, and, to my amazement, it actually worked! There was no ominous scent of scorched plastic! Corby was giddy. He had a huge grin on his face and kept opening and closing menus just because he could. The controller had been broken for months, so he hadn't been able to play anything. He challenged my little brothers to a game of *Mario Kart*. Rylee and I joined in for the last few rounds, though both of us were terrible. We competed against each other for eleventh place. (Out of twelve places, in case you were wondering.)

When Corby was done playing, I pulled the controller off his lap and neatly wound up all the cables. I glanced over at him. I was feeling strangely fond of him, almost like it was our first date again. His utter delight over a functional controller was adorable.

I was seized with a foreign impulse to hug him. I clambered over the couch arm and sat directly on his lap. He certainly didn't protest, and he didn't ask any questions. He just pulled my head into his shoulder and wrapped his arms around my waist. I kept my eyes glued to the TV to avoid looking at Rylee and Eric. This was the biggest display of PDA that had ever occurred in the Sommer household, and I wasn't sure how they would react. We sat like that for almost an hour.

After taking a shower and imagining all sorts of idealistic Corby scenarios, I almost texted him to tell him he should stop going out with other girls. But I didn't. My rational brain had been ignored enough for one day, and it wouldn't let me go *that* far. Instead, I descended three steps on my mental staircase.

The next day, Corby played *Smash Bros.* for twelve hours straight. And my mom, who had not actually seen the lap cuddles, said it was funny that Corby had brought his controller to his *girlfriend* to get it fixed. My mom had decided we were dating, even if my brain hadn't yet.

## Chapter 25

# The B-Word

*November, Thanksgiving weekend*

Christmas was coming, and I didn't have any Christmas sheet music with words. Which meant that I didn't have any Christmas music for Corby accompaniment purposes. I decided to go shopping.

I went to the tiny local music store, and I briefly considered each book in the single vocal Christmas music display before I made my selection.

I was the only person in the store other than the employee who was rummaging around behind the counter. I approached, ready to check out.

As I slid the music across the counter, I decided to seize the opportunity to try an experiment. "I need this music because my boyfriend is a singer."

I tried to say it casually, like I was accustomed to being in a relationship. I tried not to put any emphasis on the word *boyfriend*, as if I said it all the time. I glanced up at the employee. She didn't seem interested at all in my monumental confession. She just shoved the bag at me and routinely wished me a good day. I snatched the bag and hurried out to my car. I was panicking inside. Saying that phrase hadn't been as weird as I'd thought it would be, probably because Corby and I had been acting like a couple for months. But it still felt very unnatural.

I went to the Campbells' later that evening for dinner and games. After everyone else had gone to bed, I put Corby on the couch and lay down with my head in his lap. It was mostly dark; only the light above the front door was on. Gambit made a quiet mew and leaped onto the couch. He started pacing up and down my torso while we talked. That cat loved rubs but didn't ever stand still for them.*

"Hey, are you doing anything for dinner on December 7?" Corby asked while he ran his gimp fingers through my stray hair strands.

"Uh, yeah. I'm celebrating Pearl Harbor Day. Doesn't everyone?"

"Of course! We're calling our celebration "Friendsmas," though, and doing dinner with a bunch of my old roommates . . . Would you be interested in joining us?"

"Sure," I responded.

"Yay! Pen it into your mental calendar! With brain ink or whatever."

"It has been inserted."

"Permanent marker?"

"Glow-in-the-dark paint."

"Does that last?"

"Of course it does. Are you concerned about this?"

"I feel like glow-in-the-dark stuff degrades to a dull vomit-colored thing."

"Not the brain version."

Our conversation died off. There was nothing much else to say about nonexistent glow-in-the-dark brain paint.

Corby's fists paused in the pile of hair he had arranged into a fan across his lap. He looked down at me. "Tess? Do I have to keep going out with other girls?"

There was a very long pause.

"I guess not."

---

* *It's the weirdest thing. He wants rubs, so you rub him, and he starts walking until he is out of range. But then he turns around and gives you a "Why did you stop?" look and comes back. This pattern repeats until you get tired of petting an object in motion.*

"So, you will be my girlfriend?"

I hesitated. "I guess so."

And with that amazingly confident statement, I was dating Corby Campbell. For real.

At this point, Corby's legs started bouncing. Gambit, startled by the shaking, bounded off the couch. I lifted my head slightly and waited. Usually, the legs would calm down after a few seconds. When they kept on bouncing, I reached down to discover that Corby's leg bag was uncomfortably full, so I celebrated this momentous moment by retrieving the plastic pee container from the bathroom, kneeling on the floor to empty the bag, and then dumping it into the toilet.

This activity allowed enough time for my brain to catch up to what had just happened. Had I just told Corby that I would be his . . . girlfriend?! What?! This wave of realization was not a pleasant one. I knew this conversation had been coming, but I hadn't expected it right then.

I put the container back on the shelf and turned to the sink to wash my hands. My eyes started leaking. I knew it was hopeless to try not to cry, so I slowly dried my hands and walked back to the couch. Maybe I could take it back. The phrase "I guess so" was not a concrete agreement, right? Maybe Corby's dancing legs had distracted him from actually hearing my answer, and I wasn't in a relationship yet!

No such luck. I rounded the corner of the couch to find that Corby had a huge grin on his face. He was victorious, and he knew it.

I attempted to change my answer. "Can we maybe pretend this didn't just happen?"

"Hah! No! You already said yes!" He was still grinning.

I stared at him, my cheeks wet with tears.

"Look, if you still feel this way in a few days, we can take a step back again. But at least try it, okay?"

I kept staring.

"It's cute that you're crying about this." He opened his arms.

I sat on his lap, and he pulled me against his chest. I cried softly while he held me, and then I finally glanced up.

He was still smiling. "I have wanted this since March, you know."

I burrowed my head back down into his jacket collar. He was insane. Why was he so happy about having a girlfriend who was crying about being in a relationship?

I shakily heaved him back into his chair, and he took me to the door. After one last hug, I escaped to my car and tried not to think about what was happening inside that house. Corby would be telling his mom as she put him in bed. And I'm sure my tears would be a part of that story. Would Ronda think Corby was crazy too?

For an entire week, I had been pretending that I was Corby's girlfriend, and it had felt okay. Why was it so horrible now that it was official? Really, nothing had changed. We had already mostly been acting like a couple, so what was I nervous about?

I parked in the driveway and looked at the clock. It was 3:02 a.m. Maybe I was just tired? This was probably not a good time to be questioning my decisions, but I couldn't help it.

Argh! None of this was what I had pictured! Who pictures her first boyfriend in a wheelchair? Getting into an official relationship and then helping him pee and then carrying him across the living room back to his chair so his mom could put him to bed?

AHHHHHHHHHHH! I slipped inside the front door and crept up the stairs, avoiding the squeaky spots. I wanted to go back to being fifteen years old, when none of this had been an issue, and I could just focus on calculus.

Corby was still delighted with our new status the next morning.

C: Good morning, Tess. Get much sleep? It's finally snowing!

T: Is there a possibility that any of that was a dream?

C: There's a slim chance. But if so, you're still dreaming now, and you'll still be dreaming tomorrow.

T: I would be fine with perpetual dreams.

C: Oh good! I'll help perpetuate the current dream then. MWAHAHA

T: But this isn't a dream!

C: You're right! I'll perpetuate it in real life instead.

T: You aren't supposed to be excited about perpetuating nightmares!

C: I'm hoping it's more like making your kids take piano lessons even though they hate it, but someday they will be glad. PS I'm journaling about us :D

T: Are you sure you don't want to modify that entry as you write it?

C: Sure, I'll change the part where I asked, "Will you be my girlfriend?" and instead of saying, "I guess so," you say, "Yes."

T: It is hard to say yes when 90% of your brain is telling you that you are about to make the wrong decision.

C: I've worked up to 10%? That's like a 10x increase!!

T: That is still a terrible ratio.

C: Have you had a chance to process at all? I'd of course love to discuss your concerns.

T: An igloo in Alaska sounds appealing right now.

C: You dislike me more than cold? *hurt puppy dog eyes*

T: I know how to deal with cold. And stop looking at me like that!

C: *changes to seductive stare*

T: *bolts*

C: Hey! I fulfilled your request!

T: Well, how about you aim for a mature, normal look?

C: Mature? Are you sure I can pull that off? Well, if you are trying to stretch, I guess I can try to stretch too . . .

T: You do sometimes. I've seen it happen before.

C: And you cuddle sometimes. I have seen it happen before. Things can change!

## INTERLUDE NOTE THING 1

WARNING:

YOU ARE PROBABLY VERY EXCITED THAT TESS IS FINALLY DATING CORBY. DO NOT GET EXCITED. THIS PHASE DOESN'T LAST LONG.

DO NOT PASS GO.

DO NOT COLLECT $200.

## Chapter 26

# Mrs. Counselor Lady

*December*

I had finally started seeing a counselor. My goal for counseling was to figure out what I should do about Corby. But instead of talking about Corby, the counselor wanted to talk about any instances of mental illness in my family and the examples of non-Corby relationships in my life and the way I approached life in general. Essentially, we talked about everything *except* Corby. And she gave me homework! So then I had to think about everything in my life that *wasn't* Corby in addition to thinking about what to do with Corby. Not really what I wanted at all.

I drove down the freeway, preparing myself to talk to Mrs. Counselor Lady, a.k.a. Jennifer. She was nice enough, but talking to her was exhausting. And I was already exhausted. The amount of work I had with my grad school and church assignments was becoming overwhelming. The prospect of talking to some lady about my *feelings* was not a pleasant one. I had been to therapy three times now, and each time I'd gone, I had turned into a dysfunctional robot for at least two days.

Jennifer invited me into her office. "How are you?"

I shrugged and didn't say anything.

"Have you had any new insights since last week? How are things going with Corby?"

I shrugged again, looking at the floor. I didn't want to talk about Corby.

Jennifer waited a few seconds, hoping I would say something interesting. I maintained my floor stare, and she moved on.

"The last few weeks, I've asked you a lot of questions. Today, I think I will share some of my insights."

Ah! A week where Mrs. Counselor Lady would do the talking!

"I think you may be on the autism spectrum."

I looked up at her, confused.

"You told me that you have sensory oversensitivity. That is a common symptom of those on the spectrum. You also seem to have a hard time recognizing social cues and making eye contact. Now, I'm not saying that you *are* on the spectrum. You might just have a sensory disorder. Or these symptoms could just be byproducts of clinical anxiety, but you have some of the classic signs, so it is a possibility to consider."

I finally broke my vow of silence. "Well . . . can you do some tests? Give me an official diagnosis?"

"No, I am not qualified to administer those tests. But you could certainly look into it!"

What was I paying this woman for?! Using her tissues?

Jennifer kept going. "Even though you might not have a clinical condition, we can still agree that you have a significant level of anxiety, right?"

I gave her an exasperated look.

"Okay, good. It seems like one of your biggest triggers is other people's reactions, especially if they tend to overreact. Something small happens. You logically know it is not a big deal, but you worry quite a lot about what the other person will do. And if that person reacts stronger than you expected, it makes your anxiety worse. Right?"

I nodded.

"I think you have tried to overcompensate in the other direction. Because reactions are such a huge trigger for you, you try not to react at all. You pretend that things aren't a big deal. You take the blame for everything because you don't want to make someone else feel like you do. And you don't like to share your opinions or preferences. You don't want to deal with someone else questioning or criticizing your choices, so you just accept what is given to you and deal with it rather than doing what you really want."

Jennifer was making a lot of sense. Somehow, she was able to just say things simply and clearly. Like Corby could. Jennifer watched me. For the past three weeks, I had argued against all her theories, but this week, I sat and contemplated what she was saying.

She must have taken my silence as agreement, so she went on hypothesizing. "I have noticed that you are a very logical person. Let us also assume that you have a fairly severe level of anxiety. This means that you are often split between your analytical brain and your emotions, which are driven by anxiety. In most cases, the anxiety side wins. Then you systematically justify your emotional choices so that logic will fit with the emotions. For example, when I asked about all your past relationships before Corby, you told me you hadn't ever had any. When I asked some follow-up questions, you told me you didn't like any of those guys, and they all ended up moving away to college. You had some sort of story for every guy and why the relationship wouldn't work out. Am I correct in assuming that you did actually like some of those guys? But when it grew more serious, you became anxious? And then you decided not to pursue the relationship because you found logical reasons for why it wouldn't work out?"

I mutely nodded, staring at the tissue box.

"I think you have become skilled at looking for tiny flaws in all situations, including relationships, storing those flaws away until you need a reason to convince yourself things won't work out. This has never been a problem with school. You *emotionally* like school, and you *logically* do well at school, so school is a safe space where you don't feel divided. But relationships are a much different story. And your system worked until you met Corby."

Ah. Corby. I picked up the tissue box and yanked out four tissues.

"You and Corby met online. He had a creative profile. You have a lot in common. You could read his blog and imagine yourself being the girl who could finally give him everything he wanted, who could handle the unique wheelchair situation and be strong enough to make things work. Because you hadn't met Corby in person, it was hard to find reasons to convince yourself not to like him. Your two halves allowed you to move forward.

"The phone calls and texting were still not serious; you were just talking. You were excited to go on a first date, but once you met in person, you started picking things apart and finding areas that weren't perfect. But Corby was persistent. When you found logical reasons not to go on dates, Corby found logical reasons that you should. And your overanalytical brain wouldn't let you defy his logic. So you went.

"I think you have met a man who *both* your emotional and logical sides want to be with. But because you have so much anxiety around relationships, you are trying to find reasons that it won't work. You are trying to find things that annoy you so you can convince your brain to let go. You couldn't find enough reasons not to be in a relationship, so you finally said yes, but you are still looking for those reasons in preparation for when Corby wants more commitment."

The four tissues were already soaked. I yanked out three more.

"I also think you know that Corby is the strongest communicator in your life. It seems like he has helped you a lot in that area. And you know that if you were to give him up, you would lose that."*

Jennifer was right. For the first time in my life, I had someone with whom I shared everything! Well . . . half of everything. But that was still more than I had ever shared before! I finally felt connected to someone. I didn't want to lose that.

Jennifer glanced down at her watch. "Oh, it looks like we're out of time! Would you like to schedule for next week?"

No, I would not. Mrs. Counselor Lady, though her theories were interesting and had merit, had not actually given me any direction. She had neatly articulated that my soul was engaging in civil war every time I had to make a decision about Corby, but I already knew that! What was I supposed to *do* about it?

As I drove home, I thought about sensory oversensitivity. Did I actually have something wrong with me, something that made smells

---

* *I hereby award Jennifer 7,000 life points for seeing this stuff. Thanks, Jennifer!*

and lights and noises hard? I thought about how I habitually avoided people and noise and had a list of foods that had weird textures. And how hard it was to be in big groups of people and how hard it was to be touched. Was this why I liked texting Corby, but why I suddenly didn't like him in person? Was it not *Corby* I was struggling with but the *environment*? The smells and all the noise at his parents' house and the way he would brush my arm with his fist? Was *this* what my problem had been the entire time?

Meanwhile, Corby was going a little bit crazy. He knew I was talking to Mrs. Counselor Lady about emotional things—things that he was dying to talk about. I didn't want to talk about it in person, so just before leaving campus for Christmas break, I locked myself in my office and typed up an eight-page letter detailing some of the things I had learned in counseling. I emailed the letter to Corby, who was stoked about the amount of personal information it contained. Most of it was about Jennifer's insights regarding logic vs. emotion justifications and habitual underreactions. I included a bit about the sensory stuff but mentioned the autism theory only once. It was so new and unexplored that I didn't think it had much merit. Because there were so many other avenues to explore, both Corby and I mostly forgot about this potential diagnosis until years later.

*Chapter 27*

# And It All Came Tumbling Down

*January*

I spent both Thanksgiving and Christmas breaks with Corby at his parents' house. I decided to not think about the future of our relationship until the holidays were over and shoved all the stuff I had learned in counseling to the back of my brain. We watched shows and played games. We even got in a hot tub, aided by a contingency of Campbells who were on hand to lift a slippery Corby in and out of the water. I held the nearly naked Corby to prevent him from floating away for over an hour—he really seemed to enjoy that part. We assembled a Lego set, which was simply delightful. If I didn't think about the future, it was lovely spending so much time with Corby. I did such a good job that I tricked myself into being optimistic!

At the beginning of January, we went on a date to see an exhibit of expertly dissected bodies. I thought it was a great activity choice. Because of the Christmas break snuggles and all the activities we had done together, Corby was in a hopeful mood. While driving me home, he started talking about the future. He talked about his summer plans and how he would take me to Powell again. He also talked about how he wanted to take his future wife on random weekend getaways after he got married and how his nurse was willing to go on random trips to take care of stuff if his wife ever wanted to do something like that. For some reason, this conversation didn't terrify me as much as it usually would, even though there was a strong implication that he was picturing *me* in this role of "future wife."

We didn't want the evening to end. Corby parked up the street from my house so none of my siblings would see his van outside. I eased the front door open, sneaked down to the basement fridge (jumping over the creaky stairs), slid two pieces of cheesecake onto a plate, and got back to the car without anyone in the family noticing. We drove up the hill to a very scenic parking lot and ate the cake. Then I sat in his lap. This was the closest I had ever felt to Corby, and it was nice. Eventually, he had to ask me to get off his lap because he needed to get home. That was a new experience—*Corby* ending a cuddle first.*

Four days later, Corby was coming back to my house for dinner. I was about to leave campus to get home when I made a mistake: I left the protection of my personal office to use the lab printer. I ran into Rachel, a fellow student whom I didn't know very well. I didn't know any of my fellow students very well, probably because I had been avoiding them.

Rachel invited me into her tiny office closet to see her new decorations. I couldn't see a way to get out of this politely, so I went in and did my best to admire a painting of a seahorse. She cautiously started asking personal questions.

She had heard a rumor that I was dating two or three different guys. My brain burst out into hysterical giggles. Me? Date two or three different guys? I had just gotten my very first boyfriend, had never even held hands with him, and our shaky relationship was only about six weeks old. The *official* version of our relationship, that was.

I opened my mouth, intending to clear up this ludicrous rumor, but then I noticed a picture on Rachel's desk—a framed photo of her and her boyfriend, who had working legs, *hiking*. I suddenly started to cry. It was such an unexpected response that I couldn't stop it in time. I was jealous. Rachel's dates weren't cut short because her

---

* *Weird, right? I guess I should have asked her to stop cuddling more often!*

boyfriend needed to be home so his roommates could put him in bed. And Rachel could sit next to her boyfriend on a couch without lifting him first. The list grew longer. It was like my brain had been saving up a flood of thoughts, waiting to remind me of why dating Corby was a stupid idea. I wished Corby could turn pages of piano music and spin me on a dance floor and go on a walk around the block. I looked up at Rachel and choked out an apology. She smiled sympathetically.

I tried to offer an explanation. "Yeah, I sort of have a boyfriend. We have been going out for almost a year, but he is in a wheelchair, and I don't know if I can handle it . . ."

Rachel looked confused by this piece of information. "Well, if you're this sad, maybe you shouldn't be dating him? You're only twenty-one; you should find someone who you can be happy with!"

I sighed, knowing I would never be able to explain. Sure, I was only twenty-one. But Corby had made me happier than I had ever been! And I knew that I would never find anyone else like him.

I finally escaped Rachel's office. She didn't have a window in her office closet, and I was shocked to see how dark it was outside. I rushed back to my office to find a dozen texts and missed calls from Corby. I called him back.

"Sorry, I didn't realize how late it was!"

"No worries! I just wanted you to know that I left work early, and I already made it to your house. I'm at Arctic Circle getting onion rings with Rylee and Ivy."*

I could hear Ivy giggling in the background. She was probably bouncing around in the giant seatless van, having the time of her life. Both Rylee and Ivy loved Corby so much. Knowing that I would hurt my family if I broke up with Corby made everything so much worse. I hadn't even told them we were officially dating, because I didn't want to get their hopes up.

I drove home, took my backpack down to the basement, then dragged Corby inside to the kitchen table. I was grateful that my

---

* *I'm not above bribery.*

siblings were there as a distraction. Corby could tell I wasn't acting normal but didn't say anything.

The next night, we went on a double date with some of Corby's friends. We ate dinner at Black Bear Diner, the same place we went on our first date. It was surreal, walking past the parking spot we had used that day. I looked at the sidewalk, picturing me riding to the door on his lap, and then when we walked into the restaurant, I looked at the table we'd sat at, seeing ghostly images of that amazing night that had happened one year before.

After dinner, we played some card games at Corby's parents' house. When it was time for me to leave, Corby followed me to the door. I reluctantly leaned over to hug him and immediately started crying. Christmas break had been so wonderful, but something had changed. I didn't know what to do.

"I think we should talk," Corby said. "Will you come back after Mom puts me in bed?"

I couldn't talk. I could barely breathe. And I wouldn't even know what to talk about. How could we solve a problem when I couldn't identify what had happened? How had I gone from liking Corby and voluntarily sitting on his lap to being an emotional wreck in the space of four days? I mutely shook my head while slowly backing out the front door, leaving a very confused Corby sitting in the hallway.

I went home and cried for hours. And again on Sunday, and again on Monday. I wondered if my mom had noticed that the toilet paper stock was shrinking faster than average. I couldn't stand the thought of breaking up with Corby and never talking to him again, but I also didn't think I could keep seeing him.

(Looking back now, I know that I was tumbling down the side of the sensory Aztec temple that had been built over Thanksgiving and Christmas—I just hadn't learned enough about sensory disorders yet to realize what the cause was.)

On Tuesday afternoon, I had an appointment with Jennifer. The minute I sat down, I started sobbing. I was crying so hard I was almost choking. Jennifer just waited until I calmed down. Well, at least calmed enough to be shakily gulping sporadic breaths.

"Does this have something to do with Corby?"

I nodded.

"What?"

"I don't know! I just broke, and I don't know why!"

After forty-five minutes of questioning, Jennifer gave her verdict. "In addition to the sensory overload caused by Christmas break, you are constantly looking for an endpoint, when things will stop. Your brain loves endpoints because it can plan everything up to that endpoint. But with relationships, there isn't a definite endpoint. You cannot plan or predict when a relationship will end, and if the relationship is successful, there *is* no end. So your brain has decided to shut down and create its own endpoint. It seems to be a defense mechanism. I don't know what your brain is trying to protect itself from, but it is. It seemed to be triggered by Corby talking about the future. And given the amount of stress this is causing, I think the best thing to do is to end the relationship and move on."

I froze, my face buried in my hands. End it? Move on? The entire reason I was sitting in this office was because I wanted to make it work with Corby! I came to this woman for help, and she had the audacity to tell me to end it and move on? What?!

"There is no way to make this work?" I asked.

Jennifer didn't say anything. Her eyes flicked down. I followed her gaze. I had fourteen soggy tissue wads scattered across my lap. Yeah, okay. But wouldn't this happen every time I attempted to get into a relationship if my stupid brain always had to have an endpoint? How was I supposed to stop that from happening? And if I couldn't manage to do it for Corby, then what hope did I have?

Corby knew I had gone to an appointment with Jennifer. He called me that night, after he was in bed. He was in one of his persistent interrogation moods.

"Anything you'd like to discuss?" he asked.

"I think I have already discussed enough stuff today with Jennifer."

"Not with *me*! And I don't have this arbitrary 'I've already discussed stuff' limit like you do. I could discuss emotional stuff all day every day."

"Weirdo. You don't ever feel like a wrung-out rag?"

"I'm under the opposite circumstances. I feel like a wrung-out rag when I know something is wrong but have to wait for days before I can talk to you about it."

"I'm sorry I'm so terrible at all this stuff."

"Your communication is coming along great; you are not incapable of doing this!"

"Really slowly. I know that you would want it to move faster though."

"You are worth exercising patience for. You are wonderful. I care about you deeply."

"And I can't help but keep thinking that all this patience isn't ever going to pay off."

"If by 'pay off,' you mean 'result in marriage,' then yes, I think you're probably right," Corby said. "That doesn't mean it didn't pay off though. I have already learned so much from this. And created so many memories."

"Well, if you don't think it will end in marriage, wouldn't it be better to stop wasting your time?"

"I don't *know* that it won't result in marriage, and once again, even if it doesn't, it's not a waste of time. I may *never* get married. You think your concerns about dating a guy in a wheelchair and not being able to do the adventures you want to do are unique to you? You don't think I have had that problem with every girl I've tried to date in the last decade?"

"I know you have. And I keep thinking that I should be able to deal with them better than I am."

"It seems like you're doing a great job, from my perspective!"

"Yeah, great job," I said sarcastically. "I am the personification of a soggy wad of toilet paper."

Corby sighed. "Ahh, we can be an odd pair sometimes. Are you going to be able to sleep tonight?"

Ah! This was a question I knew how to answer! "Uh, no?"

"What percentage of your thoughts am I involved in?"

I liked these straightforward questions. "All of them."

"How can I help?"

"I don't think you can. I can't figure out how I flipped a complete 180 overnight, and I'm not sure I can handle this anymore."

"It really did seem like a complete 180 overnight. If what you need is for me to back off, I can try that again. Did you talk to Jennifer about this today?"

"Yes. And she thinks we should break up. But I'm not sure if backing off temporarily would help much. I know that you would hate it, and I can't guarantee that we would ever get back together officially."

"I wouldn't expect a guarantee of anything. I don't have any guarantees now. You don't need to worry about me. I'll be fine, whatever happens. I can support you in working past this if you want, or I can support you by letting go with no expectations. I sure wish you'd talk to me about it though. Crying this much isn't good."

"But never talking to you again sounds terrible!" I blindly felt around for my toilet paper roll. It couldn't be far away.

"I've known the whole time that a breakup is the most likely outcome. But I still don't think it's the only possible outcome, and I'm still willing to work with you if you're willing to work with me. Relationships aren't going to be easy all the time, just a commitment to work with each other even when things get rough. I'm still here to work on it if you can work with me too. I can also see how maybe it really will just take a lot more time before you're ready to continue trying something like this. And when I say continue, I don't mean to imply that it would be with me. No expectations. It's a decision only you can make, and I don't want you to make any decisions tonight."

Curse Corby and his stupid, elaborate, sweet speeches! I couldn't get any more words out, and it was now 2:00 a.m. My jumbo-sized toilet paper roll, which had been full just a week ago, now had only ten squares left.

Corby waited for a few moments until he realized I wasn't going to say anything else. "I care about you a lot, Tess. Don't make a decision yet. We can keep talking about this later. But I really think we can make it work. Platypus."

"Platypus," I whispered.

I hung up the phone and crawled under my table. I felt like I was giving up. Here was the perfect guy, and I was losing him because of my mental problems and his physical ones.

I crawled out from under the table and headed upstairs, but I took a detour to the freezer first, digging out some ice packs. I knew I wasn't going to sleep much anyway, so I figured that balancing ice on my face in an attempt to reduce the puffiness would be a good distraction. In a few hours, I had to teach a Sunday School lesson on the importance of agency. How ironic was that?

## *Chapter 28*

# Corby Is Not a Disposal

*February*

I was texting Corby, and I decided that I wanted to be his girlfriend again. So I drove down to his parents' house to tell him. Somehow, during those few minutes, Corby had managed to get married. To a girl with blue streaks in her hair, heavy makeup, and an obnoxious T-shirt with giant glittery text all over the front. I watched the two of them, knowing it should have been me and feeling sad I had missed my chance.

Suddenly, I was back in my bed. I had officially broken up with Corby a few days before, and he had started appearing in ridiculous dreams almost every night since. The next night, I had a dream that I was snuggled up in Corby's lap. It was amazingly vivid. I could feel the texture of his jacket against my cheek. I was a little sad to wake up from that one; it had felt strangely safe and comforting.* I was also sad that we had broken up right before Valentine's Day. I celebrated the anniversary of our first date by staying in my bedroom the entire day, pacing, crying, and retreating to the top of my mental staircase, contemplating the ever-present Corby sitting at the bottom.

I was still meeting with Jennifer. Now that I wasn't dating Corby, she had moved on to discussing how my subconscious assumptions about relationships were affecting my decisions. I found this

---

* *Nice! I at least convinced her subconscious that cuddling is okay!*

surprisingly interesting, and wrote my thoughts on little index cards, which I then taped together into a giant flowchart.

According to my flowchart, there was a point to getting married 200 years ago. Survival depended on it. Men and women contributed equally, and there were specifically defined roles. Both were needed. Today, people could survive perfectly well independently. I could get a job without the need for a man to hunt and farm and build me a cabin. And a man didn't need me to preserve fish and sew his shirts. Therefore, the only reason to get married in the modern era was to have someone with whom you were truly connected, someone you liked doing things with in your spare time. And, of course, the physical relationship. This was a reason I could not relate to. I struggled so much with physical touch in general that I didn't know why anyone would want a permanent kissing partner. But I knew it was important for other people, especially for all the male subjects I had observed.

Due to this observation, my very logical and literal brain had decided that all males were faking things in order to obtain snuggles. Males thought females were totally silly and stupid for wanting to wear certain things, wanting to shop for cute wall art, and wanting to go out on mushy, romantic dates, but they tolerated all this and pretended to like it. The better the male was at pretending to enjoy these things, the more physical affection the female would give. Eventually, they got married, and then the male stopped doing the fun relationship things because now he had found his permanent kissing partner, and she was stuck with him.

Jennifer carefully read my flowchart. She was impressed by the detail; I had never put that much work into one of her assignments before.

As usual, she had some succinct deductions. "These are some great conclusions! I agree. Part of your problem with relationships is that you are terrified that you will get married and then your husband will stop doing things with you that he did when you were dating."

"Right? I could never survive like that! What is the point of getting married if you are essentially going back to living alone, just in the same house as someone else?"

"Well, not all guys are like this. But because you are so determined to find one, you test everyone you go out with. You pull away and purposely don't touch them to see how committed they are. You want them to like you for who you are. You are good at being friends with guys since a friend is not going to con you into kissing him, but you are sabotaging every single romantic relationship that has even the slightest amount of promise because you think everyone is faking it. I also think there is another element at play here. Please tell me about your least favorite chores."

I was taken off guard. This was an odd question to suddenly ask. But it wasn't about my emotions, so I eagerly answered it. I even had an answer ready. "Cleaning the shower."

"Why?"

"I hate hair. Three girls use my shower, so there is a *ton* of hair. There is orange stuff in the corners where the water gets stuck. Between the dirty shower smells and the powerful cleaning fumes, it is awful."

Jennifer nodded. "Anything else?"

"Well . . . doing the dishes isn't bad, but I don't like running the disposal."

"Why not?"

"Because you have to put your hand in the mystery water full of nasty, soggy food to make sure there aren't any utensils that are going to slide in and make loud noises."

If it wasn't obvious to Jennifer before that I had some sort of sensory disorder, it was now.

"Okay, good. Tell me about some of the strategies you have for completing these tasks. You have to get them done, so how do you get through it?"

"Well, with the disposal, I used to use a long wooden spoon to feel around for utensils and push things down the drain. But sometimes,

I just force myself to do it without the spoon. With the shower, I take breaks when the smells get too strong."

"So you have a strategy of stepping back?"

"Uh . . . yeah?"

"You have been trying to apply this strategy to Corby. Just like with the disposal, you are forcing yourself to do things that you don't feel comfortable doing, things like touch or commitment. It worked for a little while. But when you came here two weeks ago, your strategy wasn't working anymore. The disposal is an inanimate object that doesn't care if you ignore it until you are ready to continue. Corby isn't a disposal. So instead, you have been trying ignore your own emotions and forcing yourself to continue. Now you aren't in a relationship, you have stepped back, and your brain is sorting through everything. But because the immediate threat of physical contact and a relationship is removed, you can see what you *did* like about the relationship, and you want it back."

Jennifer was right on all counts. I was sabotaging relationships, and the one time I had finally managed to get into one, I didn't know how to process it.

She continued her observations. "From what you have told me about Corby, he sounds like a very supportive man."

I nodded in agreement.

"He supports you in your education and hobbies. And he has stayed with you for a year now without requiring any sort of physical relationship. I think by now, you've realized he isn't just pretending."

I nodded again.

"Ironically, if Corby weren't in a wheelchair, you would never have stayed around this long. You associate Corby's disability with his sincerity. Since it is harder for him to have a physical relationship with someone, you know that he is going to pay more attention to the other aspects of a relationship, which you value more. And because touch wasn't a part of your relationship until recently, you stayed longer than you normally would. If Corby hadn't been in a wheelchair, you would have never stayed this long. But because he is in a wheelchair, it might be the reason why you don't stay now. Also, I think on some level, you still think he is just a really patient actor who still just wants physical affection."

Jennifer was making a lot of sense. But the problem with her was that she didn't have any concrete strategies. How was I supposed to stop treating Corby like the disposal? It was great that someone was writing the introductory chapters in my own personal textbook, but where were the equations? Where were the example problems? Was I supposed to officially date Corby but tell him not to text or call for days at a time when I needed a break? Because I knew *that* strategy wouldn't work. Corby would need an explanation every time and want to talk it out. And I did *not* want to keep discussing things.

*Chapter 29*

# A Clandestine Van Meeting

*Still February*

C: On a scale from 1–10, how would you feel if I showed up close enough to your house for you to come see me but so your family couldn't see that I was out there?

T: I like the idea, but aren't you at DnD later?

C: Well, I keep asking about DnD, but no one responds. If it's not happening, I'd love to see you. I hope it's not happening.

T: What? Corby doesn't want to play?

C: I want to see you much more, is all. Extra bad today. No idea why it's any more intense today, but it is. Looks like DnD is happening at 5, so if you wanted to meet me close to where it's at, we could spend an hour and a half together, and you could still be productive today.

T: All right, I will head down in a few minutes.

C: Thank you. I'm already on my way.

Corby and I hadn't seen each other in three weeks—since we had officially broken up. I wasn't sure I wanted to see him, but I left anyway. Thirty minutes later, I pulled into a Wendy's parking lot. Corby opened the door to his van, and I climbed onto the back seat.

I told him about a project I was doing at school. Somewhere in the middle of the conversation, I found myself sitting on Corby's lap. He held me while we talked. It was nice—and confusing. Why could I touch people when a committed relationship didn't exist? Would this happen with anyone or only with Corby? It was almost like I had a limited capacity. I could either have a relationship and struggle with everything else, or I could have everything else without the relationship.

Corby had to get to his gaming obligations. He didn't want to leave, and I would have been fine sitting in that parking lot longer. I missed him. But *Dungeons and Dragons* was serious stuff. Apparently. I didn't actually know anything about it.

I climbed out of the van, but when the door was inches away from closing, I heard Corby shout something. It sounded suspiciously like the words *I* and *Love* and *You*.* It took a second to process what he'd said since it had partially been masked by the sound of the van door snapping closed, but I looked back over my shoulder at the van, and Corby was leaning over the steering wheel to wiggle his keys into the ignition. Maybe he was concentrating on not dropping anything, but it felt like he was avoiding looking in my direction. Like he had just said something he hadn't intended to say. I suspiciously slid into my car and drove home. I certainly wasn't going to bring this incident up in conversation.

---

* *OHMYGOSH, OOPS.*

## Chapter 30

# There May Be Something There That Wasn't There Before

*March*

Something had changed.

My calendar was bursting at the seams. I was working on my master's thesis and had to collect enough data for my experiment. The end of the semester was dangerously close, so I had to run as many participants as I could before the undergraduate guinea pigs all went home for the summer. This was in addition to the research participants I had to run for one of my adviser's projects since I was his designated minion. The rest of the gaps were filled with homework and church stuff. I had somehow become a key part of three different choirs—one that I was the pianist for, one that I was conducting, and one that I was singing in. I felt like a mama bird, flying in and out of a nest only to be met by squalling, wide-open beaks clamoring for attention. And I didn't have enough worms to fill them all!

I arrived at the first practice for the choir that I was playing the piano for. A small handful of singers showed up, and I recognized one of them from church. His name was Steven. I didn't know him very well, but he came up to the piano to say hi. As we greeted each other, a very confident woman marched up to the stand, whipped out a spiral-bound music book, and thrust it toward me. The choir director had arrived! She was a force of nature. Steven quickly sat down next to me so he didn't have to walk past the scary woman to the choir seats.

I had played the piano for choirs before. Usually, first choir practices were quite boring while the singers learned their parts one note at a time. But this director sailed right in and asked me to play the full arrangement. I frantically tried to keep up. Thank heavens, Steven was still at the piano. He started flipping pages and kept telling me that I was doing great.

By the end of the first practice, we had "learned" three songs up to tempo in parts. When we finally stopped singing, I watched the choir members leave. They staggered out of the chapel looking dazed and bewildered. I was torn. That had simultaneously been the most difficult and exciting choir practice I had ever attended. And the music sounded great! Steven and I spent a few minutes gushing about the amazing harmonies among the parts, and then we kept chatting as we walked to the parking lot. And we kept talking for four hours.

Wait, what?

*Four hours?!*

I drove home, stunned. A little over a year ago, I'd thought males were an unapproachable species. They were impossible to comprehend. But I had just talked to one—for *four hours*. I had even shared some personal details about my own life. It felt wrong sharing so much with a mostly stranger. But . . . was this how "normal" people acted? Did people have conversations like this all the time? Had I actually changed that much in just a year, that I was now capable of being a "normal person"?!

Over the next few weeks, I met a few of the other singers during practice. Mostly guys. One of them asked if I wanted to get frozen custard. It had been a long time since I'd been out with anyone other than Corby. It was a bit chilly outside, so he took off his jacket and wrapped it around my shoulders. It was bizarre, watching a man with working limbs. While eating custard, we talked about some super deep topics . . . like penguins. This type of superficial topic would have been one I was comfortable with a year ago. But now? I found it . . . boring? I suddenly realized that I liked the deeper chats with Corby more. As painful as they were, talking about meaningful things and sharing opinions was undeniably more fulfilling.

Something had definitely changed.

## Chapter 31

# The Halfpipe

*A different day in March*

To my dismay, I was still meeting with Jennifer. I'd started going to counseling mostly because of Corby, but I didn't want to talk about him, so I came up with distractor topics. Just like I did when talking to Corby about Corby. I had applied all my negative dating patterns to my relationship with my counselor. It wasn't an efficient strategy, but I didn't have time to recover from one of her interrogations, so in a way, it *was* efficient. On this particular occasion, I tried to distract her by describing how homework and multichoir madness was going.

She scrutinized my face. "You seem more relaxed today. I think you thrive on excessive amounts of stress."

Well. Okay. I said nothing. I knew she would elaborate whether I wanted her to or not.

"Here is a question for you: When you get an assignment from a professor, do you think about whether or not you should do it?"

"No, I just do it. There is no option. Aren't you supposed to do all the homework?"

"I thought so. In your world, you have a designated set of 'required' tasks. When you have a lot of these 'required' tasks, like you do right now, you don't need to figure out what to do with your free time. Making decisions about free time makes you anxious, probably because you think your preferred free-time activity of cross-stitching is not worthwhile."

"Well, it is hard to argue that making tiny stitches on a piece of fabric accomplishes anything useful!"

Jennifer ignored my statement. Apparently, she did not want to have a debate on the merits and drawbacks of cross-stitching pictures of tigers while watching *Andy Griffith* reruns. Which was what I had been doing just twelve hours ago. She decided to make another observation. "Let's talk about what you said a few weeks ago about your talents being very visible. Have you thought more about that?"

I *had* thought about that question. Because it wasn't about Corby, it was a safe question to answer.

"Yeah. If you think about all the things I am good at, like school and crafts and piano, these are all things everyone can see on the outside. And it really bothers me when I tell someone about school or when they see something I knit, and they say things like, 'I could never do anything like that,' or, 'I am so bad at school.' I feel like when I do well at the things I love, it makes the people around me feel bad about themselves. I feel like I am intimidating. And I hate that."

"And do you think this has affected your behavior?"

"Yes. I think that I purposely don't work on the things I don't do well and try to make those things more visible so people can say things like, 'Well, yeah, she is great at math, but she doesn't have any friends.' And I like that response better because then the person can feel good that they have friends instead of feeling bad that they aren't very good at math. Which, I might point out, they just need to practice. I don't understand why everyone keeps informing me that they would never be able to knit. How many of them have actually *tried* it?"

Jennifer ignored that question too. She stood and went over to a whiteboard on the far wall of her office. She drew two big circles on the board, one on top of the other. Like a giant eight. She then started writing words in each circle. In the bottom circle, she wrote things like *crafty*, *smart*, *no relationships*, *no physical touch*, and *musical*. In the top circle, she wrote words like *courageous* and *empathetic*.

She finished writing and turned around. "The bottom circle here is what you think people see you as right now." She clicked her marker against the board.

I nodded. It was really difficult to hide that I was crafty and went to school.

Jennifer jabbed the marker lid at the top circle. "This is what I see in you. Who you actually are."

I stared at the words she had written. I vehemently disagreed with the top circle. *Courageous*? Hah! *Empathetic*? Anything but! I would have never used a single word on her list to describe myself. And how had she decided on *those* words by watching me cry for four months in a row?

She didn't wait to see if I agreed with the words. She knew I would try to argue, so she forged ahead. "You used to spend all your time in this bottom circle, but Corby created an environment conducive to the top circle. For the first time in your life, you admitted to having opinions, dislikes, and problems. You let someone know who you really were instead of creating someone you wanted them to see. You really like being in the top circle. But it is so uncomfortable not to be in the bottom circle that you jump back down. But then you miss the feeling of being authentic, so you climb back into the top circle. For the last few months, you have been jumping between these two circles. And it has gotten more intense over time. You might be switching circles multiple times a day. You have tried to leave Corby a handful of times now, but you always go back and pick up in the same place."

She finally stopped clicking her marker against the board and sat down. She looked at me.

"What do you think about this pattern? Does it seem accurate?"

I didn't agree with her choice of top circle words, but the analogy did make some sense. I didn't feel like I had to pretend as much around Corby. And I didn't try to hide the stuff in the bottom circle. Corby wasn't intimidated by the things I did.*

---

* *Yeah, I'm not. Knitting is hot.*

"I agree with some of it. But I would say that I'm actually in a halfpipe, not in a circle."*

"If it is easier to picture halfpipes, that works too."

She really didn't want to debate today.

"Okay, good. Because I feel like one minute, I think everything will work out with Corby. I try to hang on to the side of that pipe, but eventually, I slide down and go up the other side."

Jennifer was excited. This was the first time I had engaged with one of her silly analogies.

"Good! And there is an audience throwing snowballs at you! The audience in this case represents distractions, like homework and choirs!"

Uh, okay? She got way too excited over visualizations and analogies. I didn't understand the snowball thing, but it made her happy. And for the first time ever, I hadn't cried in an appointment.

---

* *The discovery of the halfpipe analogy was great. It became a useful way to ask how Tess was feeling because she felt like she could answer.*

## Chapter 32

# Genuine Practice

*April*

Corby worked for a company that owned fancy private boxes at local sports arenas. The company gave tickets to various employees as rewards or incentives, and Corby had received tickets to a basketball game. He asked me to accompany him.

After my chat with Jennifer, I decided I should consciously try being authentic. On all our previous dates, I hadn't wanted to encourage physical contact by initiating it right from the start. Even if I'd wanted to give Corby a hug, I had held back until he'd asked for one. But today, I *wanted* to give him a hug, so I resolutely marched up the ramp and into the van and sat on his lap. Corby was stunned. I climbed off a few minutes later, when a family member pulled into the driveway. My newfound authenticity had limits.

The game was just okay. I had never bothered to watch basketball, so I didn't fully understand what was going on. It was more fun watching people in the adjacent boxes lose their brains every time the ref blew his whistle.

Corby didn't have any trouble being authentic. He kept his arm around my shoulders the entire time, even though a dozen of his coworkers could see us.

After the game, we drove back to my house. Corby turned the car off and pulled his chair into the center of the van. I clambered over my seat and into his lap, then wrapped my arms around his shoulders and hugged him tighter than I ever had before. Corby whipped his arms around my back and wiggled his fists into my hair. We sat like that for several minutes. Then I felt Corby's lips on my neck. It was strange. This wasn't happening to me. I was reading a paragraph in a book and just imagining it, right? I had given an inch, and Corby was trying to run a mile, as usual. There were drawbacks to being authentic.

My brain started working again. I slid off his lap and onto the back seat. I was glad it was dark. I didn't know what to think.

"It's late. I should really get inside. You have work tomorrow," I said.

"I guess so. But this is *way* more fun!" Corby was delighted. This was more voluntary snuggling than he'd had in years.

"You'll be tired . . ."

"Meh, this was worth it. But okay." He opened his arms for one last hug and snuck another kiss on my cheek. "Thanks for coming with me tonight. I really had a good time."

While I was brushing my teeth, I glanced in the mirror. There was something on my neck. I spit out the toothpaste and leaned in to investigate. It was a speckled red mark.

No.

It couldn't be.

I had heard of these before but never seen one in real life.

I, Tessa Sommer, had gotten my first hickey. I decided that tomorrow would be a great day to wear a scarf.

## *Chapter 33*

# An Unspoken Goal

*May*

Corby, Ronda, and I were playing a board game. Just as the game ended, Corby's catheter clogged. His body got *angry*. All his muscles twitched involuntarily, his blood pressure shot up, the skin on his neck turned red and blotchy, his eyes started to water, and he stopped making his usual funny quips.

Scott lifted Corby onto a bed while Ronda pulled out a catheter kit and handed me a roll of paper towels so I could supply them as needed. She pulled discolored tubing out of a hole below Corby's stomach and slid a fresh one in. As soon as the new catheter reached the right place, urine streamed out of the end into a plastic container. The transformation was miraculous. Corby's muscles stopped twitching, his skin returned to a normal color, and he recovered his ability to make jokes. But the episode had left him drained and a bit lightheaded, so Scott moved him to the couch so we could watch a movie.

After the movie ended, I turned off the TV and put my head in Corby's lap. "Are you still working on your talk for Sunday?" I asked. He had been asked to give a talk on missionary work in church, and I knew he had been prepping.

"Yeah. But it isn't going very well."

"Why not? You usually don't mind talking in front of people."

"I don't know. I just don't have as much to say about missionary work, I guess."

"Just because you weren't able to serve a full-time mission yourself doesn't mean you don't know how to be a missionary. You do missionary stuff all the time! You should adopt your usual attitude of confidence that you have with everything else and just say what you think about it."

Corby looked down at me. "Tess, you just called me out on something!"*

"Uh . . . sorry?"

"Don't be sorry! Besides the title, we really act like we're in a healthy relationship right now. It's not like at first, where I was constantly pushing you to be more like a partner. Like, being willing to state your opinion or admit you like me or share your feelings or call me out when I'm being dumb. Have you noticed I don't push you nearly as much with things like that lately? It's not because we're not an official couple. It's because you hardly need pushing anymore."

Yet again, I contemplated just how much I'd changed in the past year. As if to cement this change, I sat up, threw my arms around Corby, and buried my face in his neck. He raised his arms and gently stroked my back.

After a few minutes, he turned his head and whispered in my ear. "I sure love you."

I chose not to say anything. But I didn't pull away. We just sat there.

After a few more minutes, I finally broke the silence. "Uh . . . remember that time I met you in the Wendy's parking lot before you went to DnD? Did you say 'I love you' then too?"

"Mm-hmm," Corby replied. He had wiggled his face into my hair.

"*Aha*! I thought so. But I wasn't sure." We sat for a few more minutes. I decided to ask another question that had just occurred to me. "Since when have you felt this way?" I wasn't sure I wanted to know the answer . . . but I did.

He leaned back so he wouldn't be eating my hair. "Since last November. Before we started dating the first time. Well, the only time

---

* *Honestly, it was something I always wanted! People being doormats for each other doesn't help either party.*

we *officially* dated. Because we have been dating this whole time, you know."

I was shocked. And not shocked. Of course he felt this way. He wouldn't have stuck around this long if he hadn't. But he had felt this way for that long? And hadn't said anything? That was very uncharacteristic of Mr. Conversation.

We talked about a few more things, but it was 3:00 a.m., and I needed to get home and do some homework before bed.

Corby softly kissed my cheek. I slid off his lap and put my shoes on, then walked down the hall and tapped on Ronda's bedroom door to let her know it was time to put Corby in bed. I stole back down the hallway and out the front door as soon as I heard movement.

As I drove home, I made a goal. I decided that I would be in an official relationship with Corby Campbell by the end of June. He had invited me to go to Lake Powell with him again this year, and that was in July. I thought it would be nice if I went as his actual girlfriend this time instead of as an abnormally close friend-who-was-a-girl. I hoped that I would be able to fulfill my new goal; it was only six weeks away. But a timeline was supposed to help with goal keeping, right? I decided not to tell Corby about my goal because I didn't want to get his hopes up. I sat on my mental staircase, counting the stairs between us, trying to make a plan to conquer them. Unfortunately, the angelic cheerleading squad had their own plans, and I wasn't going to like them.

## Chapter 34
# The End

*June*

I was frantically running around a desert, desperately trying to get away from a giant spider that was chasing me.

"Eric! Help!" I shrieked.

We were playing Minecraft. My brothers had joined forces with Corby to convince me to play a video game, and I was not doing very well. After running around in circles and experimenting with all the buttons, I managed to build a tiny dirt structure that would supposedly protect me from the monsters that would spawn at night. Except I forgot to close my shack door, and a zombie invaded my tiny hut.

I hollered frantically, sprinted out into the wilderness, got lost, and died. I sheepishly handed my controller over to Eric so he could find my stuff and get me back to the zombie-contaminated dwelling.

Corby said that he needed to get home early, so I maneuvered him down the scary ramps and back into his chair by 10:00 p.m. I was ready to go back inside and leaned over to give him a hug when he said the ominous phrase, "We need to talk."

Crap. I felt my muscles get all tense. I sat on the van seat, dreading what was coming.

"We need to figure out where this relationship is going. I have been thinking about this for weeks now, and as I see it, there are three options: First, date for real. You would be my girlfriend. Second, keep going as we are now. Except that I would have to get used to initiating dates and kissing you even though we aren't in a committed relationship, which isn't my favorite thing. Third, we break up. This means that I wouldn't be able to contact you for at least a month so that I could get over you and move on with dating other people. No texting, no emails, nothing. I can't move on until I get over you, and I can't do that if we keep talking all the time."

I sat for a moment in silence. I didn't know what to say. He had told me that he loved me just a few weeks ago. I had a goal to date him by the end of the month! How had he spent an entire day building a virtual Minecraft house with me, planning what we were going to build next time, knowing that he was going to drop this bomb?*

I decided to stall. "What do you think we should do?" I asked.

I was sitting on the back bench in the van. Corby was just a shadow. The shadow was silent for a moment.

"Option three."

My spine hunched over. And my eyes started leaking. Again. This man had the potential to hospitalize me for dehydration. Although the timing was a surprise, the decision wasn't. I was still shocked that it hadn't happened sooner.

Corby asked me what I was so afraid of. The darkness made me bold. Well, bolder than usual. Tears rolled down my face as I haltingly tried to tell him how I felt in very short sentences. I was clearly able to *date* Corby, but I still couldn't picture us being married. I didn't think that I could be his primary caregiver,** especially when it came to the physical demands of bowel care and showers. The list went on—things I would have to give up, things I would feel obligated to do. I

---

* *Compartmentalization! It's this thing men seem better at doing, where you decide to not think about something, and then you successfully don't think about it. It can be useful and dangerous.*

** *While Tess is still more of my caregiver than I'd hoped, I do have neighbors come almost every morning and evening to help get me dressed, get in and out of bed, and even do bowel care and showers. These people are all angels, and if they aren't going to heaven, I'm going to get into an argument with God.*

was crying so much that I started to feel sick. I was gulping air like a fish out of water, trying to prevent huge, ugly sobs.

I knew Corby really wanted me to pick option one, and even though I had a goal to get there, my brain refused to form the words. I knew that if I started dating Corby, we would probably get married, and I just couldn't accept it.

"How long would I have to stay away?" I asked.

"Probably six weeks. I know that I sort of invited you to Powell already, but if we start talking again before Powell, I will bring you, and we will just end up like this again. I need to move on. I wish you could pick option one. I can't do this halfway thing any longer."

We sat in silence for a few minutes. I attempted to dry my face with my sleeves, but they were already covered in snot and soaked through.

Corby was clearly not happy with this choice. He kept smacking his limp fist on the ceiling of his van. It was weird. This was only the second time I had seen him get frustrated.

He continued. "Maybe I'm the one who needs the six weeks. I have been thinking about what *you* need this entire time. Not what I need. And I promise this isn't the end. We will still be friends. We will still talk. And six weeks isn't that long."

Sure, not that long. Only long enough to miss most of the summer.

"You know, I had a goal to date you by the end of June," I admitted.

Corby slapped the ceiling again. "Please don't say that. I have been praying about this for weeks, and this is really what I feel like we need to do.* I'm sorry that I can't honor that goal, and I'm sorry that this is going to hurt so much."

---

* *I know it's weird and frustrating that even after she told me she had a goal to date, I still decided to move forward with the breakup plan. Leading up to this, I felt a surprising amount of peace coming to this decision, and I didn't want to second-guess myself in the moment of high emotion. Seeing how things worked out in the end, it still feels like an inspired decision, even if it was a bumpy ride.*

The angelic cheerleaders were behind this?! What were they playing at? And how was I supposed to convince Corby that this idea was stupid if he had angelic backup? Nothing I could say would matter anymore.

I stood up to leave. My legs felt shaky. Corby held open his arms, and I crawled onto his lap. He held me for a few minutes, and I soaked it in, knowing that this might be the last time.

I leaned against his chest in silence, gripping his shoulders.

After a few minutes, he had another question. "Tess? Can you kiss me before you leave? For real? I waited for so long, and this might be our last chance."

Corby sounded so sad, and I felt so empty. I tilted my head up, and he gently pulled my face toward his. After one and a half years of fake dating, I finally kissed Corby Campbell. In our traditional fashion, it was entirely unromantic. He was abandoning me for six weeks, and my face was soaking wet with a salty hint of snot. I hoped Corby wouldn't notice that bit.

The entire experience was bizarre. I had never kissed anyone before, so I just copied everything Corby did. And it was no brief peck.

Eventually, we pulled away.

Corby let out a very heavy sigh. "Thank you."

I couldn't say anything. I slid off his lap and waited for the van door to slide open, then I ducked out of the door and slowly walked away. I felt shaky and sick and lightheaded. The textures involved with kissing were decidedly off-putting, and I thought I might throw up right there on the lawn. But I held it together and stoically walked up to the porch.

I was going to slip through the front door in a dignified manner, but the universe really wanted to put an exclamation mark on how awful this night had been. I was locked out. Corby, being the chivalrous man that he was, hadn't left yet. He saw my shoulders slump in defeat and rolled down his window. I shakily yelled that the door was locked, and then he got to watch me stagger around in the dark until I found the hidden key.

I headed straight for The Zone, grabbing a new jumbo roll of toilet paper before I collapsed under the table.

I stared at the unfinished wall studs for ages, trying to figure out what had just happened. Eventually, I opened my laptop and started writing. There was so much in my brain. Things I wanted to tell Corby but hadn't been able to say because I had such a hard time talking. And now I couldn't say them to him because he was gone. So I said them all to an obliging Microsoft Word document.

I wrote about things I had talked about with Jennifer. I listed the things I was frustrated about. Things I was confused about. Things I was scared about. I admitted things I had been trying to bury for the last year. I wrote for pages and pages. About halfway through, it turned into a letter to Corby.

> I think about you all the time. Every time I practice the piano on Sunday afternoons and play a song from *Hercules*. When I drive past your office and wish that I could come in and sneak one of your meal tickets. Or when I see a spray bottle and wish that you were there telling me to date you. Every time I drive down the freeway and see the billboard that says the estimated time to 10600 South is seventeen minutes. The next time I finish my lectures for class early, but you won't be there to celebrate with me. The next time I walk upstairs and see Eric and Kyle playing Minecraft and wish we could add that second floor onto our treehouse. Or even tonight, when I go upstairs and get into bed under that super fuzzy blanket we bought together. And when I wake up tomorrow when my alarm goes off, but there won't be a text with a stupid cat meme. Really, what is the point of going to bed? It is now 5:06 a.m., and I probably won't be able to fall asleep.
>
> I tried not to let this happen. I didn't want you to get associated with every single aspect of my life. But

> you did. Even the grass on my lawn? You peed all over it! I let you meet my family. I told you about church and the people at school. I have never done that with anyone before. I even stopped caring about crying in front of you, even though I did probably look kind of scary. But you didn't care about that. And it was lovely. That is what I will miss the most. Not the crying. But the familiarity and the acceptance.* I have never experienced anything like that before. I already miss you. I'm sorry for making you feel guilty and for not telling you about my plan to date you. I love you. Night, Corbs.

I looked at the clock. It was now 5:30 a.m., and my Word document was twenty-five pages long. If this were a mushy romantic movie, I would have gotten a mug of something steamy, walked out onto a beautiful deck with an ocean view, stood in the perfect light of a half-risen sun, and let the ocean breeze cool my tear-stained cheeks while gently blowing tendrils of my perfectly groomed hair. And then Corby would have driven up along the sand in a convertible and proclaimed his love and . . . Never mind. This wasn't a movie.

I leaned back in my office chair and glanced over at the window. A faint glow shone around the edge of the cobweb-covered blinds. I gathered the wads of used toilet paper and tossed them into the trash can. Then I tiptoed up the stairs, past my sleeping sisters, and plugged my phone into the charger.

There were no texts from Corby.

---

* *Yay relationships! Why is everyone always worried about looking ugly while crying? The trust shown by crying in front of someone else always feels like an honor. Who cares about looks at a time like that?*

# INTERLUDE NOTE THING 2

*Dear Reader,*

*During the beta reading process, it quickly became apparent that our dating story elicits feelings of frustration. Multiple readers expressed the desire to stop reading or, in some cases, slap me.*

*In some ways, this is good because it means I accurately conveyed what we were experiencing. I was frustrated. Corby was frustrated. I, too, would like to slap past me. It is okay if you feel this way.*

*Also, Corby apologizes for being such a cuddle-starved monster. He is deeply embarrassed about how often he brought it up. He would also like to slap past Corby and understands if you agree.*

*Thank you for your persistence.*

## *Chapter 35*

# Unsent Emails

*Every single day for six whole weeks*

Dear Corby,

I'm not going to send this email, but I'm writing it anyway. Then I can pretend to send it and imagine your responses.

I drove down to Provo tonight. I went swing dancing for the first time in over a year. It totally wasn't worth it.

I left the dance early. I drove to your house. Your van was parked out front. That made me rather pleased. If it hadn't been out there, I would have been freaked out that you might pull up behind and catch me. It also meant that you weren't on a date. I circled the block twice before going to the gas station. I wanted to text you and surprise you with the news that I was literally sitting two blocks away. But I couldn't. I thought about driving by your place again, but I got on the freeway instead. Driving by twice was creepy enough.

* * *

I have discovered that I get a lot more done without interruptions. I even gave a lecture on it. I almost used you as an example: "I broke up with my boyfriend a few days ago, and now that I'm not texting him, I get lecture videos done much more quickly." But I didn't. Sharing details like that with students probably isn't appropriate.

* * *

Well, that break lasted all of twenty minutes. I can't believe you have been doing this for a year. Wanting me but always having me run. I hate being on the other side. Come back. Corby!! I miss you!!

* * *

Aaand . . . I'm back again. The song "I Want You Back" keeps running through my head. I thought about emailing you the link, but it is kind of about wanting a girl back. And you aren't a girl. But now I understand what the lyrics mean. A lot of breakup song lyrics suddenly make a lot more sense. Have you changed your mind yet?

* * *

Your initials are *CC*. I could have been calling you Carbon Copy for the last year. What a missed opportunity. I should stop thinking about you and try to get some sleep. I guess. Night, Carbon Copy. Platypus.

* * *

I'm mad at you right now. When I woke up this morning, I was imagining all the things that I would say to you when you got back. Things that would make you feel guilty for leaving. I know I shouldn't. I know you probably thought you were doing the right thing. But I don't see it that way. I don't think I will be able to pick back up where we left off. You are missing all my favorite activities. When it gets colder, I can't invite you to things because you can't get inside anyone's house. You are missing everything! And this was your choice! So yes, I do think that this is going to hurt our relationship. I am not going to run back to you in three weeks.

The whole day is over. Tomorrow night will be three weeks. I'm still mad. Why was this the thing you had to enforce? Why, of all things, did you have to choose this one?

* * *

It's July now. And you aren't here.

## Chapter 36

# Corby and the Other Woman

THE FOLLOWING CHAPTER IS WRITTEN FROM THE PERSPECTIVE OF CORBY. THEREFORE, I=CORBY, NOT TESS.

Dating Tess was not logical.

If any other guy came to me and said, "I've been trying to get together with this girl, but she's told me multiple times that she's not interested and that I should move on. What should I do?" my advice would be pretty straightforward: "Move on!" However, that was what Tess was saying to me, and for some reason (I feel like it was divine intervention), I was inspired with the patience and perseverance to hang around.

Why? One logical reason I came up with was that I saw an opportunity to help. Back in high school, the girls I often pursued had low self-confidence. In contrast, I was overflowing with possibly unjustified self-confidence. So I would tell these girls how great they were, hopefully building them up. I felt good about helping someone else grow.*

---

* *If you're a girl I dated in the past and you feel like this definition doesn't fit you, it probably doesn't. I said "often" the girls I'd pursue, not exclusively. Also, hi! I hope you're doing great!*

My needs changed post-breakneck. If I had some medical emergency, I couldn't afford to be paired up with someone who would collapse under the pressure. I realized I needed to start dating girls who also had confidence.

Tess was an enigma. At the time we met, she was far above average in academic and get-things-done experience. She was twenty years old and finishing her bachelor's degree! However, she was significantly undeveloped socially. So she was this weird mix of the confidence I was looking for and the need for help that I was subconsciously drawn to. Also, she was very attractive.

Looking back on the first year of knowing her, these were the reasons I hung around. I clung to the memory of our first date—the Tess I'd met that night who had willingly climbed onto my lap and shared information. I knew that version of her was buried somewhere—I just had to figure out how to bring her back.

I didn't *want* to fake break up our not-relationship. But we had been in her halfpipe for well over a year. I had tried dating other girls for months, but since I was already emotionally invested in Tess, I couldn't connect with someone new. I logically decided that during the six weeks off, it would either give me enough time to clear her out and connect with other people, or I would come away from it knowing more than ever that I should stick with her.

It occurred to me that if we didn't get back together afterward, I would have essentially dated a girl for over a year but never kissed her. At that moment, it felt inexplicably important, so I asked her if she would kiss me. She did. Our first kiss. And she was crying. And that was all my fault. I'm such a guy.

Several weeks later, it was the Fourth of July, and I looked up into Trisha's face.

I met Trisha online in May, after I resumed one of my dating profiles. She had been a potential candidate for a weekly pre-Tess-date date. And she was nothing like Tess. I had learned more about Trisha in one week than I had learned about Tess in six months. Trisha was very outgoing and animated. She had recently beaten cancer but was still recovering from chemotherapy, and she was not opposed to physical touch.

At this moment, Trisha was standing behind me, her arms resting on my shoulders as we watched the fireworks from a mountainside overlooking the valley. It had taken months for Tess to let me put my arm around her, but Trisha had put her arms around me.

I had talked to Trisha about Tess. In fact, Trisha had her own Tess, but his name was Jordan. Trisha and Jordan were in a sort-of relationship, and she didn't know what to do about it either, so we often talked about our fake relationships.

Trisha, unlike Tess, was not afraid to ask difficult questions.

"Corby, do you love Tess?" she asked.

I thought for a moment. "I think so. People have various different definitions of 'love,' but the way I feel about her and the history of our relationship closely matches what I think love should be. That doesn't necessarily mean it's right for us to be together though."

"My situation with Jordan is almost identical. He said he wasn't sure that my cancer was something he could handle in a relationship. If I hadn't gotten cancer, we would probably be engaged by now."

"I guess a difference between these stories that still has me debating is that while Tess expressed that she was not sure she could handle my challenges, she never quit trying to work on them with me. In addition to working on a lot of other things at the same time."

Trisha had opinions about this. "In my mind, if Tess can't handle the hardships that would come with marrying you, that should be a huge sign. You deserve a woman who doesn't think it's a big deal. She's had plenty of time to figure it out. Yes, it'll take work, but you just do it. It's simple."

"Half true and half false still. I don't think I can adequately convey how much she has grown in just the one year I've been in her life. She went from being unwilling to discuss anything to talking freely. From hating hugs to wanting to cuddle. From strictly independent to allowing me to help. It was more growth than I've seen in any other relationship. Partially because I've never dated anyone who has started at such a low point, but still. She is not everything

I want yet, but I don't really expect a relationship to be everything I want. We have both consistently adapted to each other's needs, and I feel like that's more likely to make a relationship work than coincidentally matching from the beginning. So while the chair is still a struggle for Tess, it is *way* less so than it used to be, and I've already seen her get over things that were a struggle for her before, so it seems entirely plausible that we could overcome this together too. But there is no guarantee. She certainly won't get over it if I distance myself from her."

"How does she make you feel? Does she love you enough?"

"Yeah, I felt loved. I've certainly been in relationships where the women were better at communicating their appreciation for me. But once again, this is an area where Tess has improved a lot. It would be so much clearer if she just stopped progressing. But I haven't seen that happen yet. In just the last few months, she had started to be emotionally supportive and call me out on things."

Trisha paused for a long moment. "Your mind is a difficult place. One minute, I think one thing based on something you say, and then something opposite two minutes later. I feel like this should be simple and easy."

"Well, I think I've correctly conveyed where I'm at then. I've never had my mind in such a difficult place in regard to a relationship. I also feel like this should be simple."

"I don't envy your position."

"Yeah, but it was a good processing session. Thanks!"

"It was a roller coaster."

"*I know, right*?"

During the last week of the "breakup," I went to Lake Powell with my family. While Powell was fun, I was more excited for the next week. When I would get to see Tess.

When I got home, I did a mind dump in my journal. I listed the things I liked about Trisha and the things I liked about Tess. Logically, Trisha made more sense for me to date. But I still had a connection with Tess that didn't feel resolved. I felt extra peace about pursuing Tess when I was at church; that was a good sign.

Eventually, I came to this conclusion: While having Trisha made Tess's absence a lot easier, I did still miss and want Tess specifically. A relationship with just any girl didn't adequately fill the gap. This felt far from comprehensive, and even though it was not straightforward, my gut feeling was that I should choose Tess.

Now I just had to see if she still wanted me back.

## *Chapter 37*

# Meanwhile . . .

*July*

The six weeks were almost over. Corby was sleeping under a gorgeous starlit sky at Lake Powell at this very moment. I stretched my arms back over the top of my office chair, contemplating the unfinished basement ceiling. Wads of faded pink insulation poked through rips in the paper lining. What a contrast.

I sighed and opened my email account, scrolling through my unsent drafts folder. I had written hundreds of messages to Corby. There were sad messages and angry messages written in all caps and boring messages where I told him about school and nonsensical things that my grandma had said. Sometimes I tried to imagine his responses, but Corby messages were hard to fill in. He liked catching me off guard. I missed that.

I looked at the clock. It was well past 2:00 a.m. I thought back on my evening. I couldn't remember doing anything useful. I trudged up the twenty-eight stairs to the shower, not skipping a single stair. I no longer cared about being efficient.

Forty minutes later, I dropped my head onto my pillow and pulled out a flashlight. Then I opened the Bible and found the story of Jesus healing the lame man who was lowered from a hole in the ceiling by his friends. I had a lot of questions about this story. For instance, getting a limp Corby up a ladder didn't sound feasible, even with four dudes helping. And did those four dudes fix the hole they'd made in the roof after their friend was healed? Or did they just abandon the mess they had made in all the excitement? After letting my mind drift along these lines for a minute, I pulled it back. The *real* question I had was for God. Why did He heal that random man over 2,000 years ago, but He wouldn't heal Corby? I knew that He *could* do it. So what did I have to do to get that to happen? What was the point of dangling these tantalizing stories in my face if they couldn't happen again?

I glared up at the dark ceiling. I wasn't feeling too friendly toward God. I started a very informal prayer, asking if He would heal Corby if I showed more faith. Like, if I told Corby that I would marry him to prove to God that I would accept Corby even in his broken state, then could Corby be healed?

I spent the rest of the night trying unsuccessfully to fall asleep, as I imagined Corby pretending to still be paralyzed up until our wedding day, but then we would shock everyone when he *walked* out after the ceremony was over. It would be perfect. No one would think it was weird that a videographer was hanging around, and we would have everyone's reactions on tape! Then my wedding would actually feel like a celebration and not the death of my hopes and dreams!

The next morning, I woke up feeling empty. I had felt empty a lot lately. At first, I missed Corby so much that it hurt. Especially when I was driving to school and those silly breakup songs came on the radio. But for the last two weeks, I had mostly felt . . . nothing. Completely unmotivated. Exhausted. I had done the bare minimum to get by, and I had wasted an awful lot of time. I had never just sat and done nothing this much in my entire life. I didn't feel like me. I drove up to campus anyway. It was summer break, so the campus was also empty. The setting was appropriate for my mood.

Several days earlier, I had entirely given up on being useful and had brought a massive jigsaw puzzle to campus. I had shoved my computer monitor under the table so I could utilize every available surface. I wasn't using the monitor anyway—schoolwork was something the old me did. The air-conditioning at school had been broken for weeks, so I sat in the sweltering office for hours in complete silence, methodically clicking the pieces together.

I heard a rustling noise from the hallway. My door was cracked open a few inches in the hopes of catching a tiny draft of air, and I saw one of the office secretaries delivering an envelope to a neighboring office. As she stood up, she glimpsed my puzzle through the crack in the door and did a double-take, her eyebrows making a quizzical shape. I guess she had never seen any ambitious grad students doing 1,000-piece puzzles in their tiny office closets.

I quickly looked down. After a long moment, I heard her back out of the hallway toward the elevator. Thank heavens. I didn't want to talk to anyone. I reached out with a toe and pushed the door closed.

I worked on my puzzle until it got dark. Reaching over to flick the light switch felt like too much work. I leaned back in my chair and stared at my pale reflection in the window, trying not to think about what would happen next week. Corby might not come back. Surely he had met someone and finally realized that he had wasted his time on me. Even if he hadn't met anyone, I wasn't sure I wanted him to come back. I didn't want to make more decisions.

As I sat there in the dark, I thought back to the previous night when I'd attempted to bargain with God so I could play pranks on people with a walking Corby. Suddenly, echoes from my high school psychology class started to tickle my brain. *Bargain with God*? Wasn't that one of the stages of grief?

I found my phone and did a quick Google search. Sure enough, *bargaining* was a stage of grief. Along with *denial*, *anger*, *depression*, and *acceptance*. The dusty wheels of my brain started to slowly turn. Was I stuck in an endless cycle of grief over the loss of the future I had planned with someone who could walk? Had this six weeks of silence opened up the space for grief to fully invade? Is that why I suddenly didn't care about anything? The idea seemed sort of ridiculous. Could you feel grief for something you had never experienced in the first place? I had certainly yelled at Corby a lot in my unsent emails. I had tried to make virtual Corby feel guilty. I had tried to bargain with God just last night. And I felt like I had been in denial of all sorts of things since the day I found Corby's dating profile. If doing puzzles in a closet at school didn't indicate some level of grief-fueled depression, I didn't know what would. I curled up in a ball at the top of my mental staircase, completely exhausted from all this thinking. And I didn't care if Corby was sitting at the bottom.

# USEFUL

## Gratitude

The last few chapters have been rather dismal. (I know, I know, I promise it gets better soon.) But at this extremely low point, everything just felt . . . broken. My mind refused to think of anything other than that bruised inch of Corby's spinal cord.

Today, Corby no longer feels broken. He is just Corby. And I am incredibly grateful for so many things that came with that bruised spinal cord. I made a list of some of my favorites. Some of them are admittedly quite frivolous, but this book could use some frivolity at this melancholic juncture.

1) Our shower will always be gigantic. We installed a massive 4 x 6 ft shower in our current house. Yep, we have a twenty-four-square-foot roll-in shower. The back corners don't even get wet. It is big enough to contain Corby's bulky PVC pipe shower chair. When I take a shower, the shower chair can remain in the back half of the shower, where it becomes a handy footrest for leg-shaving purposes.
2) Corby doesn't wear clothes out very fast. Which is good, because neither of us is fond of shopping.
3) Snuggling! (Which is a weird thing to read at this point in our story, but I do eventually adapt to Corby snuggles.) Every night, I curl up against Corby's side and hug one of his arms after covering his very prominent collarbones with a pillow. One of our neighbors was really surprised when Corby said that we snuggle all night. She said something like, "Just wait until you've been married longer. That will stop." I was slightly confused until it occurred to me that other men roll around while they're asleep. Corby doesn't. He can't get up to pee. He can't steal the covers. So he is my body pillow. Literally. I can shove my cold feet under his legs, and he doesn't complain because he doesn't know they are there.

4) I have a very compelling reason not to hoard stuff. I mean, I wasn't planning on it anyway, but Corby needs an uncluttered floor. It is nice to have that built-in accountability.
5) Corby is my literal man-purse. I rarely carry things because I can hang them on his chair or throw them on his lap.
6) Riding on Corby's chair is one of the true joys of our relationship. Sometimes I perch on the back, balancing on the antitipper wheels. Sometimes I put on rollerblades and hold onto the back of his chair so he can whip me around the neighborhood at max speed (7.5 mph). But the best ride of all is when I climb onto Corby's lap—the "permacuddle." Almost every night during the summer, we go on a stroll (stroll = stride + roll). But sometimes, instead of walking home, we permacuddle. Corby holds me with one arm and drives with the other. And there is nothing else quite like it. Snuggled in my husband's arm, silently speeding down the middle of the road on a perfect summer evening in the dark. It is quite romantic. The looks we get from other drivers and pedestrians is very entertaining. Permacuddle works while stationary too. We keep puzzle books in Corby's backpack, and if we get stuck in a line somewhere, I climb onto Corby's lap, and we do crosswords together.
7) The Vanborghini! (Aptly named because of its terribly high price tag.) I hate driving, and since Corby is the only one who can drive his van, I have a great excuse to never take a turn driving anywhere! The van itself is great too. Because the middle seat is missing, it is a good, spacious place to hang out. And once Corby is locked into his place, I can load a *ton* of stuff in that middle area.
8) House shopping is kind of a pro and a con. Obviously, there are not a lot of houses designed for wheelchairs. That can be hard. But when we started house shopping, it actually ended up being kind of nice. I just looked at the pictures of the master bathroom, which is the hardest thing to adapt. If that looked okay, I would look at the entrances. Those two pictures alone eliminated 98 percent of the listings. I wasn't overwhelmed by dozens of options, and I didn't have to go to endless open houses. The process was quite efficient!

9) Corby can't really reach many things in the house, even though we have made it as accessible as possible. While this is sometimes troublesome for him, for me it is great. When I put something down . . . it stays there! I can find it again later!
10) It is very easy to hide things, such as Christmas gifts and surprise projects I am working on. I just throw them in the middle of the floor—upstairs! Corby never goes upstairs, for obvious reasons. I don't think he is aware of quite how much craft stuff I have since he can't see it all. I just take it upstairs, and he doesn't know anything about it! *evil cackle*
11) I'm not sure how to phrase this, but we have a higher incentive to have a very friendly, nonargumentative relationship. It would be disturbingly easy to get mad, throw him in bed, take his phone, and walk away—and he wouldn't be able to do a single thing. It is very uncomfortable taking care of someone else while being angry or ignoring each other, so the few times we have had an argument, we have made up very, very quickly. Thankfully, neither of us gets mad easily, so it isn't really an issue.
12) I still knit a lot, and I make a lot of scarves. Because Corby is always frozen, he wears those scarves year-round, which makes my hobby useful and, therefore, means that I am *totally* justified in making large yarn purchases.
13) As a couple, we have so much to look forward to. So many firsts! Either the first time we are able to do an activity at all or the first time we are able to do an activity standing up. I believe in the resurrection, and I believe in eternal marriage. I know that one day, Corby and I will be a proper walking couple. We have an unofficial Resurrection Bucket List for whenever that happens. My top activity is dancing. I miss dancing so badly. (Yes, I know I could technically abandon Corby for an evening and dance with other people's husbands, but that is weird. Therefore, I am waiting to relearn dancing when we can both do it together.) I am also looking forward to the first time *Corby* gets out of bed to turn off the light. And the first time he puts on his own pants or takes a shower on his own or hugs me *standing up*. All the other couples we know have already experienced pulling weeds together, and

> it probably wasn't significant enough to remember. But I am going to remember! I might frame the first weed Corby pulls just to commemorate the occasion!* And I get to anticipate and get excited for all these things!

It's easy in life to focus on the downside of any circumstance. But as we look, we can find upsides too. This is a skill that needs practicing (I obviously did not possess it while we were dating), but it can be learned!

---

* *I am also looking forward to this a lot! We have done a good job of splitting the duties of life into categories that make sense, given our circumstances. But I'd love to contribute more directly to the physical responsibilities someday, like weeding and laundry.*

## *Chapter 38*

# The End of the End

*July continued*

The six weeks were over. At 7:00 a.m., I heard a tiny buzz come from my phone. Just like it had in my previous lifetime. The life that had abruptly ended just six weeks ago. I snapped my head up and looked. There was a text from Corby. But was it a real text? Or a dream text?

C: Good morning, Tess. I miss you.

T: Corby? I miss you too.

C: Can I come see you today?

Ugh. I knew Corby would want to see me soonish, but I wasn't expecting him to want to *immediately*. I was still empty. And empty people are not capable of relationships. Also, I was mad at him.

I guess I wasn't *completely* empty.

T: I guess it depends. Last time we talked, it didn't turn out so well.

C: I know, I'm sorry. Sounds like I've damaged your trust pretty bad. :(

T: That day was not good. It was like being pushed off a cliff. I was SO

CLOSE to being your girlfriend. My goal was the end of June. I think I would have made it.

C: I'm so sorry :(. I know I've grown a lot and learned a lot about myself in the interim. The question is, Can we discuss it in person, or do we have to just text today?

T: I know. I tried not to be mad about it. And I didn't mean to make it harder for you. Maybe I could see you later.

C: So I can't use seeing you as an excuse to leave work early? :(

T: Didn't you just take an entire week off for Powell?

C: Yes, I did take a week off, but I can still take today off. I told them I was going to.

T: You were already taking today off?

C: Yes. To see you, if you'd let me. I miss you. I'm pretty sure I led out with that point.

T: Yeah, you did. It just seems risky. I could have had a 17-hour meeting.

C: I told them I'd "probably" take off early. I'm still telling them that haha. Apparently, I'm more excited to get together than you are though :P Can I please come up now? I just finished my last task, and it's a perfect stopping point to leave for the day.

T: Fine.

By this point, I had gotten dressed and driven all the way to campus, planning to work on my puzzles some more. I was sitting in the car in the parking lot. I knew that if I didn't see Corby, he would just keep bugging me about it.

My phone rang. It was Corby.

"Hello?"

"Hi. I'm leaving. Can we meet at my parents' house?"

It was strange to hear his voice again. But not strange. It had only been six weeks.

"Sure. I can leave now." I turned my car back on and started to drive.

Corby didn't want to hang up. "What have you been up to?"

"Not much. Mostly making lecture videos. I finally finished them all and got them uploaded. Oh, the air-conditioning in my building has been out for the last two months. I installed an app on my phone to measure the temperature, and it gets up to ninety-five in the afternoon."

Corby offered his condolences, and then asked follow-up questions, just like he used to. I told him about how the blood-drive people can really mess up your arms and about how we had been spreading tar on my grandpa's warehouse rental roofs at 5:00 a.m. on the weekends. He told me some of the stories from Lake Powell—the board games they played and the cute things the kids had done. It felt like a normal conversation.

I pulled in front of the house. Corby's van was in the driveway, and he was already sitting at the bottom of the ramp. I climbed out of the car, and he opened his arms. I gave him a long hug, and then we went to Chick-fil-A.* I had never been before. We just kept talking as we went through the drive-thru. Then we drove to a park and found a picnic table.

---

* *Tess is so oversensitive to textures that she doesn't really notice taste as much. This gets even more pronounced when she is overloaded. I didn't realize how extreme it was until this Chick-fil-A visit when I got all the sauces and made her try them. Tess, upon trying the honey mustard and the ranch, informed me that the only difference was that the honey mustard tasted "stickier." Stickier isn't a taste!*

After we were done eating, Corby started getting serious.

"I really am sorry for breaking up with you."

I glared at him. "I still don't understand why you had to do it."

"I don't know either. But I think it was for me. I couldn't emotionally get over you and date other people if we kept going like we were before. I had to try something different. And full disclosure, I met a girl."

My heart sank. Why had he rushed back and bought me chicken nuggets so soon if he had met a girl?!

I built a tower out of the remaining waffle fries, not wanting to look at him.

He continued. "We went out a lot and texted. We even held hands and cuddled a bit. But even though I had the opportunity to date her, I realized that I didn't want a relationship with her. I want one with you."

I didn't say anything. He was being all mushy again, just like a scripted movie character. He wrapped up his little speech. "I actually thought about coming back two weeks ago, but I decided to finish out the full six weeks. And I was way more excited to see you again than I was about going to Lake Powell."

I shook my head. "I really tried not to be mad at you. But I was. And I am so tired of everything that I don't know what I want."

"How about we go back to my parents' house and play something?"

Thank heavens! I didn't want to talk anymore.

Corby got a bit lightheaded on the way back, so when we got inside, I hauled him onto the couch and reclined the back slightly so he could take a nap. I had a giant backpack with me, full of tasks I had been ignoring while doing jigsaw puzzles. While Corby napped, I pulled out my laptop and started grading assignments for the class I was teaching.

When he awoke, I helped sit him up, and he began reading the questions over my shoulder. And somehow, my laptop ended up sliding onto the cushion next to me, and I was in Corby's lap. Kissing him.

During the six weeks, I had read a "how-to" article about kissing. I still didn't particularly enjoy it, but treating kissing like a homework assignment made it easier to approach.

The article must have helped because a few minutes later, Corby pulled away and asked, "Are you sure you haven't kissed anyone before?"

A sliver of smugness slithered through the empty void. I may have been absolutely terrible at relationships and communication and commitment, but I could learn anything from an article. I just wished that someone would write an article about how my stupid brain worked.

## Chapter 39

# Soggy Cheerios

*August*

I swirled the milk in my bowl, watching a few Cheerios chase each other in a circle. I was at a church activity for single adults. I didn't want to be at this activity. I didn't want to do much of anything. Over the last month, my anger toward Corby had faded. We had gone out a few more times, and he had started asking if we could date again. He seemed to think that we could move on as if those six weeks had never happened. But they had happened. And now the mere idea of making any more decisions filled me with dread. Why bother working on our relationship if he was just going to leave again? I had worked so hard to change so much about myself over the past year, and it hadn't been enough. Why would it be different this time? Why should I want to be with someone who expected so much? I sat by myself, urging the Cheerios on in endless swirls.

A few of my fellow ward members sat down at my table. I barely glanced up.

One naively asked a most dangerous question. "Tessa! How are you?"

Up to this point, I had been pretending that everything in my life was fine, not telling anyone about Corby and the roller coaster we were on. But pretending was exhausting, and I couldn't do it anymore.

"Oh, I'm all right. Just trying to figure out what to do with this guy I'm sort of dating."

"You're seeing someone? How long have you been going out?"

"For like a year and a half?" I didn't feel like explaining the nuances of how we had been dating but also not dating. I idly popped some milk bubbles with the tip of my spoon.

My pronouncement was met with silence. I finally looked up. The entire table was looking at me in shock. I had interacted with all these people at least once a week for an entire year and had never mentioned that I was seeing anyone.

One of them recovered his ability to speak. "That's . . . great? Tell us about him."

I gave the shortest explanation possible, returning my attention to the disintegrating Cheerios. "We met online, and we see each other every week. He wants to be in an official relationship, but he is in a wheelchair, and I don't know what to do."

There was another long pause before one of the older choir dudes spoke up. "Look, you're only like twenty-three, right?"

"Twenty-two." I sighed.

"Ah, twenty-two. You're so young! And you have so much potential! You shouldn't throw all that away for someone like him! You should find someone else who actually cares about you!"

Anger flooded through me. *Someone who actually cares about me?* How dare he suggest I was throwing my life away on Corby when this guy hadn't even met him! I suddenly remembered why I liked Corby so much. I had never met another man who cared more about me or who constantly encouraged me to live up to my potential! I thought about arguing, but the terrible speech wasn't over yet.

"If you were thirty, I would tell you to go for it. But you have plenty of time to find someone else!"

This man was nuts. I tried to defend my actions. "But what if he is the right person for me? We broke up earlier in the summer, and I was completely miserable. And I have tried to give him up a few times, but I can't!" I stood up, threw away my soggy Cheerios, and stomped out to the parking lot.

I relentlessly prowled the edge of the parking lot. How did any of this make sense? Once you are "too old," you should just settle for anyone who would take you? If someone has a physical disability, then they don't have any potential? If choir dude were friends with Corby, would he be telling Corby to just take anyone he could get because he was too old and too disabled? I was fuming. If choir dude got to know Corby, I was sure he wouldn't be saying these things. I may not be right for Corby, but I knew Corby was right for me!

*Chapter 40*

# The Consequences of Miscommunication

*September; Corby's perspective*

C: Fun fact: When you slid me up in bed last night, my underwear totally didn't move with me. I put my arms down at my side and didn't feel any cloth and was like, "Uh-oh!" I sat up the bed and got them mostly up, but if I had been rolled over, there would have been much bum.

T: I am super skilled at unintentionally getting all your clothes off, aren't I?

C: Twice in 18 months isn't all that frequent, but I guess it's still twice more than everyone else.

T: See? Mad skills.

C: Honestly, this makes you better at taking my pants off than I am at getting my pants off.

T: And I wasn't even trying . . .

Tess was being infuriating. Nothing the woman did made any sense. She was usually so logical, but not when it came to relationships.

About a week into the six weeks of silence, Rylee had texted me saying that Tess wished that she had picked option one. The day I came back, she even kissed me. But I had been back for over a month, and she had reverted to her usual patterns of not touching me or saying much—it was even worse than before I'd left. When I tried to ask, she just kept saying that she was "empty." I knew I'd hurt her by breaking up, but I thought that the six weeks would have changed *something.* I wasn't sure how much longer I could do this. It felt like we were just casual friends.

Even though I didn't think Tess would talk to me about this, I decided to ask her anyway.

C: Will you be shattered if we officially clarify friends status?

T: Did you meet someone else?

C: No, I haven't. My mind isn't 100% made up, and we can definitely still talk about this. I just don't feel very "wanted" in the relationship, emotionally or physically. Everything we currently do, we can do as friends.

T: I guess I have been confused about what I should be doing physically since we're not in a relationship. You said you didn't want to cuddle if we weren't dating, so I was trying to help you enforce that.

I read Tess's message a few times. She had actually given a legitimate response, which she hadn't done in a while.

It suddenly occurred to me that Tess's behavior *had* been logical. Well, the physical aspects anyway. I thought back on some of the things I had said before. I had previously made it quite clear that:

1) I liked snuggling. Tess knew that physical touch was my primary love language. I had made that embarrassingly clear.
2) I didn't want to kiss someone unless we were in an actual relationship. Things tended to get complicated if I crossed that line.
3) I had repeatedly told Tess that I wanted to be with someone who helped me enforce my commitments.

Tess was doing exactly what I had asked her to do. We weren't in a relationship, so she was trying to help me enforce my commitment not to make out. In a way, Tess was showing me that she *did* care. And I had put her in a weird situation, where I needed physical touch to feel love but then asked her not to touch me and then complained that she wouldn't cuddle.

I felt stupid. I thought communication was one of my strongest skills, but I had really messed this one up.

Tess came to my parents' house on Labor Day. She slipped in the door, gave me a really brief, awkward hug, then nervously backed up and leaned against the doorframe, shoving her hands into her pockets. She didn't seem to want to look at me.

"Do you have any thoughts about what we should do about our relationship?" I asked.

She gave a typical Tess deflection. "What do you think?"

"I think we should act like a couple, just for today. And then start being just friends again."

She took a deep breath and nodded. That single phrase was magical. Suddenly, Tess *did* know what to do. I had told her that we should act like a couple for the evening, and it quickly became apparent that she understood what I meant by that. I had given her a verbal commitment, which gave her permission to throw out my no-touch-without-commitment rule. She was free to show me love in the way that I liked best. She cuddled up next to me on the couch and kissed me. Later, she even held my hand under the table while we were playing a game with some of my friends.

It was *amazing.*

The version of Tess who I met on our first date—the one who had willingly sat on my lap—was back for the evening. I knew she was capable of doing what I needed. This was the most physical she had been in the entire year and a half I had known her.

Something was changing. Including the way we communicated. I was slowly starting to figure out how I needed to phrase things for her to understand—clearly defined parameters. I began to realize that Tess was terrible at comprehending nuances. She categorized everything into just two or three concrete mental categories that were never allowed to mix. In her mind, she could either touch me, or she couldn't. And I had unintentionally muddled up those categories and made a huge "gray zone" that she was just not good at navigating.

A week later, I asked my institute teacher if I could buy him lunch. (Institute is like an extra Sunday School class held during the week.) I didn't know Brother B. personally, but he was an amazing teacher. I felt the most confident about dating Tess while I was sitting in his class every Thursday. More importantly, he had mentioned several times in various lessons that he had married someone with anxiety, and the decision had been really difficult. From the little he had shared, Brother B.'s wife sounded quite similar to Tess. So I took him to In-N-Out for lunch and told him about my situation. He had a lot of great insights.

Tess came over that evening. She was sitting on my bed, and I was in my chair—she was following the rules of the "just friends" category very effectively, totally avoiding touching me.

"So, I had lunch with Brother B. today. I'd like to tell you about it, if you're open."

Tess pulled her legs to her chest so she was in a little ball. She didn't look happy about my sudden change in topic. She probably thought I was going to break up with her again . . . which wouldn't have been totally unexpected, given how dissatisfied I had been the last month.

"Brother B.'s wife has super-high anxiety. Worse than you, believe it or not."

"Oh, I know my anxiety isn't *that* severe. It has just been extra bad the last few months. Since July 6, if you want to be exact," she responded.

"I guess you're right; I didn't really even notice it the first year I knew you. Anyway, the two of them scheduled their wedding seven different times. And she broke it off six of those times, I guess pretty close to the actual wedding dates. I asked Brother B. what his biggest regret was. He said that he wished he hadn't pushed her so hard and that he should have just waited until she was ready."

Tess stopped twisting the corner of my pillowcase and slowly looked up, a cautiously hopeful expression in her eyes.

"I know I have certain expectations about how a relationship should look, about how it should be official, and about how I want to keep the physical aspects only when I'm in a committed relationship, but maybe that isn't what you need. I choose you, and instead of pushing you to meet my expectations, I am willing to wait as long as you need. I'm not going to force you into making any decisions until you tell me you are ready. Our relationship is still good right now, even if it isn't what I pictured."

"You mean, we can act like we did last time I was over here?" she clarified.

"Yep."

"Even though we aren't actually dating?"

"Yep."

I guess she liked my decision, because she clambered off the bed, launched herself into my lap, and voluntarily gave me a giant kiss.

## Chapter 41

# Officially Official

*October*

For the first time in months, I was no longer curled up in a ball at the top of my mental staircase. I had sat back up, and was again contemplating Corby. The staircase seemed a lot smaller now. My motivation was slowly returning. I managed to get stuff done at school that didn't involve jigsaw puzzles. And it was really nice being able to talk to Corby without being in constant fear that he would want to suddenly break up again. We spent a lot of time together, continuing to hone our Minecraft building skills and creating a costume for Corby for comic con. He wanted to go as a Roman "chair"iot, so I made him a leather vest, we spent an evening buying stuffed horses at a toy store, and I built a lap-sized chariot shell out of cardboard boxes.

Was I still unsure about the future? Yes. But something magical had happened. I started doing things like buying wheelchair-accessible symphony tickets for a performance that wouldn't happen until *April*—six months away. Now that I wasn't trying to stay with Corby just so I wouldn't lose him, it seemed that my brain was finally okay with acknowledging that he would likely be around for at least six more months.

One morning, as I was wrestling my legs into two layers of fleece-lined tights, I glanced up at my closet shelves and thought about how

I should probably get rid of some of my old clothes in the next few months so I wouldn't need to move them.

Wait.

Did I just casually think about moving?

I froze, trying to recollect what my brain had just generated. Why was I planning on moving?

To be with Corby. Of course.

The thought was so frightening and so natural at the same time. Somehow, I had finally come to terms with Corby. To the point that I was planning on getting married and moving in with him. *In a couple of months*. I guess if we were getting married soon, we might as well be in a relationship. I again started referring to him as my boyfriend in my constant mental dialogue. In just a few short weeks, I had crept down my mental staircase. I was now sitting on the bottom stair, looking directly into Corby's face. But he didn't know I was there.

My mom had independently decided that Corby wasn't leaving any time soon. She and Rylee found some used wheelchair ramps that just happened to be the perfect size for the porch. They folded in half and could be easily stored. Mom reassured me that if we ever broke up, it was just fine. The ramps would be useful as her parents got older and could no longer ascend the two stairs into the house. The ramps were very nice, *much* lighter than those metal slabs in Corby's van, and they were wide enough that he could stay in his power chair! The acquisition of these ramps meant that he started showing up at my house more often.

At the end of October, I had to fly out to California to present one of my research papers. I gave my presentation, watched some other boring presentations, and took a bus to the beach so I could see the ocean for the first time. I wrote the word *platypus* in the sand and texted it to Corby. After riding a bus back to the hotel, I leaped onto the bed and discovered a Corby text on my phone.

> C: I'm not debating any ultimatums or anything, but I am unsure where our relationship stands from your perspective, and I'd like to

discuss sometime. Just thought you might like advance notice to gather your thoughts.

T: We're dating, aren't we?

C: We're dating, but you aren't my girlfriend. You haven't let me know you accept the title anyway. We're still just unofficially dating.

T: Oh, in my head, I've been your girlfriend for a month now. I guess the word "official" just makes everything seem so serious and irrevocable.*

C: Really? I've still been referring to you as "this girl I'm dating" or just as "Tess" because I didn't think I could call you my girlfriend.

T: Yeah. I've told people that I'm dating someone. I just thought you weren't calling me your girlfriend because you know I don't like that word.

C: I thought we were still building up to you being comfortable with it haha. Is that not a goal? I can keep phrasing it, "We're dating," but we both know we're not dating others. I love our relationship; thus, I don't need any ultimatums.

T: I know that you haven't been going out with anyone else for weeks now. And I'm still not totally comfortable with it yet, but yes, it has been a goal, and I'm definitely getting there.

---

* *WHAT!?! I'm quite proud that I responded calmly at the time. I didn't feel at all calm when I sent this. I was ecstatic! And incredulous! And I didn't want to startle Tess. Haha.*

C: I don't think we need to be doing anything else. My only real worry was I didn't think we were exclusive in your mind.

T: Well, that's good. 'Cause I don't think I can do much more than I'm doing now.

C: This, to me, is all the things a healthy, normal relationship is.

T: Well, good.

And with that romantic text exchange, I was officially dating Corby Campbell. Well, I had been dating him in my mind for weeks, but now he knew about it. And this time, I didn't cry.

## Chapter 42

# Bling

*March (Yes, six whole months later)*

C: Tesseract.

T: Tessellation.

C: Diatessaron.

T: I didn't realize there were so many words with my name in them.

C: Agreed. But there totally are. My name is not word friendly. Corbeil?

T: What is that? A crab species?

C: "A sculptured ornament, especially on a capital, having the form of a basket."

T: . . . that was my next guess.

C: Should have been your first. Everything about me SCREAMS ornamental basket.

Dating Corby was going well. In fact, it was going so well that by the end of December, we had started looking at rings. Wedding rings. You know, the kind of ring that you wear after getting engaged to someone? It was strange. It took me nearly two years to finally date

Corby. And now that I was . . . well, nothing had really changed. We still texted all day and went out on weekends, but now it was less confusing. The biggest change was that I had started holding his hand regularly.*

In December, he moved in with his parents full-time. Ronda taught me how to do catheter changes and other medical things that I would need to take over after we got married. Sometimes I slept in Corby's parents' guest room instead of driving home. Since I never knew where I would be, the back seat of my car now looked like a chaotic closet full of wrinkled outfits.

The ring-buying phase took a solid three months. Corby was taking it slowly. He didn't want to overwhelm me with scary, significant decisions. I had moments where I questioned what we were doing. But instead of hiding from Corby, I ran to him and did my best to talk about it. He had become a safe place rather than a confusing place. Mostly. I was still not very good at communication.

I picked the ring that would be the least inconvenient while knitting. The decision had been made. That moment of texting Corby about officially buying a ring was the moment that I officially made the decision. I sat in my office closet and hit the tiny Send button.

We were getting married. *We were getting married.* We had decided to *buy a ring.* Even though the decision to purchase an expensive piece of jewelry was not a legally binding decision, it had the same weight. I wasn't going to back out now.

A few days later, I went to Corby's place. We were going to see a Brian Regan comedy show that night, and it would be a logical night for a proposal, but he knew I didn't want an overblown public proposal with lots of spectators.

---

* *Did you pick up that we were kissing regularly before we were holding hands regularly? I still find this fact very amusing. Tessa's hands are her safe place, where she knits and cross stitches and does puzzles. For Tess, holding hands was a bigger deal than kissing.*

As we walked out of the garage toward the van, he said, "Hang on, there is something in a box in my backpack that you might want before going."

I, of course, assumed that it was the ring. But it was Corby, so you never knew. I looked into the backpack and found a ring box. I pulled it out and sat on Corby's lap. He got all serious and said, "Tessa Sommer . . ."

"Yes, Corbinealious Brycetholomue Campbelliticus Maximus Danger the III?"

He paused for dramatic effect, looked into my eyes, and said . . . "Would you like some fruit snacks?"

I opened the box. There really was a package of fruit snacks compressed into the tiny ring box. I looked at him suspiciously, but he didn't say anything else. I graciously fed him some of the fruit snacks while we were driving.*

A few days later, I was back at Corby's house. It was a gorgeous spring day. I climbed onto Corby's lap, and we snuggled while we talked about our days.

As I was climbing off, Corby said, "Oh yeah, there is something in my backpack for you."

This routine felt familiar. There was a ring box in the backpack. I looked at Corby's face and realized it was another joke. I opened the ring box and found that he had stuck a goldfish in the little ring slot. I ate it with an exaggerated amount of exasperation and was about to walk away, but Corby stopped me and told me to grab the shiny bag in the bottom of his backpack.

While I pulled it out, Corby started reciting a string of puns that he had clearly written especially for this occasion. "I hope this isn't too cheese-cakey, and I know it puzzles you that it took me so long, but you are my favorite kind of fruit snack, and I would goldfish with you every day. I made sure there was no one to documentary this, but

---

* *Having people feed me in my hospital bed when I first broke my neck was not my favorite. But having someone feed me snacks while I'm driving is the best!*

I'd love to knit my life to yours, and I will never Lego. Will you marry me?"

I reached into the shiny gift bag and pulled out a ring box. But this was a special ring box. It was made out of blue and orange Legos. Blue and orange were our wedding colors, a detail that had been decided months ago so my mom could reserve tablecloths or some other trivial wedding detail that I didn't care about.

I opened the box. The ring had been built right into the box; I had to pry up a Lego to get the ring out. The construction was very clever. I found out later that Corby had recruited his mom to be his hands and had directed her on how to build it.

I put the ring on my finger and of course said yes. I then gave in and agreed to take some selfies so Corby would have proof that this event had actually happened. We then proceeded with our usual evening activities—eating french toast and watching *Megamind*.

Somewhere in the middle of everything, it occurred to me that I should probably tell my own parents that I had gotten officially engaged, so I texted a picture to my mom. Evidently, I had chosen to text her while she was attending a piano recital, so she couldn't cheer or show anyone until it was over. She stayed awake until I got home so she could see the ring in person.

## Chapter 43

# Mechanical Hugging Machine

*July*

I looked out from behind a wall of strangers who all wanted to *hug* me. All I could see was a long snaking line of even more strangers. The night of our wedding reception had arrived.

I didn't really want to be at this wedding reception. Sure, it was *my* wedding reception. Well, sort of. It was Corby's wedding reception. He was the one who had always been excited to get married. And Corby had invited 80 percent of the attendees, who, as previously mentioned, all wanted to hug me. He had sent out over 450 invitations. Based on the bit of the line I could see, all of them had shown up. The line went around the gym, through the foyer, and out the door of the church building. We found out later that some people drove by, saw the line, and never even bothered to park.

We held the reception in the gym of a church building. It wasn't the most beautiful venue, but it was free. And we could bring our own food, so we wouldn't have to pay to cater food for this massive crowd. We opted to have a Rice Krispie bar. My mom recruited an army of aunts to make dozens of pans in six different flavors. I had seen the table earlier in the evening but hadn't tried any of them, and it wasn't likely that I would get one at this rate.* The cake was also made out of massive blocks of Rice Krispies.

The line was moving faster than average. We had typed up several posters detailing our very long dating story and hung them on the wall. Almost everyone got to the front of the line, said, "Your story was so great! Congratulations!" and moved along. I was grateful that we'd hung those posters up; I didn't fancy being interrogated by all these strangers.

The other unique feature at our reception was the decorations. They were almost exclusively made from Legos, down to the topper that adorned our cake. Making Lego decorations had been a bright spot in an otherwise onerous task of planning a reception. The cake topper even had a Corby minifig in a tiny wheelchair.** It was perfect.

I robotically hugged person after person, making zero effort to remember any of the names. I wasn't going to remember anything about this night. I could feel half my brain slowly losing control from all the hugging and the noise.

A girl came through the line who I actually recognized. She had gotten married about a year before, and when she opened her arms, I stiffly leaned in for yet another hug. As she gave me a squeeze, she said, "Marriage is the best! You're going to love it so much!"

I heard myself saying, "Yeah, it's going to be great!" That was on the outside. On the inside, my sensory-plagued brain was losing its cool, and it yelled, "*You'd better *&%^$ be right about that*!" I reprimanded my brain for using naughty language, then mechanically reached out to hug the next person, plastering on my calm, smiley persona. It was a good thing Corby was doing most of the talking. He was thrilled with the amount of hugs he was getting.

---

* *Tess had experimented with the flavors in the weeks leading up to the event though. It was a really rough job, having to try different Rice Krispie recipes. :D*

** *Which the Lego company sent us* for free *when we asked where to get one. Lego fan for life!*

Hours passed. Finally, I could see the end of the line. I could also see the rest of the room for the first time since setting it up; a surprising amount of people were still hanging around.

After the final hug, we whisked into action. Some of Corby's friends transferred him to his manual chair while I ran into a tiny classroom usually used for Sunday School and swapped my long wedding skirt for a short tulle one. We then headed to the dance floor. Corby and I had learned to dance. Sort of. Over the past few months, we had started going dancing together, and some of the other dancers had helped us cobble together a series of dance moves. Corby led by using eye rolls, eyebrow wiggles, and very specific glances. I preferred dancing with guys who had functional legs, but it was cute that Corby was trying to learn. I had come to this reception for him. And he had learned dancing for me.

The reception guests who were still hanging around gathered at the edges of the dance floor. "Love" by Nat King Cole came from the speakers. We didn't have any connection to this song—we had actually forgotten to plan this particular detail and it was the first song that popped into my head when the DJ asked what he should play. I grabbed Corby's fist, and we started to dance.

In typical Corby and Tess fashion, our first dance was kind of a disaster. Corby had never worn long sleeves when we were practicing, and they kept getting snagged by the wheels; plus, our eyebrow system was not foolproof, and I wasn't the best dancer to begin with. I studiously avoided looking at any of the people, instead staring intently at Corby's eyebrows. But I was aware of the audience. They were strangely quiet. Some of them were making suspicious sniffling noises.

As the song finally ended, Corby tried to dip me. In the process, his sleeve got snagged again, so on the last note, I slid off his lap, onto the footrest, and almost to the floor. What a finish! The audience gave us a round of applause anyway, and they flooded the dance floor for several more songs.

The next morning, we were married for time and all eternity in the Draper Utah Temple. I don't remember much of what the sealer said, though as part of his remarks, he looked at me and said, “I’ll bet Tessa has been planning this day for years.” I wanted to say, “No, but Corby has!” but it didn’t seem appropriate, given the gravity of the situation, and I didn’t want to throw off his speech. So I mutely nodded while glancing sideways at my almost-husband, who was smirking. I knew he was thinking the same thing I was.

We went up to the altar, where the bench on one side had already been moved so Corby’s chair would fit. It was hard to say yes because my throat was so tight, but I squeaked it out, and just like that, we were married.

Corby’s friends had decorated the van by taping little brides to the back of Corby’s chair on all his van logos. It was perfect. We got into the van and drove off amid our families cheering and chasing us. It had been a great morning. And being married didn’t feel any different at all. Corby and I were driving off in his van, like all the hundreds of times we had done so in the past two and a half years. We just looked a lot more attractive than normal.

We went home to our new condo, and I went to the bathroom and nearly strangled myself trying to get out of my wedding dress. Sure, Corby was there and would have probably *loved* to help me, but his gimpy fingers were useless in the face of corset lacing. So I wiggled out myself and put on normal clothes. We then proceeded to do very typical newlywed things: We played *Minecraft* all afternoon, then started a jigsaw puzzle, excited to finally utilize our counter-height table. Because he could finally reach the pieces, Corby’s enjoyment of jigsaw puzzles tripled. It felt just like a date. But it wasn’t. We were married. And my mental staircase was gone.

# USEFUL

## Bowel Care

Time for another useful chapter! This time about the trials and tribulations of pooping! Which is *exactly* the topic you expected to follow a wedding, right?

Bowel care is the single biggest inconvenience of being in a wheelchair. Not being able to walk is easily solved. We pay a bunch of money and get a fancy wheelchair.* If someone puts Corby in the chair, he can get around just fine. But we can't pay a bunch of money and make it so that he doesn't have to poop. Which is unfortunate, because we would pay a *lot* of money to get rid of bowel care.

Normally, the bowels all work together in a very organized way. Certain muscles tighten, other muscles relax, and you can consciously choose a convenient time to let everything out. Unless you have food poisoning or something.

For people with SCI, everything is messed up. Sometimes, everything stays tight all the time. These people cannot consciously choose when to poop. Other people have the opposite problem. Everything is loose all the time, and I will leave it to you to imagine what that means. Neither situation is ideal.

In either case, having a regular bowel-care routine is key. You have to poop on a regular schedule, both to get your body into a routine and to keep things from getting backed up and causing embarrassing accidents. Some people even have special diets because they have discovered that eating certain foods makes it significantly harder to manage their poop.

God designed bodies with lots of backup systems. Many people who are tight all the time (such as Corby) make good use of the bowel reflex. When a certain part of the bowel is stimulated in a circular motion, the anal sphincter relaxes and lets the poop out. This is called "digital stimulation." And yes, it is exactly what it sounds like: using

---

* *Actually, insurance pays most of it. Insurance can be trouble, but this is one situation where they usually help.*

your finger to stimulate the sphincter. Over and over again until everything is out. For Corby, this takes sixty to ninety minutes, so he spends four and a half hours a week pooping. With a buddy. In bed. Cute, right?

There are many methods of doing bowel care. Paraplegics, who have full arm and hand function, can usually do their bowel-care routine themselves. Some quadriplegics have even figured out setups for doing it themselves, but that is less common. Many SCI patients are able to do their bowel routine while sitting on the toilet, but Corby is not one of those. He gets extremely lightheaded during bowel care. If he tried to sit up on a toilet, he would pass out within about ten minutes and fall to the floor. So he stays in bed and lies on his left side.

The process looks like this:

Every day, Corby takes stool softeners. The night before bowel care, he takes laxatives. At 5:00 a.m. on bowel-care days, a bowel-care angel comes and inserts a suppository with even *more* laxatives and waits twenty minutes in a different room. Then, every two minutes, the angel comes back into the bedroom and does the digital stimulation thing ten to fifteen times, sometimes more. Usually the bowel-care people look nothing like angels, but anyone who is willing to do digital bowel stimulation at 5:00 a.m. for over an hour definitely has some saintly qualities and is deserving of the "angel" title.

These angels come because Corby doesn't want me to deal with his literal crap. And I don't want to. Since getting married, I have taken on a lot of Corby's care. But this is the one thing he has never let me help with. Could I do it if we were desperate? Sure. Corby has a document with instructions and pictures, so if there were an emergency, I could technically do it. But Corby doesn't want to cross that line. He is independent in our relationship because he finds people to help him who are not me. And I am grateful.

Bowel care will need to be done every Monday, Wednesday, and Friday morning for the rest of our lives. We don't have a choice. It began just two days after we got married. I heard the front door of our condo open, and I rolled to the other side of the bed. That first morning, I just listened and pretended to be asleep. I have now gotten very good at sleeping through everything. Bowel care is not a very nice thing to listen to.

Corby's medications can change his bowel-care routine. Some medications have side effects of either diarrhea or constipation; both are very exciting. One time, we were playing around with some medication doses. Corby hadn't taken a certain medication for a few weeks, but then we decided to add it back in, and neither of us considered that he should probably take a smaller dose for a few days and work up. A couple of days after taking this innocent-looking tablet, the bowel-care guy—DeLynn—showed up. Corby and I were asleep, facing each other on our sides. DeLynn inserted the suppository and went into the bathroom to wait for twenty minutes.

About fifteen minutes later, I started hearing little spurting noises. The ominous sounds grew in intensity. I opened my eyes. Corby opened his. We stared at each other for a minute, slowly coming to the realization that those increasingly loud noises were coming from Corby, and then we started to giggle. The room was dark, the only light coming from underneath the bathroom door. Whatever was happening, it was too late to stop it now.

DeLynn eventually came out of the bathroom. He took a couple of steps into the room and then stopped, staring at something we couldn't see. I decided I should probably get up and help. That little pill had had quite an unexpected effect on Corby's bowels. The mess covered an impressively large area of the bedroom.

I turned on the light, and let DeLynn decide what to do with Corby while I lugged the new portable carpet cleaner we'd received as a wedding gift out of the laundry room. The inaugural use of that carpet cleaner was memorable, to say the least. And Corby has never taken that particular medication again.

# USEFUL

## The Honeymoon: Aka . . . Can you have Sex?!

This chapter should probably consist, in its entirety, of a single sentence. Something like, "Some things are better left unsaid." But of all the questions we get from complete strangers, the ones most often asked are 1) "Can you have sex?" and 2) "Can you have kids?" I will now answer those questions in a very clear-cut, clinical manner.

Short answers:

1) Yes.
2) Probably?

Everyone, men and women, have two physical arousal pathways: psychogenic and reflexogenic. The reflex response is pretty straightforward: touch = arousal. This response is a reflex, so the brain is not really involved.

The psychogenic response is driven by the brain. When the brain gets excited, it sends messages down the spinal cord to the genital area. These messages usually work together with the reflex response to generate and maintain an aroused state. These messages don't ever get past Corby's injury site, which means he can't voluntarily maintain an aroused state, no matter how much physical stimulus there is. Therefore, sex for us is different. We are intimate in other ways, and it works for us.

For the first few years of our marriage, I couldn't figure out why Corby wanted to have sex at all. I know that *I* can feel what is going on, but Corby *cannot*. It is still hard for me not to feel weird about that. Corby has tried every approach he can think of to explain to me that it doesn't matter that he can't feel it. He gets pleasure and feels like a man when he can do something for me. I counter this by saying that I don't *need* sex. So I am doing it all for him, and he is doing it all for me . . . It gets confusing. It is really difficult not to fake pleasure just to make Corby feel like a great husband. It is an area we have both had to work through. And over the years of our marriage, our version of intimacy has continued to evolve. It is nothing like I thought it would be. And that is okay!

The very first night we were married, I put Corby in bed. I knew how to do that. I had been helping with that for months. Then I went into the bathroom and got myself ready for bed. A couple of people had given me lingerie at bridal showers, but I had hidden it in the back of the closet with deep reluctance. Instead, I put on what I always wore to bed: stretch pants and an oversized T-shirt. I acted like we still weren't married. Mostly. Before today, I had crawled behind Corby and stayed on top of the covers to hug him from behind before sneaking out the door and driving home. But this time, I got *under* the covers. And stayed there. It was nice not having to drive home.

We just lay there for a good while, enjoying this feeling of not having to leave. And then we started kissing. At some point, I pulled on his shoulders so he was sitting in an upright position. This was a position that I had never pulled him into before. I sat on top of his legs, and his legs were *not happy*. They got really tight and started to shake, and Corby started to tip sideways—toward the edge of the bed.

It happened so fast that I didn't react in time. I dove off the side of the bed to at least break Corby's fall. It sort of worked. I slammed into the side of the wheelchair, and Corby landed on top of me, so he was protected from getting stabbed by the foot rests. No one was seriously hurt, so we lay on the bedroom floor and laughed for a minute. But then I had to figure out how to get Corby back up onto the bed. I could barely lift him out of his chair, let alone off the floor. It took thirty minutes to drag him over to the wall, hoist him onto my lap, and use my legs to inch my back up the wall with Corby in my arms. I was glad it worked, because I didn't want to sleep on the floor. That incident remains the only time Corby has ended up on the floor. Thank goodness.

So . . . question #2—Can we have kids?

This question doesn't have a universal wheelchair answer. Reproduction after a SCI is not fully understood yet. What we do know is that following a SCI, most of the sperm also act paralyzed. They no longer swim—they just lazily float and occasionally twitch—so they aren't about to embark on a treacherous journey up a fallopian tube.

Corby's case is a bit more complicated. Several years ago, before I met Corby, there was an incident where a nurse inflated a catheter balloon in the wrong place. Let's just say that there was a lot of blood, and now Corby's urethra is completely blocked by scar tissue. No sperm are getting out the normal way. But before you get all upset about that, I am actually delighted with that scar tissue. It means that we have never had to fool around with birth control! Wheelchair perk!

About five years after we got married, Corby went to a fertility specialist. She did a sperm extraction procedure and found that Corby has "a surprising amount of sperm." Not sure what that means, but she was pleased. Even then, the success rate of IVF following SCI is lower than for non-SCI couples. And that is assuming that there is nothing wrong with me.

Now that I am happily married, having children is a question I agonize about all the time. Would I be able to take care of Corby *and* kids? After having a baby, I would be the sole caretaker of an infant while simultaneously taking care of Corby for at least the first four years. Corby can't pick up a baby without help. He can't prep bottles or change diapers. And to top it all off, babies are a minefield of sensory input. Until we can figure out better ways to mitigate my debilitating physical response to noise and smell, we will probably not be having kids. But we reserve our right to change this decision if the angelic squad from our first date returns and starts cheering us on.

So *can* we have kids? Maybe. *Will* we? We are still deciding. And before you send us an email asking if we have ever heard of adoption, yes, we have talked about it. But adopting comes with its own challenges. So who knows what will happen in the future. Whatever the case, it will be an interesting adventure.

# USEFUL

## Normal Day

This is the chapter I wanted to read all those years ago when I found Corby's profile. I just wanted to know what a normal day looked like. Keep in mind that this is how *our* days are. This will not match any other wheelchair couple on the planet because we are all different.

5:00 a.m. (M, W, F): Bowel-care person comes. They let themselves in with the door code. I roll to my side of the bed. If all goes well, I stay asleep until bowel care is done. If not, I pretend to sleep and listen to someone else rummage around in my bathroom and closet. The M and F guys also give Corby a shower. The whole routine ends around 6:30–7:00 a.m.

6:30 a.m. (T, Th): On nonbowel-care mornings, the morning person comes at 6:30 a.m. They spend twenty minutes helping Corby get dressed, get out of bed, and gather the things he needs for work.

7:00 a.m.: Corby rolls into the bedroom and over to my side of the bed. I groggily climb into his lap, nuzzle my face into his shoulder, and keep sleeping for a minute while he soaks up his morning cuddle. I then crawl back into bed and go back to sleep for a couple more hours. Corby then drives himself to work. Or he makes the treacherous six-foot commute to his home office that is maturely decorated with Spider-Man murals.

9:00 a.m.: I wake up and head upstairs, where I operate some small businesses. I also run errands, do yardwork, and clean the house. If Corby is working from home, I get him lunch. Could I have a full-time job? Sure. I tried to work a traditional job for the first few years of our marriage. But on several occasions, I had to leave and speed home to save Corby from a clogged catheter or other wheelchair emergency. It is easier to work from home on my own projects so I can be available to help him when he needs it.

4:30 p.m.: Corby gets home from work. He usually texts me when he gets in his van so I can get dinner ready by the time he rolls in. I sit on his lap and snuggle for a minute.

5:00 p.m.: We eat dinner. I cut up some of Corby's food and stack things in certain ways so he can pick them up easier, but he feeds himself.

5:30 p.m.: Corby reads me scriptures while I clean the kitchen and do the dishes.

6:00 p.m.: During warm months, we usually go on a stroll. We talk about what we did during the day, or we talk to random neighbors we run into. After we have strolled as far as we want, I climb onto Corby's lap and permacuddle on the way home. Sometimes, I put on rollerblades, and he pulls me around the neighborhood instead.

7:00–9:30 p.m.: Once a week, we try to have a dinner or board-game night with friends. They always come to our house since their houses have stairs. Other nights, we play board games with just the two of us. We also have a number of video games we like. Sometimes, we sing at the piano or do Lego sets. Sometimes, Corby moves one of his armrests, and I drape myself over the edge of the couch and onto his lap so he can brush my hair. On Saturday, we work at the temple for most of the day. On Sunday nights, we go to one of our parents' houses for Sunday dinner, and we play games there too.

Once a week, we have what we call a "useful night." It sounds ominous, but it is an attempt not to act like irresponsible teenagers *every* night. Lately, I have been using "useful nights" to write this book. Corby uses these nights to work on church-calling stuff or update the budget or make calls to insurance companies. Sometimes, he uses the time to learn new coding languages or work on other projects. We always feel very mature after a good "useful night."

9:30 p.m. (Sun–Th): Nighttime guy shows up. They knock once and then let themselves in. Regardless of whether we are in the middle of a board game or movie, we stop what we are doing, and Corby goes to bed. We aren't going to make the night guy wait for us. Sometimes it's frustrating to have to stop something when we are five minutes away from finishing, but it's better than having to transfer Corby myself. Sometimes I stay for the bedtime routine, and sometimes I hide upstairs.

10:00 p.m.: I crawl into bed behind Corby, kneel behind his tailbone, and attractively drape myself over his torso so he can wrap his free arm around my back. We talk about plans for the next day and say a prayer together. Then I turn out the lights and go upstairs to work for a few more hours.

12:30 a.m.: I head back downstairs. I get ready for bed, then roll Corby back. (Because Corby sits in one position all day, we need to give his skin a break at night. The night guy rolls him on his side, and I roll him to his back after a few hours.) I've tried to go to sleep at the same time Corby does, but I find it difficult to wake up, roll him back, and then fall back asleep. Also, going to bed early makes it harder to sleep through bowel care. After joining Corby, I snuggle up against his left side until the next morning guy comes in and kidnaps him.

And that is our routine! Is it a bit different? Sure. But we have it set up so that everything runs pretty smoothly. The morning and night guys enable me to have sick days or make plans that don't involve Corby because I don't have to be around every second to help him. It also gives Corby a feeling of independence since his life isn't completely reliant on a single person.

## INTERLUDE NOTE THING 3

WARNING: THE FINAL THREE CHAPTERS IN THE BOOK ARE CALLED "LESSONS." YOU PROBABLY THINK THEY ARE MEANT FOR BOOK CLUBS AND, CONSEQUENTLY, MIGHT BE BORING, BUT THEY ARE JUST AS EXCITING AS THE TIME I PULLED CORBY'S UNDERWEAR OFF IN FRONT OF MY SISTER.

Over the course of our marriage, Corby has convinced me to participate more in his motivational speech things. This has forced me to look back and think about the lessons I have learned since marrying him, and I have written about them here. I actually wrote these chapters first, then realized they would have a greater impact within the context of our dating story, which is why the rest of this book exists. I hope you get something out of them.

## *Lesson #1*

# Accept Service

One day, when I was about ten years old, my mom put two pans of enchiladas in the oven. Several minutes later, we heard a strange noise. Mom opened the oven door to find that one of the glass pans had shattered. Enchilada sauce was pouring into the bottom of the oven, where it started to burn. Mom started yelling for us to get some towels. But upon reflection, she must have decided that she didn't actually want her small children helping with a project that involved broken glass and boiling-hot sauce because then she started yelling at us to stay in the hallway.

Right in the middle of all this chaos, there was a knock at the door. I answered it. A young man who lived a few doors down the street was standing on the porch because his mom had sent him over to drop something off. His name was Shawn, and he was about seventeen. I invited him to step in. He obviously heard the noise coming from the kitchen and asked if everything was okay. I told him what had happened, and he asked if he could help. I told him I would check.

From the safe spot in the hallway, I said, "Mom, Shawn is here. He wants to know if he can help!"

Mom immediately looked up and said, "*No*! Just have him wait. I'll be there in a minute!"

I went back to the front door. Shawn and I stood there for several minutes, breathing in the smell of burnt tortillas. It was awkward. Eventually, Mom came out with her "company face" on. Shawn asked if everything was okay, and Mom smiled and assured him that everything was just fine. She got him out the door as quickly as possible, and after Shawn left, the "company face" disappeared, and Mom resumed her frantic cleaning.

My mom is not alone in behaving this way. Most people don't want their neighbors to see their kitchens right after they make enchiladas, even when the oven *isn't* overflowing. I would say that most of us want to be the ones giving service. We don't want to be the ones being served. We don't want other people to see us when we are vulnerable. We want to appear independent, strong, and capable of handling anything.

When I met Corby, I prioritized self-sufficiency. One of the biggest obstacles to my choosing Corby was that I wasn't sure if I could take care of him *on my own*. But Corby knew how much care he needed. Long before I met him, he had decided that his future wife would *not* help with his bowel care. I help with everything else, but even after nine years, Corby has not let me help with bowel care a single time.

A few months before we got married, Corby and Ronda started searching for a new bowel-care person. Up to that point, he had been able to find former nurses who just wanted a part-time gig while raising young kids. But this time, he couldn't find a nurse. Instead, a member of our church volunteered (initially, with quite a lot of "encouragement" from his wife). He was a prison guard with no medical training. But bowel care isn't complicated. We set up a payment arrangement, and Ronda trained him just in time for our wedding day. DeLynn was the first angel I met. He was Corby's sole bowel-care person for the first two years of our marriage. We also had eight regular night/morning people. Nearly all of them were either teenagers or young, newly married men who lived in our condo complex.

At first, it was *so* weird having people constantly coming and going through our bedroom and bathroom—places that are usually the most private. It was uncomfortable and inconvenient. Years later, I still worry about making sure all the right supplies are there, and I worry about keeping the house at least sort of clean. I know for a fact that Corby's routine has often been an inconvenience for his caregivers, interrupting their house projects or family events. Is it stressful trying to find people to help? It certainly is. And I feel so lazy when I keep sleeping while someone else interrupts their own sleep to help my husband. Could I get up and get Corby out of bed myself? Yeah, I could. Have I thought about taking over so that we won't be an "inconvenience" to anyone else? I certainly have. But for my physical health, Corby's mental health, and the sake of our relationship, I had to learn how to let other people help. And this has become one of the biggest pros of being married to a guy in a wheelchair.

Two years after getting married, we found a house with no stairs in the garage. We weren't even really looking for a house. It just magically fell into our laps at the right time. About a month before moving in, we went to the church we would be attending. We introduced ourselves to a few people and let them know that we were going to need some ongoing help after we got settled. The day we moved in, the whole neighborhood showed up. There were so many helpers that they weeded our whole yard, set up all the shelves, and even hung up most of our art. By the time we went to bed, it looked like we had been living in the house for months. As great as that was, the best part was that they had brought a completely filled-in sign-up sheet. Each morning and evening slot was filled with a different person, including three people who had volunteered to learn how to do bowel care—without even knowing who we were. I still get chills just thinking about this.

The very night we moved in, the first helper showed up and introduced himself. We met a new person every night and every morning for a week. By the end of that week, we felt like we had lived in the neighborhood forever. None of the helpers expected anything in return*—not even the ones who were coming at 5:00 a.m. We have now lived in this house for over six years. There have been more than twenty different helpers from just this neighborhood; eight have done bowel care. Some have been helping since the day we moved in. And

---

* *Or even allowed us to pay when we offered.*

every time someone moves out or their work schedule changes, another person steps up within a couple of weeks. Apart from these regularly scheduled people, I can easily think of at least two dozen other people who have helped in other ways, with car repairs, sprinkler repairs, yard projects, and everything else that comes with owning a house. Every time we have needed help, we have been able to find it. It has just been a matter of reaching out and asking.

When we got married, I sent out eighty reception invitations. Corby sent out 450. He is older and far more social than I am, so it makes sense that he knew more people, but now that I have experienced Corby's routine, I understand why so many people wanted to come support him. He has been the recipient of service for twenty years, and the relationships that are formed through giving and receiving service are so much stronger than other types of relationships. Many of the people who come over to help Corby have become close friends. Some of the caregivers are not as outgoing or social, so we never would have gotten to know them if they hadn't volunteered to help. If Corby suddenly didn't need help anymore, we would miss feeling this connected to the people around us. We are privileged to experience this level of long-term service, and it has been wonderful.

I guess I have gotten a little bit better at letting people serve me. But it is still sometimes difficult.

When I am struggling to accept help from someone, I remind myself of how I feel when someone asks me for help. Even if it is inconvenient, I am flattered and honored that a friend or neighbor thought of me when they needed something. I will do anything to help that person. And I'm sure the people around us feel the same way when we call and ask them for help.

So to wrap up, there are two main points I hope you take with you from this chapter:

1) Service is a way to build a relationship. If you are struggling to connect with someone, consider asking *them* to help *you*. Even if you don't need help, the shared experience will be a great memory. For example, do moms *need* help from their toddlers when baking cookies? No. But you let them help anyway because it builds the

relationship and creates fun memories. And this principle applies to everyone, not just small children. Pause for a minute and ponder who your closest friends are. Chances are, one of you helped the other in some significant way early on in your relationship, or you have become closer by helping each other.

2) Accept service. This second takeaway is actually a challenge: I challenge you to always accept help from another person, especially when that person has offered to do something specific. Accept this service even if you don't need it.

This will not be easy. I still struggle to accept help. But every gift that is offered to us is an opportunity to build or strengthen a bond of love. When we are good and grateful receivers, we open a door to deepen our relationship with the giver of the gift. So learn to ask for help, receive help when it is offered, and don't feel guilty about it. Receiving service has been one of the highlights of our marriage.

*Lesson #2*

# Dreams and Expectations

Everyone has dreams. Not the kind you have when you are asleep but the kind in which you picture how something will be in the future. Other words could be *hope* or maybe a *goal*. Dreams are what drive us to action and give us things to look forward to.

But sometimes, or maybe even most of the time, our dreams don't work out exactly how we pictured them. And sometimes, they don't work out at all.

A dream is not a tangible thing. The event or person or object or experience that we dream about and plan for doesn't actually exist. Yet we still invest our time and emotion in them. The more time and emotion we invest, the harder it is when they don't pan out. But it feels a bit silly (or a lot silly) when you are disappointed about something that never existed! So we try to brush this disappointment away, telling ourselves that we are being stupid.

Ivy is my little sister. She absolutely *loves* birthdays. Most kids do, but she has been above average in this department. She would start planning her birthday in great detail about four months in advance, so when her birthday finally arrived, we knew Ivy had been eagerly anticipating and planning this day for weeks. In other words, she had created a dream of her perfect birthday.

On her tenth birthday, her dream was working out pretty great. The whole family came for dinner, mom cooked the meal of Ivy's choice, and there were presents on the table. Ivy was a happy little girl.

After dinner, my dad pulled some pie out of the fridge. He started cutting the pies into pieces so he could serve them, not realizing that they were the substitute for the normal birthday cake. Happy little Ivy walked into the kitchen and saw that her birthday pie had been cut before the candles had been blown out, and her face fell. She quickly left the kitchen. My mom realized what was happening and stopped my dad. We found Ivy on the stairs. She was trying not to cry, making strangled attempts to laugh it off. She was perfectly aware that she was crying over something silly—who cries over a pie being cut too early?—but she couldn't articulate why that marred whip cream topping was so devastating. I have a guess though. Those cuts didn't fit into her dream. Every birthday, my mom takes the birthday kid's picture, with the kid smiling from behind a dessert with lit candles. Ivy had pictured this moment, but she hadn't pictured ten candles crowded onto a single piece of pie or a picture of her face above a chocolate pie with messy cuts through the middle. Luckily cream pies are forgiving. You can smooth them over and still salvage the birthday picture.

This type of thing happens all the time. Most brides have some sort of breakdown at some point during their wedding, especially if they are the type of girl who has been planning her wedding since she was six. Inevitably, something happens that wasn't part of the dream, and they get upset for a moment. In extreme cases, they turn into a bridezilla, desperate to salvage an experience that doesn't yet exist.

You can also see this pattern in various TV shows. Take *The Great British Bake Off*, for instance. If you have seen even one season of that show, I guarantee that you have seen some contestant crying on camera because Paul Hollywood told them their cake was undercooked or too dry or had no flavor. They will even vocalize the phrase, "I can't believe I'm crying! It is just a cake!" So you know they feel silly. And then they will follow it up with the phrase, "But it's not just a cake." And it isn't. That hopeful baker spent the entire week making a dozen practice cakes, worrying over their granny's ganache recipe, and the whole time, they were picturing themselves getting compliments from the judges and possibly even receiving a Hollywood Handshake. So are they crying over the cake? No. They are crying over the dream that didn't become reality.

Even I fell into this baking-dream trap! I enjoy experimenting with various recipes for fancy desserts. One week, I tried making fruit tarts that would be worthy of any high-end bakery display window. I looked at pictures of potential fruit arrangements and read up on the best glaze and bought some special perforated tart rings to guarantee success. I pictured presenting a gorgeous tray of stunning tarts to my family for Sunday dinner. I had a minor tart dream.

I even mitigated this dream, telling myself in advance that the tart shells had a very high chance of failure. But they didn't fail! I achieved tart-shell perfection! I also made a perfect filling from scratch! On Sunday afternoon, just before we needed to leave, I pulled out all the components, thrilled to finally be able to decorate my cute little tart shells with stripes of artistically carved strawberries and shiny glazed raspberries. But when I opened the plastic containers of berries that I had bought just two days before, I was horrified to discover that they were covered in fuzzy, white mold.

My Sunday afternoon was temporarily ruined. My dream of tart perfection, which I'd thought was on the home stretch, had come to a full stop. My twenty-six-year-old self attempted not to cry as I looked at the mold and tried to decide just *how* dangerous it was. I knew I was being silly. Who cries over tarts? Me, that's who.

Corby was smart and didn't tease me about it. Nor did he try to give alternate suggestions. I quicky covered all the tarts with peaches so we could make it to dinner on time, and they were of course delicious. But deep in my heart, I knew the berries would have made far superior tarts.

These are pretty low-level examples. We obviously all have dreams and expectations that are much more serious than fruit tarts.

After Corby broke his neck, one of the therapists at the hospital pulled Ronda aside and advised her to have a funeral for the dreams she had built up for her son: dreams about his future wedding, graduation, and career. None of those things were going to look the way she had pictured. Again, it sounds silly to have a funeral for a dream version of Corby. The real Corby was very much alive and already coming up with wheelchair pranks to play on people. But it was a necessary step in moving on.

So, are dreams real? I think they are. Do they impact our decisions? I think they do.

As hinted at earlier in this book, I am convinced that I spent almost two years grieving over the man I'd thought I would one day marry. A man who had never existed. I had never pictured what he looked like or sounded like, only that he was a faceless figure whom I would one day go on a camping trip with and dance with and have children with.

For two years, I tried to ignore this man. And "the Man" did not appreciate it. Whenever I tried to step forward with Corby, that dream man would creep up in the background, reminding me that Corby wasn't what I was looking for. "The Man" had working legs. He was able to get himself ready for bed and walk up the stairs into my parents' house, and dish up his own plate of food. But if I tried to acknowledge "the Man," it meant criticizing Corby, a real man whom I had so much love and respect for.

So for two years, I painstakingly grieved over someone who didn't exist. Someone who had enormous influence on all my dreams for the future without me consciously knowing what was happening. For two years, I bounced around the stages of grief.

There are five stages of grief: denial, anger, bargaining, depression, and acceptance. I didn't go through these stages in order, and I most certainly did not go through them one time each. There were many, many nights that I stayed up late, desperately looking for any shred of hope that a cure for paralysis would be available in the near future. I knew it was extremely unlikely that a complete fix for SCI would ever be discovered, but I didn't want to accept this difficult fact.* I didn't want to marry a guy with such a permanent defect. I would often beg God to intervene, but He never did.

I tried to hide all my anger and frustration from Corby. I knew he was already feeling discouraged about ever getting married. He was acutely aware of all the things he couldn't do, and I didn't need to rub them in. I also realized that some of the things I was mad about were insignificant. I knew that in the long run, the ability to camp and hike and dance were not important. I knew Corby had the qualities that actually mattered, like solid communication and financial skills. We had the same religious beliefs. He was everything I had ever wanted—with one major flaw.

There were moments of acceptance while we were dating. One of the best dates we had was when I fixed Corby's massive game controller. Instead of dwelling on the should-have-beens, I accepted Corby's limitations and helped him be able to play *Smash Bros*. This might have been easier because I was not as emotionally connected to video games as I was to other things, so my expectations of a future husband's ability to play *Smash Bros* wasn't really a significant portion of my dream. But still. It was nice.

Trying to bury these emotions was not a healthy long-term strategy. It did not encourage healing or acceptance. When I bottled up my emotions and didn't ever address them, eventually they'd just kind of explode. Instead of doing the healthy thing and discussing my concerns and letting myself be mad and sad, I tried to ignore them. I didn't do a very thorough job. Corby wrote in his journal multiple times about how he felt "persecuted" around me. I always looked at the negative. I pointed out all the things he wasn't able to do instead

---

* *It may be interesting to note that I don't follow studies or technology advances for helping with disabilities at all. The time I spend daydreaming about what I'll do once X thing restores Y functionality is time not spent finding things that I can do here and now. Plus, if some surgery or device ever reaches the general market, there's no way I won't hear about it.*

of focusing on the things he could do. (Optimism is so natural for him that I don't think he fully realizes how difficult it is for other people.)

Anyway, looking back now, I was just stuck in the grief cycle. I was trying to convince myself that Corby was not for me and would never be for me, and I was logically and rationally trying to put together an ironclad and unemotional case for why we should break up. I was even trying to convince Corby that I wouldn't fit with what he needed. With logic on my side, it wouldn't be painful. We would calmly and rationally move on and find people who matched the silhouettes in our heads. It was an unsuccessful attempt.

A big explosion took place after Corby left for the Six Weeks of Silence. Suddenly, I could write down all my feelings. I could even write them down as if I were talking to Corby, and I could be honest because an unsent email wouldn't be read. As those six weeks went by, more and more of my bottle lids popped off, and the contents suddenly started overflowing. I began to allow the grief process to occur completely uninhibited. I was mad. I wanted Corby back. I never wanted to see Corby again. I loved Corby. I hated Corby. I was angry with God but grateful that He had guided me to Corby in the first place.

Corby showed back up right in the middle of this process. I didn't want to see him, and it was so bad that at one point, he felt like he had to write a letter defending the fact that he could write legibly. I hate that letter. At the time, that weak, wiggly Corby scrawl represented so much of what he couldn't do. Why on earth would I want to marry someone who was not capable of writing more legibly than a third grader? Did it matter? Well . . . no. But if he couldn't write, then what else couldn't he do? *Everything! That's what!*

My final arrival at the acceptance stage was a combination of a few factors. The biggest one was when Corby decided to give me space. He told me he would wait. And suddenly, that gave me permission not to squirrel away my emotions in bottles, scared that they would lead to another breakup. Instead, I let myself have hard days. If I told Corby I needed space, he gave me space. He didn't even demand that I explain why, though he made it clear that I could talk to him about anything.

I have all our texts from the day we met up to the day we got married. Between the time we got engaged and the time we got married, I have plenty of examples of days where I questioned everything we were doing. I'd tell Corby, and he'd just listen. Slowly, Corby became a safe space, even when I was struggling with him.

Are there still moments when I hear a fun song and miss dancing? Yep! There will always be moments like that. I'm sure that if we ever have kids, pieces of this grief cycle will be repeated as I encounter bits of dreams related to raising children that just aren't going to work out with Corby's limited physical ability. But it will never be as bad as it was for those first two years.

If your mood suddenly changes and you don't really understand why, maybe sit down and have a good think. Did your mood change because something is actually wrong? Or is it because something doesn't match a dream you didn't know you had? This is especially important if you are the type of person who visualizes things weeks in advance. I suspect that our expectations and dreams play games with our emotions far more than we realize.

## *Lesson #3*

# Everyone Is Lame

I have a pet peeve. Corby shares this pet peeve, though he is a wheelchair veteran, so it doesn't bother him as much. We hate it when people say things like, "You are *so* inspirational!"

Do we understand where this is coming from? Sure, I guess. But it is hard to fathom why someone thinks we're inspirational when they see us eating hamburgers at Denny's. The way I look at it, if we're sitting in Denny's, we're setting an example of laziness by choosing to eat out. One time, someone thought Corby was inspirational because he went to Walmart. Corby is not an inspiration for going to Walmart. If we are equating inspiration to difficulty, the woman who brought her two-year-old twins to Walmart is far more inspirational than the dude who doesn't even have to stand up in order to purchase a large bag of crispy M&Ms.

When somebody makes the statement, "You are *so* inspirational," it implies that something about us is compelling or surprising. The random guy at Walmart looked at Corby for fifteen seconds, saw the chair, and decided that his very visible disability made him compelling. But what does that imply? If Corby surprises people by purchasing crispy M&Ms at Walmart, it implies that some people don't expect to see a wheelchair user at Walmart. They must have the erroneous impression that people in wheelchairs rarely venture outdoors. They picture wheelchair users sitting next to the window all day, wistfully watching people with functional legs walking their dogs and retrieving their mail, wondering if life is worth it.

We have met a lot of people in wheelchairs. And we can think of only a few who have the "life is over" attitude. The rest have jobs or have joined wheelchair sports teams or do other normal activities, like shopping and eating out. When Corby decides to shop at Walmart, he simply drives to a wheelchair parking spot, which were designed for people like him, rolls through the automatic doors, which were designed for people like him, and grabs what he wants off the shelves. If something is on the top shelf, he has to ask for help, but store employees or other shoppers are always happy to assist. Society has literally written laws about designing things for disabled people, yet we celebrate when they use those things! It doesn't feel right.

The other phrase that bothers me is "I could never be in a wheelchair. I would rather die." Or, "I can't believe you married a guy in a wheelchair. I could never do that."

Again, I sort of understand where these statements are coming from. But whenever someone says things like that, I feel like my choices have made them feel bad about themselves. Like watching me live my life has made them feel inadequate because they aren't strong enough to deal with what I do. Well, you have now read pretty much this entire book. I hope you don't still think I'm some sort of hero. Marrying Corby was not an easy choice. I could not immediately look past the chair and accept Corby for who he was. I was mad and confused and upset for two years. Two entire years!

I think a better description for Corby is that he is unusual. And our relationship is unusual. Let me put it in terms of an analogy. Let's say that you have a son, and he decides to play the trumpet in the high school band. Your neighbor also has a son who joins the same band. That young musical student chooses to learn the mellophone. (For your daily gee-whiz collection, the mellophone is a variant of the French horn specifically designed for use in marching bands.)

When you see these two boys march together in the band, do you look at the boy holding the less-common instrument and think, *He is inspirational*! Of course you don't! It's the same thing for Corby. He has dealt with what life threw at him. Life threw him a challenge that is visibly different, so it attracts more attention. But that doesn't mean he is "inspirational." When it comes down to it, he's just a dude who works a nine-to-five job and plays video games at night. Nothing inspirational about that!

He does give motivational/inspirational presentations on occasion. This is an interesting phenomenon in our culture. For some reason, we look at people with visible disabilities and think that because they manage to go to Walmart in their condition, they must hold some deep, powerful secret to life. We call this effect "double story points." If I go to Walmart and tell you about it, you're like, "Great. You get a story point. I'm so glad you were able to get your backup lightbulb stash replenished. Whatever." But if Corby goes to Walmart and buys the same package of lightbulbs, for some reason, he gets a bunch of story points. Because he went to a store! And bought lightbulbs! In a wheelchair!

If I make a PowerPoint about choosing to be positive and choosing to be grateful and building constructive beliefs (some of Corby's common speaking topics), you would politely listen and think, *Sure, maybe some of those ideas have merit.* But if Corby rolls up and gives the same, exact speech, it holds a lot of extra weight. If the dude with the gimpy fingers can be grateful, so can I! Would you have read this book if it hadn't featured a wheelchair? Anyone could write a compelling book about what they have experienced and learned. But for some reason, we like visually obvious experiences.

Let's return to Walmart. I know you enjoy being there. There are a lot of different types of people at Walmart. Corby happens to be in a wheelchair. You can glance at him and, within a few seconds, make a decent guess at the sorts of things he might be struggling with in his life. But what if you glance in the next aisle and see me? Ordinary thirty-one-year-old. Wearing jeans and a sweatshirt, buying toilet bowl cleaner. If you look at me, you have no way of knowing what I went through that day or that week or that month. After reading this book, you know some of the things I struggle with. Such as ridiculous overreactions to physical stimuli. But you wouldn't be able to tell from looking at me. If I am actually buying toilet bowl cleaner, chances are I'm holding my breath and moving as quickly as possible because the cleaning aisle is the worst sensory experience in the whole store and must be avoided at all costs. (In reality, I purchase unscented cleaners online just to avoid this aisle.)

Let's leave Walmart and go to your neighborhood or your family. Or even you. What struggles do you and your loved ones have that would not be readily visible to a random passerby? I will start a list. Do you know someone who has struggled with infertility or had a miscarriage? What about mental illnesses, like anxiety, depression, or OCD? Do you know someone who has an addiction or who is going through a divorce? Do you know any families where a son or daughter died by suicide or lost their life in a tragic accident? You can't see those things on the outside, but they are all legitimate struggles.

The things on that list are generally negative. I think we can all agree that addictions and death are bad. But something on *your* list may not necessarily be bad. Maybe it's just hard. For instance, having a spouse in the military isn't bad. But is it hard? Sure! Same with having a spouse who has to travel a lot for work or who works really odd hours that are hard to plan around. Maybe you got divorced and have since remarried, and now you are trying to combine two families. Do you love all your children from both families? Sure you do! But is it hard to make everything work out in a blended family? Of course it is!

Maybe you have dug a hole for yourself. Maybe you accidentally got into a lot of credit card debt, and now you are trying to pay everything off and get yourself on the right track again. Is that challenge any less difficult because you caused it yourself? No, it isn't. In fact, it might be more difficult if you're blaming yourself for your current position.

I could try to rate some of these challenges on a scale from easiest to hardest. Personally, if I had to choose the easiest thing on this list, it would be "disabled husband." I have now experienced it, so I know it isn't as hard as everyone thinks it is. Corby's problem is pretty easy to solve. We throw a lot of money at getting wheelchairs and caregivers. You can't do that with things like anxiety or addiction. I myself have thrown a lot of money at various counseling services and random supplements in an effort to solve my sensory issues, but none of them have worked.

In the end, rating challenges is pointless. Everyone will rate them differently based on their life experiences and perceptions. The real point I am trying to make is that everyone has a thing. That thing might change over time. If you went to Walmart and saw a little bubble floating above everyone's head, stating exactly what their thing was that day, I wonder if we might treat each other differently. If there were a bubble over Corby's head, it probably wouldn't say anything about the wheelchair. Most days, I think he worries about me, especially when I'm at home, curled up in a ball because I visited the toilet-bowl-cleaner aisle.

If you happen to believe in God, or some other higher power, I challenge you to look for ways that you were intentionally created for *your* "things." I believe God specially designed me to be with Corby. And He designed Corby to both be in a chair and deal with me. We have actually written out lists before, and it was a great exercise. I think I find dealing with the chair easier than someone else would because I was meant for it. It also means that you were made to withstand your challenges as well.

The original title of this book was *My Husband Is Lame.* It was a great title with an excellent pun, but the silly publishers thought it was potentially offensive or that it sounded like I hated men. We tried to soften the title by changing it to *My Husband Is Lame . . . And So Am I.* They rejected that idea, too, but it does perfectly sum up this chapter. My husband is literally lame. I am figuratively lame. And that is what I think about when people say, "I could never do what you do." Well, guess what? You already have. Because everyone is lame! We are all dealing with lame things every day! Hopefully, we look back at a time when we were lame and see how far we've come, grateful that we aren't lame in that particular way anymore. And hopefully, we keep moving forward, knowing we can tackle the next lame thing when it comes. Because everybody is lame. And being lame is wonderful.

# Epilogue

Murder.

I do realize that the word *murder* is not generally a good word to end a book with. For most readers, the word *murder* is probably rather alarming, especially after a happy ending. Fear not, this ending has nothing to do with actual murder. That would be awkward.

I stood on a chair, wearing a bright-teal Pakistani wedding outfit I'd bought off a sketchy foreign website. Twenty-four people were in my living room, which I had draped with silky fabric panels. They were wearing equally elaborate costumes, staring at me while I proceeded to explain the rules for how they could attack each other. They had come to our house for an Arabian Nights murder mystery party. Corby and I were dressed as genies, ready to run the game.

As everyone started interrogating each other, trying to solve Aladdin's murder, I looked across the room at Corby in his muscle suit and blue turban. We had just celebrated our seventh wedding anniversary a few months before. I thought back to the afternoon of the day we got married, when we did a jigsaw puzzle in our quiet condo. The Tess of that afternoon *never* imagined that one day I would be wearing gold lipstick and massive sparkly earrings and be directing two dozen people on game mechanics.

I am not the same person I was when I made that dating profile in 2014. People who meet me now can't believe I used to pace around like a caged tiger, sobbing, just because Corby wanted me to share opinions. I now share opinions with lots of people. I am still not totally comfortable doing it, but I do it. And although I still prefer being alone, I regularly do things like host murder mystery dinner parties. I plan weekly board-game nights and DM for DnD sessions. I've discovered that I'm a pretty good long-range assassin in video games. You know, important life skills. (And yes, Corby achieved his goal of transforming a random girl into a trophy nerd wife. It's a strange combo with the knitting.)

It was interesting to look back at all my old journal entries while I was writing this book, especially the ones where I was clearly terrified of the concept of marriage. A few weeks after getting married, I came to the conclusion that marriage was *wonderful*. We did the same things we had for the previous two and a half years but in our own little condo. Without all the stupid discussions.

Did I give up some things? Sure. I no longer dance or camp or hike. But I gained so much more. A Corby, who unquestioningly supports me in everything else I want to do and follows me around the house and yard like a happy mechanical puppy. I help him with his disabilities, and he helps me with mine. Because of this support, I have started a few tiny craft businesses. I have discovered new hobbies that I can do with him. And we talk about everything. Somehow, I went from being torturously reluctant to share anything to sharing everything with another human. We go on walks and drives and talk for hours. It now feels weirder *not* to tell him things.

If pre-Corby Tess could see who I am now, I don't think she would recognize herself. And that is largely due to Corby. He is the kindest, most patient man in the whole world. I still can't believe he waited for me, and I still think he could have found someone so much better. The decision to marry him is the best one I've ever made. I wouldn't change it for anything. In fact, if someone came up to us right now and offered to heal Corby—a 100 percent guarantee of a complete recovery—for *free*, I'm not sure I would say yes.* I absolutely love our life together. I have never known Corby outside of his chair, and now that I have accepted him the way he is, I don't want him to change. Being a wheelchair wife is part of my identity, and I wouldn't have it any other way. Marriage is wonderful! Corby makes me so, so happy, and I love him so much. Platypus.

---

* *Tess is not sure she likes the idea of a Corby who can come upstairs and disturb her crafting supplies. But I'm sure she'd find walking Corby loves her just as much as chair Corby. And I love her so much!*

# Book Club Discussion Questions

## Disability

1. Have your views on physical disabilities changed at all after reading this book? In what way?
2. Have your views on mental disabilities changed at all after reading this book? In what way?
3. How do you decide when to accept a limitation versus try to overcome it? Can you think of a time you did one or the other?

## Everybody Is Lame!

1. In what ways are you "lame"? Are they visible, or would others be surprised to learn you struggle with those limitations? (Remember, these challenges might not be permanent disabilities like the examples in this book. They might be a temporary situation impacting your life right now.)
2. In what ways is your partner "lame"? How have you supported each other or built your relationship to accommodate each other's needs?
3. For religious groups: In what ways did God prepare you for your "lameness"? Have you been blessed with talents

or personality traits that have helped you get through your unique challenges?

4. Have you ever avoided growth because it felt too uncomfortable? What helped you push through?

## Accepting Service

1. Have you ever asked for service from someone else? How did it change your relationship with that person?
2. Think about your closest friends and the way your relationships started. Did either of you ask the other for help? If so, did it strengthen the relationship?
3. How do you feel when someone else reaches out to you for help? Do you question whether or not they actually *need* the help? Do you resent being asked? Are you always happy and willing to help someone else? What if it is someone you don't know very well?

## Expectations

1. Think of a time when something didn't go how you expected—big or small. Did you grieve over what was "supposed" to happen?
2. Are there unmet expectations from your past that you are still having trouble accepting?
3. Are you the type of person who visualizes and plans for the future? Do you think that unexpected changes to your plans upset you more than other people around you?

## Relationships

1. Tess and Corby have pretty opposite personality types. Do you and your partner have similar or different personalities? Have you been able to use each other's strengths to balance out the challenges you struggle with?
2. For married readers: What was on your "list" when you were looking for a partner? Did you find someone who matched

everything on that list, or did you have to give up some of those things? Was that hard for you to accept? For single readers: What is on your "list" for a future partner? Are there less-important qualities or traits that may be holding you back from potential relationships?

3. Have you ever married/dated someone with a love language different from yours? How did you navigate your preferences in expressing/receiving affection?

## Silly

1. What's your favorite "wheelnote" or silly moment in the book? Did any make you laugh out loud?
2. Would you swipe right on either Tess or Corby based on their dating profiles? Why or why not?
3. Which moment would you cast in a rom-com, and who would play Corby and Tess?